# METAPHYSICAL ODYSSEY INTO THE
# MEXICAN REVOLUTION

# METAPHYSICAL ODYSSEY INTO THE MEXICAN REVOLUTION

## FRANCISCO I. MADERO AND HIS SECRET BOOK,

### *SPIRITIST MANUAL*

**C.M. MAYO**

paperback
ISBN 978-0-9887970-0-0

hardcover
ISBN 978-0-9887970-3-1

Dancing Chiva Literary Arts
Palo Alto www.dancingchiva.com

An excerpt from this translation first appeared in
*Sol Literary Magazine.*

By permission of the artist, the cover incorporates the painting by
Kelley Vandiver, "Gerbara and Eye." www.kelleyvandiver.com

Maps of the Burned-Over District and Mexico by Bill Nelson www.
billnelsonmaps.esva.net

ALSO BY C.M. MAYO

*Sky Over El Nido*
(winner of the Flannery O'Connor Award for Short Fiction)

*Miraculous Air: Journey of a Thousand Miles*
*through Baja California, the Other Mexico*
(travel memoir)

*The Last Prince of the Mexican Empire*
(novel)

*Mexico: A Traveler's Literary Companion*
(anthology editor)

*For Agustín Carstens, como siempre*

*and for all who would wonder at
the marvels of Mexican history*

# TABLE OF CONTENTS

## ABOUT C.M. MAYO

C.M. Mayo is a novelist, travel writer, poet, and literary translator. Her most recent work is *The Last Prince of the Mexican Empire* (Unbridled Books), an historical novel based on a true story of mid-19th century Mexico. Named a best book of 2009 by *Library Journal*, it is based on extensive, original archival research, about which Mayo has lectured widely, including at the Library of Congress, the Center for U.S. Mexican Studies UCSD, and the Harry Ransom Center at University of Texas Austin. The Spanish translation by Mexican novelist and poet, Agustín Cadena, was published by Random House Mondadori Grijalbo as *El último príncipe del Imperio Mexicano* in 2010.

Her previous book, *Miraculous Air* (Milkweed Editions) is a travel memoir, rich with research and original interviews, of Mexico's Baja California peninsula, from Los Cabos to Tijuana. Her first book, *Sky Over El Nido* (University of Georgia Press) won the Flannery O'Connor Award for Short Fiction.

Mayo's translations of Mexican contemporary literature have appeared in numerous journals and anthologies, most recently, *Three Messages and a Warning: Contemporary Mexican Short Stories of the Fantastic* (Small Beer Press) and *Best Contemporary Mexican Fiction* (Dalkey Archive). Her own anthology, of 24 Mexican writers, is *Mexico: A Traveler's Literary Companion* (Whereabouts Press).

Born in El Paso, Texas and raised in California, Mayo was educated at the University of Chicago. She has been a resident of Mexico City for over 20 years.

Her website is www.cmmayo.com

## ACKNOWLEDGEMENTS

This book and the accompanying translation would have been flat-out impossible for me to have completed without the constant support and encouragement of my husband, Agustín Carstens. I am also deeply indebted to José Ramón San Cristóbal, Martha López Castillo, Carlos Múgica, José Francisco Hernández Sánchez, Maria Josefa Valerio, Inés Avalos, and other staff members in Mexico's Ministry of Finance for their assistance with this project, most especially in providing me with a xerox copy of the original *Manual espírita*. My most sincere thanks also go to other staff in other archives, among them, the Centro de Estudios de Historia de México CARSO, where Susana Morales never left me waiting for more than a few moments for any book; the New York Theosophical Society Library; and the House of the Temple Library in Washington D.C., where Larissa Watkins was a true "library angel."

Ideally, a book should have many readers before it goes to press, and though I claim responsibility for any and all errors, many other eyes have caught errors, confirmed doubts, and added surprising new information, among them, historians Luis Cerda, Manuel Guerra de Luna, Heribert von Feilitzsch, KimiQuiztli SeLuZha and Yolia Tortolero Cervantes, without whose work, *El espiritismo seduce a Francisco I. Madero*, I surely would have been wandering lost in the woods. And a special gracias to Carlos González Manterola, whose enthusiasm in many conversations over many months was especially sustaining, and who, among so many other things, brought to my attention Jorge Luis Borges' devotion to Swedenborg. Bobby Clark and Mary O'Keefe helped me "de-dizzify" chapter one.

Thanks to Eva Hunt, *Sol Literary Magazine* published an excerpt (in which editor Cazz Roberts, thankfully, caught some slippery typos), and thanks to them, to PEN San Miguel, and Susan Page and the many volunteers at San Miguel de Allende's Literary Sala, I had the priviledge and the delight of being able to talk about the translation (and so clarify my own thinking about it) to two English-speaking audiences far more sophisticated than most about Mexican history.

Editor and poet Diane Fouts—thank you, Dawn Marano for sending me to her—gave me invaluable suggestions and caught more typos than I thought possible in my book-length manuscript, *Metaphysical Odyssey*.

A big hug of a thank you to my many friends, *aficionados* of Mexican history—Alfonso and Ana Guerra, Mílada Bazant, Sophie Bidault, María Teresa Fernández Acevez, Sandra Gulland, Rev. Stephen A. Hermann, John Kachuba, Ileana Ramírez, Deborah Riner, and Rose Mary Salum—who lent their encouragement and support in so many other ways. And thanks, Sam Quinones, for sending me your spine-tingling essay on Dr. Grinberg-Zylberbaum.

Thank you also to Jana Anna and Rose Rosetree for some very special insight.

Artist Kelley Vandiver gave his permission to incorporate his painting, "Gerbara and Eye," on this book's cover.

Rose Quinn, an eagle-eyed wizard with Adobe InDesign did the formatting.

Amron Gravett prepared the index; Bill Nelson, the maps.

Finally, and crucially, *muchísimas gracias* to Rubén Pacheco for his expert assistance and his saintly patience with all my digital endeavors.

*La política no desplaza al espiritismo: nace de él*
*(Politics does not displace Spiritism: it is born of it)*
—*Enrique Krauze,*
*Francisco I. Madero: Místico de la libertad*

*The roots of all things are connected*
—Chan K'in

*Be not bewildered, be thou not afraid*
—Bhagavad-Gita, 11:49

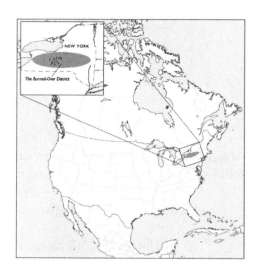

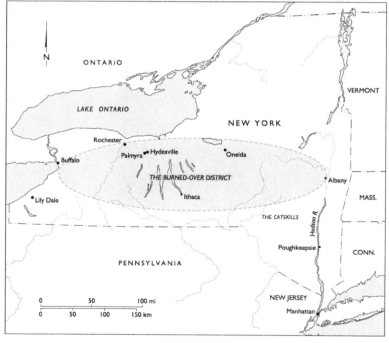

The Burned-Over District, an area approximately between Albany and
Buffalo, got its name from the fiery passions of its nineteenth-century
religious revival movements.

# ROOTS, ENTANGLEMENTS, ENCOUNTERS

## Francisco I. Madero's Secret Book

When Halley's comet, that star with the quetzal's tail, flared across Mexican skies in 1910, it heralded not only the centennial of Independence, but a deeply transformative episode, the Revolution launched by Francisco I. Madero on November 20, what Javier Garciadiego calls "the true beginning of a process, the birth of the modern Mexican state." The great chorus of Mexican historians agrees. And yet, almost unknown and curious as it may sound, a vital taproot of this revolution lies in the Burned-Over District of New York state.

As a writer of both fiction and nonfiction, I have learned to appreciate that fact can be stranger than anything one might imagine. Before returning to the Burned-Over District, a word about Francisco I. Madero and how I came upon his *Manual espírita*, this until now obscure and yet profoundly illuminating book—at the very least for understanding Madero himself, why and how he led Mexico's 1910 Revolution, and the seething contempt of those behind the overthrow of his government and his assassination.

Madero was a Coahuilan rancher and businessman without whose daring and passion the Revolution might not have begun when it did, and without whom modern Mexico might not have been able to rightly call itself a republic. Francisco I. Madero was none other than Mexico's "Apostle of Democracy," who rejected a stolen election and took up arms to bring down

Porfirio Díaz, the military strongman who had ruled Mexico directly and indirectly for more than three decades. When Díaz fled to Paris in 1911, Madero did not seat himself upon the presidential throne; with an interim government in place, he once again campaigned throughout the country to become Mexico's democratically elected President, and only after unequivocally winning that election did he take office later that year. In 1913, but fifteen months into his term, Madero was overthrown in a coup d'état engineered by a cabal of conservatives (and the influence of a meddling U.S. ambassador) and then, with shocking casualness, executed. The Mexican Revolution then exploded into a new and more violent phase, churning on until 1920 with Alvaro Obregón's presidency or, as some historians argue, the end of the Cristero Rebellion in 1929.

Popular imagery of the Mexican Revolution usually features rustic characters in bandoliers and washtub-sized sombreros, such as smoldering-eyed Emiliano Zapata, with his handlebar mustache and skin-tight trousers, or Pancho Villa, who always seems to wear the smirk of having just quaffed a beer (though he was a teetotaler; more likely it was a strawberry soda). Less often are we shown Don Francisco, handsomely-dressed scion of one of Mexico's wealthiest families—usually bareheaded, occasionally in a top hat—for he was and remains a confounding figure. He was a Spiritist, and what the devil is that? I had no idea. And until 2008, it had not occurred to me to wonder.

I had just finished writing *The Last Prince of the Mexican Empire,* a novel based on several years of original archival research into an episode during Mexico's French Intervention of the 1860s, the so-called Second Empire under Maximilian von Habsburg. I mean to say, spending an afternoon delving into an archive, I am happier than a cat after mice. At that time, my husband was in Mexico's Ministry of Finance, which has a number of archives, among them, Francisco I. Madero's. His archive is available to the public, but thanks to my husband's invitation, I had the immense privilege of viewing it in private with the curator, Martha López Castillo.

When we arrived, she had arranged a selection of the most outstanding items on a table that spanned nearly the width of the room: Madero's masonic regalia; photographs; documents. We went down the table, as she explained the importance of each piece.

Years earlier, on a tour of the National Palace, in one of its parade of ornately decorated rooms (I couldn't have told you which) I had seen the bureau that still bore the bullet hole from the shoot-out between General Victoriano Huerta's men and the presidential guard that ended with President Madero and Vice President, Pino Suárez, taken prisoner. If I knew anything about Madero it was because I had been living in Mexico on and off for two decades, and in Mexico, Madero has a stature comparable to Abraham Lincoln's—in the political-historical sense, not the physical, for Madero was short, with a balding pate and a neatly trimmed triangle of a beard. In portraits, Madero appears kindly yet dignified—one can easily imagine him managing a prosperous complex of farms and factories (as he did). The few moving pictures of him reveal a theatrical, embracing energy. Madero was also distantly related to my husband's family: a paternal uncle had married a great niece of Madero. In sum, what I knew then about Madero amounted to little more than the barest gloss over the story Mexican schoolchildren learn, but certainly I was vividly aware of his transcendent and deeply respected role in Mexican history.

Not halfway through this presentation, my gaze fell on a little book, *Manual espírita* by "Bhîma."

"Who was Bhîma?" I asked.

"Madero himself," the curator answered.

I had picked it up and was already leafing through it... *Los invisibles, Chrishná, Mosés, La doctrina secreta...* it seemed a farrago of the Bible, Madame Blavatsky, and Hindu whatnot.

"Really?" I said. "Bhîma was Francisco Madero?"

"Yes."

I knew, instantly and absolutely, that I had to translate this book into English. Had it been translated?

"No."

"Are you sure?" This, too, seemed too extraordinary.

"I assure you, it has never been translated."

Within the week, I had received a xerox copy of this strange little book, and I began my self-appointed task—which turned out to be a Mount Everest more than I imagined.

### From Rapping with the Fox Sisters of Hydesville To D.D. Home Afloat Among the Chandeliers of Paris

Why had I leapt at it? Apart from an intuition, as a translator of poetry and literary short fiction, I knew how little Mexican writing appears in English, and translating Madero's relatively simple vocabulary and syntax, in a work barely big enough to merit a spine, seemed a lark of a project. Oh, maybe a couple of weekends? Yet not three pages in, I was dumbfounded. I had no context for such ideas. Frankly, it gave me the creeps. So instead of translating, I started reading—four years' worth of reading. And this, for the moment, brings us back to the Burned-Over District of New York state.

Once the heartland of the Iroquois nation, this approximately 50-by-500 kilometer swath of verdant Yankee farmland between Albany and Buffalo got its name not from any fire but from the fiery passions of its nineteenth-century religious revival movements. Traveling preachers filled billowing tents with celebrants, and Mitch Horowitz writes in *Occult America,* "[f]or days afterward, without the prompting of ministers or revivalists, men and women would speak in tongues and writhe in religious ecstasy. Many would report visitations from angels or spirits." A few outstanding figures in the long list of those who traveled through, settled in, or departed from the Burned-Over District include Jemima Wilkinson, aka "The Publick Universal Friend" who called herself a channel for the Divine Spirit; the utopian Oneida Community; the Millerites, who sold their worldly possessions in expectation of Judgment

Day in 1844; Shakers; Quakers; Joseph Smith, founder of the Church of Jesus Christ of Latter-day Saints, who claimed to receive instructions from the Angel Moroni to unearth the golden plates of the Book of Mormon; and, most relevant to the story at-hand, the Fox sisters of Hydesville.

The Foxes, a Methodist farmworker family, the father a blacksmith, moved into their cottage shortly before Christmas 1847. There would have been snow pillowing up to the windowsills, and a pre-electricity sky spectacular with stars. On their straw-stuffed mattresses, the family would have been bundled in blankets and quilts. But through the cruel winter nights of 1848, their sleep suffered with odd noises, crackles, scrapings—as if of moving furniture, bangs, and knocks. By springtime the children had become so frightened by the "spirit raps," they insisted on sleeping with their parents. As Sir Arthur Conan Doyle (yes, of Sherlock Holmes fame) recounts in *The History of Spiritualism:*

> Finally, upon the night of March 31 there was a very loud and continued outbreak of inexplicable sounds. It was on this night that one of the great points of psychic evolution was reached, for it was then that young Kate Fox challenged the unseen power to repeat the snaps of her fingers. That rude room, with its earnest, expectant, half-clad occupants with eager upturned faces, its circle of candlelight, and its heavy shadows lurking in the corners, might well be made the subject of a great historical painting. Search all the palaces and chancelleries of 1848, and where will you find a chamber which has made its place in history as secure as this bedroom of a shack? The child's challenge, though given in flippant words, was instantly answered. Every snap was echoed by a knock. However humble the

operator at either end, the spiritual telegraph
was at last working.

Kate Fox, eleven, and her sister, Maggie, fourteen, determined that the spirit they called "Mr. Split-foot" was that of
a peddler who had been murdered and buried in the house.
Conan Doyle, who went so far as to reprint the sworn April 11,
1848, testimony of both parents, was one of many Spiritualists,
as they came to call themselves, who considered the events in
the so-called "Spook House" of Hydesville "the most important
thing that America has given to the commonweal of the world."
And whether one laughingly discards, ardently accepts, or finely
sifts and resifts ad infinitum the evidence of the existence of
said murdered peddler and any communications from beyond
the veil, the fact remains that whatever happened in Hydesville
ignited an enthusiasm for "spirit" phenomena evoked in the
ritual of the séance—from channeling to table tipping to pencils
and chalk stubs writing by themselves, or by communication by
means of a planchette; clairvoyance; flashes of light and floating
orbs; levitation; ectoplasmic hands, feet and faces oozing out
of velvety darkness; and "spirit photography"—throughout the
Burned-Over District, north to Canada, out west, south, to
England and Ireland and, at full-gallop, across the European
continent into Russia.

The Fox sisters received an avalanche of press, which
only increased after P.T. Barnum put them on display in his
American Museum on New York City's Broadway, charging a
dollar—then more than a tidy sum—to communicate through
them to the ghost of one's choice. (As science historian Deborah
Blum recounts in *Ghost Hunters*, among those who paid their
dollar were the novelist James Fenimore Cooper and Horace
Greeley, editor of *The New York Tribune*, both of whom left
convinced that they had heard from spirit.) Scores of mediums now emerged, claiming to communicate with spirits as
diverse as a drowned child, Egyptian high priests, and "astral"
beings; seeking them out in darkened rooms came legions of

the bereaved, curiosity-seekers, skeptics on a mission, and quite a few intellectuals.

Among the celebrated mediums in this period were the English Florence Cook; Nettie Colburn, who gave séances for Abraham and Mary Todd Lincoln in the White House; and Scottish-born American Daniel Dunglas (D.D.) Home, who toured France in the 1850s, which, according to historian John Warne Monroe, "seemed to mark the first step in the spread of this second, metaphysical American Revolution." According to magic historian Henry Ridgely Evans, "No man since Caglisotro ever created so profound a sensation in the Old World."

Home's séances, like his audience itself, attained a new level of glamour, a world apart from the Fox sisters. Attended by royalty, including the Emperor Louis Napoleon and his Empress Eugénie, and high society of all stripes, according to Janet Oppenheim in *The Other World*, an evening with Home might feature a spine-tingling cornucopia of phenomena:

> [F]urniture trembled, swayed, and rose from the floor (often without disturbing objects on its surface); diverse articles soared through the air; the séance room itself might appear to shake with quivering vibrations; raps announced the arrival of the communicating spirits; spirit arms and hands emerged, occasionally to write messages or distribute favors to the sitters; musical instruments, particularly Home's celebrated accordion, produced their own music; spirit voices uttered their pronouncements; spirit lights twinkled, and cool breezes chilled the sitters. If Home announced his own levitation, as he did from time to time, the sitters might feel their hair ruffled by the soles of his feet.

Let us float down from the ceiling for a moment, back to the grittier question of roots.

### The Seer of Poughkeepsie

This sudden fashion for communicating with spirits, and the congruent appearance of the movement that came to be called Spiritualism, had meshes of roots, many also entangled with Occultism, and from Greek, Egyptian, Arab, and Jewish philosophies and concepts filtered through the Renaissance (in particular, the *Corpus Hermeticum*, writings attributed to Hermes Trismegistus / Thoth, and the Qabalah, a tradition of Jewish mystical teachings developed in the twelfth and thirteen centuries); Gnostic Christianity and mystic Catholicism (the latter notably familiar with visions, apports, and levitation); alchemy; the "angel conversations," held in daylight with a crystal ball, of polymath and astrologer to Queen Elizabeth I, Dr. John Dee; English and Celtic magic and other European folk traditions including those of the German Hexenmeisters; Mesmerism (forerunner of hypnotism, introduced by Viennese doctor Franz Anton Mesmer and brought to United States by French enthusiasts, among them the Marquis de Lafayette); and a New World grab-bag of African and indigenous American influences. But if Spiritualism as it emerged in the Burned-Over District in 1848 had a prophet, it could be said to be Andrew Jackson Davis, the "John the Baptist of Spiritualism," or "Seer of Poughkeepsie," Poughkeepsie being a town a short sail up the Hudson River from Manhattan.

Born in 1826 to working-class parents, Davis received boyhood training in tailoring from a Mesmerist who recognized his psychic talents. Soon Davis was well-known in the region for his clairaudience (psychic hearing) and clairvoyance (psychic sight), which he used for making medical diagnoses. One day in 1844, he claimed he fell into a trance and woke to find himself in the Catskill Mountains, some 65 kilometers northwest of Poughkeepsie, where he conversed with the spirits the Greco-Roman physician and philosopher Galen and the Swedish mystic Emanuel Swedenborg, who had died more than 70 years before. Subsequently, over a period of little more than a year, by entering a trance and allegedly channeling the words from spirits, Davis wrote a book. Published in 1847 when he was twenty one years old, his nearly 800-page opus, *The Principles of Nature, Her Divine Revelations and a Voice to Mankind,* foresaw the explosion of Spiritualism in the following year. The famous quote:

> It is a truth that spirits commune with one another while one is in the body and the other in the higher spheres. . . and this truth will ere long present itself in the form of a living demonstration. And the world will hail with delight the ushering-in of that era when the interiors of men will be opened, and the spiritual communion will be established such as is now being enjoyed by the inhabitants of Mars, Jupiter, and Saturn.

Davis' *Principles of Nature* was a best-seller of its day—according to historian Mitch Horowitz, it sold nearly a thousand copies in its first week. For many readers the "proof of the pudding" that this was genuine communication from beyond the veil was that its author was not only so young but unschooled. Davis himself claimed he'd read almost nothing in his entire life. A professor of Hebrew at New York University, one George Bush, assured the *New York Tribune* that he had heard the entranced Davis quote Hebrew correctly and "display a knowledge of geology which would have been astonishing in a person of his age, even if he had devoted years to the study."

It did not go unremarked, and Davis readily acknowledged, that his *Principles of Nature* echoed much that was in Swedenborg's works. And here we must dig a little further and examine one more root of roots: Swedenborgianism, which had arrived on American shores in the late eighteenth-century, when an Englishman brought Swedenborg's books and their stunning revelations to Philadelphia.

## The Solace of Swedenborg

Emanuel Swedenborg was a man with two lives, in a manner of speaking. Born into a well-to-do Lutheran family in Stockholm in 1688, he graduated from Scandinavia's most prestigious, the University of Uppsala. He studied Isaac Newton's works in England, and made his career as a mining engineer, becoming a member of the Swedish Royal Academy of Science, a government minister, and respected author of a book on metallurgy, among other works on astronomy, chemistry, geometry, and even portfolios of mechanical inventions including a submarine and a flying machine. He seemed to be, as historian Catherine L. Albanese puts it, "a veritable Leonardo da Vinci of the north." Had Swedenborg done nothing more, he would have been remembered as one of eighteenth-century Europe's most wide-ranging and pioneering scientists, but at the age of 53, one night in London, he received a visit from Jesus Christ (whom he had earlier spied in a corner of a tavern in a mist of snakes). Jesus Christ informed him that he, Swedenborg, would reveal the true spiritual meaning of the Bible.

Perhaps one wonders whether Swedenborg could have benefitted from a dose of modern pharmaceuticals. Later, after his books on the Bible and the spirit world began to circulate, some called him insane; clergymen accused him of heresy; and Immanuel Kant made jest of his ideas in *Träume eines Geistersehers*. But as Swedenborg scholar Jonathan S. Rose writes, concurring with other biographers, "Contemporary reports, however, attest that [Swedenborg] was intelligent, clear-headed, reliable, and kind. There is abundant documentary evidence that he was physically, politically, and intellectually active until his death at eighty-four. If this was insanity, it was an illness strangely beneficial."

After that visit from Jesus Christ, Swedenborg found himself seeing into the spirit worlds and easily conversing with angels and spirits about all manner of mysteries from the Mind of God and the creation of the universe to the nature of the Trinity and what happens after we die. As Irish poet W.B. Yeats put it, Swedenborg processed such mystica "as if he were sitting before a large table in a Government office putting little pieces of mineral ore into small square boxes for an assistant to pack away in drawers." In other words, Swedenborg authored a vast and punctilious oeuvre, eighteen books in twenty-five volumes, all in Latin (then the lingua franca of the educated western world) and published at his own expense, at a remove from Swedish censors, in London. The works include *Arcana Coelestia* (Secrets of Heaven), a multi-volume study of Genesis and Exodus, along with a tour of the myriad spirit realms; *Heaven and Hell*; *New Jerusalem and Its Heavenly Doctrine*; *The Last Judgement*; and, in addition to several others, *Other Planets*, introducing spirits, angels and inhabitants of Mercury, Venus, Mars, Jupiter, Saturn, and the moon.

To cram all that ouevre into a nutshell: There is one God, pure love and wisdom. In Jesus Christ, God, until then purely spiritual, became physically human. God created two worlds, the physical and spiritual. He created man in his image. Man is an immortal spiritual being who lives in the physical and the spiritual realms, the latter being the more real and multi-leveled from the depths of Hell to the sublime heights of the divine. Love is the source and essence of life. Human beings have will and intellect. The spirit worlds and the human world are intimately connected, each affecting the other—as below, so above. If we are to enjoy our afterlife in some level of Heaven, not Hell, while on earth we must reject evil and do good, though it is not God who judges, but we ourselves. And finally, to paraphrase Swedenborgian theologian Jonathan S. Rose, the Catholic Church took a wrong turn before the Nicean Council of 325, for the Pope and clergy do not hold the keys to heaven, and the Protestant churches born of the Reformation, while an improvement, are dead wrong in asserting that faith alone could save anyone.

Though Swedenborg made no effort to promote an earthly church, his concepts of morality, the afterlife, and the spirit world found purchase and, especially after his death, spread quickly, first in England and then the United States where a Swedenborgian church was established in 1817. By 1852, a congregation had sprung up in San Francisco. And if true believers such as Henry James Sr. (father of the novelist and of psychologist William James), remained a tiny minority, a large number of leading American, English, and European figures of the nineteenth-century were influenced by Swedenborg's ideas, among them, Honoré de Balzac, William Blake, Fyodor Dostoyevsky, Ralph Waldo Emerson, Johann Wolfgang von Goethe, James Joyce, and Helen Keller. The Spanish speaking world also had its admirers, such as the great Argentinean writer Jorge Luis Borges, who said of his readings of Swedenborg, "I was astonished."

Swedenborg first flagged my attention in an unlikely place: the New York Public Library's Manuscript and Archives Division, where, as part of the research for *The Last Prince of the Mexican Empire*, I read the diaries of the U.S. envoy to France John Bigelow. What drew me there was curiosity about Bigelow's motives and role in aiding his countrywoman Alice Green de Iturbide in regaining custody of her infant son, whom she had, to her bitter regret, given up to the childless Emperor Maximilian von Habsburg as his heir presumptive in September 1865. She and her husband, Don Angel de Iturbide, a Mexican diplomat and son of Mexico's first Emperor, turned up in Paris that November, hoping to influence Louis Napoleon, whose army occupied Mexico, to oblige Maximilian to return their child.

Apart from a fascinating account of Bigelow's meetings with the Iturbides and his communications with U.S. Secretary of State Seward and French Foreign Minister Drouyn de Lhuys, I learned that there was a reason his compassion for the Iturbides might have been unusually fierce: he had recently lost his own four-year-old son. Day by day, through a hot Parisian summer, Bigelow had recorded his child's fever and decline in heartbreaking detail. On several nights, he turned to the Bible. And he mentioned reading Swedenborg for solace.

## Incidents in the Year 1891

The earth orbits the sun twenty-six times, *et voilà*, we arrive in a Paris dominated by a preposterous arrow poking the sky— the Eiffel Tower, the tallest building in the world. It is 1891: Maria Slodowska (later Marie Curie) enrolls in the Sorbonne, Paul Gauguin disembarks in Tahiti, and the city bubbles with wonders, such as this: in a hotel, for a few coins, you can pick up the *théâtrophone* to listen to live music in the Ópera. Let us alight now, and peer in a window as young Madero pulls down a magazine, falls into a chair, and begins to thumb through it with rising astonishment.

Nineteen years old, Madero has been educated by the Jesuits in Saltillo; briefly, St. Mary's College near Baltimore; more rigorously, the Lycée in Versailles, and now, in the École des Hautes Études Commerciales where, in his words:

> One not only studies accounting and short-hand... but very interesting studies of commodities, methods of manufacturing all kinds of things, the most modern machines and apparatuses, the places one can find raw materials, markets for manufactured goods, pricing costs and, in general, whatever information could interest a person who would like to set up an industrial or mercantile business. Furthermore... [there are] very complete courses on Political Economy, Commercial Geography, Applied Mathematics, and all kinds of financial operations; the Civil and Commercial Code; Fiscal Legislation...

He is the oldest of sixteen children and grandson of a wizard of capitalism whose far-flung interests range from ranching and banking to cotton, wine making, textiles and trading. In the early 1880s he had served as governor of the state of Coahuila.

This still vigorous norteño grandfather who had formed, in the words of his biographer, Manuel Guerra de Luna, "one of the most prestigious and wealthiest families in the history of Mexico," was Don Evaristo Madero: a bull-necked patriarch of such Brobdingnabian standing that for any heir to flourish outside his shadow would have called for a most original and more than formidable personality—which we know Francisco I. Madero did have, to his grandfather's dying consternation.

Though aristocratic titles had been abolished along with Maximilian's reign in 1867, it could be said that what we have here, thumbing through his father's copy of *La Revue spirite*, is a Mexican prince.

And speaking of Mexican princes (trust me, I'm going somewhere with this), let us return for a moment to Agustín de Iturbide y Green, that toddler Maximilian von Habsburg had wrested from his parents back in 1865. As Madero would have read in the news from Mexico, Iturbide y Green spent 1891 in jail.

By this time, Iturbide was twenty-eight years old and an officer in the Mexican Cavalry. Tall, reddish-haired like his famous grandfather, "the Liberator," the erstwhile heir to the Mexican throne was very handsome and fluent in English, French, and Spanish, having been educated in Belgium, and England, and at Georgetown University in Washington, D.C., where his mother's was one of the "old families," descended from Revolutionary War hero General Uriah Forrest and Governor Plater of Maryland.

Scandal-plagued and ephemeral as it was, Agustín de Iturbide y Green's embrace by the court of Maximilian lent him cachet with the portion of Mexican society that remained sympathetic to the Catholic monarchist cause and spellbound by even the faintest perfume of royalty, as even many Liberals were. In sum, any American newspaperman visiting Mexico was sure to want an interview—in fact, after his visit to Mexico in the early 1880s, to scout for railroad investors, John Bigelow himself published a profile of young Iturbide for *Harper's New*

*Monthly Magazine.* But all that said, many Mexicans, especially Mexico's dictator, Porfirio Díaz, nurtured vivid memories of the cruelties of the French *contreguerrilla* and the blood-soaked battles to crush Maximilian's empire, and they viewed the likes of "Prince" Iturbide with a gimlet eye.

I discovered young Iturbide y Green's dangerous penchant for speaking freely in the Matías Romero archive in Banco de México, many years ago on the hunt for different prey. For a letter-to-the-editor that criticized Porfirio Díaz, Iturbide y Green earned himself a court-martial and a year in prison. On his release from that Mexican jail, Iturbide y Green sailed for Washington, never to return. But the smoking crater of his article "Mexico Under President Díaz," published in the prestigious *North American Review* in 1894, provoked an anxious kerfuffle of correspondence among Romero, by then back in Washington as the head of the Mexican legation, Porfirio Díaz, and other high-level figures.

With the rhetorical elegance of the winner of Georgetown University's Merrick Debate Medal that he was, Iturbide y Green said that Porfirio Díaz had risen to power as chieftain of a band of *chinacos*, or bandits; that "general plunder [was] an essential feature in the government's policy"; and that foreign investors should not be fooled: millions "had been borrowed in European markets 'for the conversion of public debt,' 'for the liquidation of subventions,' for anything but the real purpose, which was to have an ample supply of funds for Caesarism." Díaz's reign was enforced by "money and murder"—murder most commonly in the authorities' heavy-handed application of the *Ley Fuga*, or fugitive law, which allowed them to shoot any prisoner attempting to escape. Iturbide y Green's article went on like a battering ram. "[T]he people think now that, under the present government, peace costs more than it is worth... A general feeling of impending collapse is noticeable throughout the country." But he concluded on a John-the-Baptist note: "I have implicit faith in the integrity of a new generation and, consequently, see in the approaching fall of Díaz the solution of our difficulties and an assurance of national prosperity."

Agustín de Iturbide y Green, as far as I could determine, never met Francisco Madero nor had anything to do with his 1910 Revolution. A devout Catholic, Iturbide remained in Washington, where 1910 would find him plagued by chronic tuberculosis of the bone and living a quiet life as a translator and professor of French and Spanish. I would like to call him the Mexican Revolution's John the Baptist, but that title, if someone must have it, more justly belongs to a Colegio Militar-trained topographical engineer, zealous anti-Porfirian and Spiritist named Lauro Aguirre.

Spiritism: we must leave that word, bright butterfly, in mid-air. And as for Paris, for just another moment, let us mute those carriage-wheels rumbling over the boulevard outside, freeze that page of *La Revue spirite* upright, in mid-turn, and leave young Madero, leaning forward in his seat, eyes dagger-fixed upon the next.

In this same year of 1891, in the Maderos' neighboring state of Chihuahua, in a valley of the rugged Sierra Madre, a half-starved village called Tomóchic erupts in gunfire. A furor spreads across the northwest as the rebels take up the banner of "La Santa Niña de Cabora," a mestiza folk saint and healer named Teresa Urrea. She is nineteen years old—born, as no one notices at the time, in the same month of the same year as both Francisco Madero and "Porfirito," the dictator's son. For her talents as a medium and healer, Teresa attracted a following of thousands—and the enthusiastic admiration of the leader of a nearby Spiritist circle, that same Lauro Aguirre, about whom we will hear more.

The governor of Chihuahua tried to paint the Tomochitecos as "Indians" and "bandits" (neither of which they were); and while they did insist they would obey no one but God and Teresita, as historian Paul Vanderwood details in his magnificently researched *The Power of God Against the Guns*, there was provocation in a town and region already polarized after consecutive years of drought. It took the Mexican army multiple confrontations and until the end of the following year to kill the rebels, along with many women and children, and pound and burn and altogether crush Tomóchic. As one of his own generals wrote Porfirio Díaz, "the true story of Tomóchic is horrible beyond belief; one could write a novel about each of its episodes."

Someone did write a novel about Tomóchic, signing himself "An Eyewitness," and it caused such a sensation in Mexico City when it appeared in installments in *El Demócrata* that Porfirio Díaz ordered the newspaper's editor and the suspected author, one Lieutenant Heriberto Frías, arrested and held incomunicado. The editor, Joaquín Clausell, took responsibility, claiming he had modeled *Tomóchic* after Émile Zola's *La Débâcle*, the international best-seller about the fall of Louis Napoleon. But the authorities, having rifled through his papers, suspected otherwise. The little hothouse of the Mexican literary world speculated, could the author be Zola himself? An edition of *Tomóchic* printed on the Texas side of the border, in Río Grande City, made its way to Mexico City bookstores where it went like proverbial hotcakes. Not until 1899 did the author—it was Heriberto Frías, now a journalist—reveal himself. But that was more than a decade before Porifirio Díaz would leave power. As Mexican historian Antonio Saborit writes, Frías "was the owner of a speaking mask that one day spoke under the name Heriberto Frías."

More than a century later, someone wrote a splendid novel about Teresita—her great-nephew, Luis Alberto Urrea, with *The Hummingbird's Daughter*. And at the 2009 Texas Book Fair in Austin, in the Senate Chamber, a weirdly cavernous venue, I found myself on a panel, as the author of *The Last Prince of the Mexican Empire*, with him.

As the saying goes, *México es un pañuelo*, Mexico is a handkerchief—that tiny.

But too, I think of a second meaning for that flash of white cloth: a magicians' prop. Nothing in Mexico is quite what it seems.

## Enter Allan Kardec, *Chef du Spiritisme*

Though an energetic evangelist, Francisco I. Madero schemed to conceal his Spiritism from the public—his personal letters during his presidential campaigns and his administration make this clear—and, over the several decades after his death, few Mexicans in public positions have had the incentive, the metaphysical context, or the wherewithal to begrudge more than a glancing mention of it. As early as 1915, any public discussion of Spiritism became taboo—historian Yolia Tortolero Cervantes uses this word, and quite rightly, even while Spiritism was being practiced "in secret by many public figures," as she also notes. There is more to say of this thundering silence about Spiritism in Mexico, which has persisted to this day with a very few notable exceptions, but to properly comprehend the term we must hie back to Paris of 1891. Reanimating our scene, we let that page of *La Revue spirite* fall. And—Francisco licks his thumb—another.

This magazine Madero is reading belongs to his father. His mother and other family members are Catholics and, as he surely knows, the Church had declared diabolical the main ritual of the Spiritists, the séance. Decades earlier, the Pope had slapped the works of Allan Kardec, founder of *La Revue spirite*, on the Vatican's Index Liborum Prohibitorum.

Allan Kardec: this elbow-sharp and magnetic nom de plume, supposedly taken from one of his other lifetimes as a Druid priest, belonged to a French educator named Hippolyte Léon Denizard Rivail, who died in 1869. From his stern-looking portrait, with his knob-chin and kingly pose, one might take Monsieur Rivail for a mightily conservative banker. "Kardec" was an unlikely guru. According to his English translator, Anna Blackwell, he was "grave, slow of speech, unassuming in manner, yet not without a certain quiet dignity." Further, and somewhat frighteningly, "he was never known to laugh." Yet anyone who doubts his influence can visit Paris's Père La Chaise cemetery and find, among the stone angels and sarcophagi and mausoleums of the likes of Chopin, Collette, Victor Hugo, La Fontaine and Molière, Kardec's megalithic tomb ever-heaped with flowers.

Rivail had been educated by the Swiss Johann Heinrich Pestalozzi, who, radically for the time, emphasized freedom of thought and direct observation. According to John Warne Monroe in *Laboratories of Faith: Mesmerism, Spiritism, and Occultism in Modern France*, Rivail had been a longtime student of Mesmerism when in 1853 he learned of the baffling phenomenon of the *tables parlantes* or table tipping, from a friend who said he had managed to induce a table to lift itself off the ground and turn, and more: like the Fox sisters of Hydesville, he was communicating with spirits through the table by means of raps and knocks.

Though skeptical, Rivail determined to study this phenomenon. He soon moved on to observing mediumistic writing, in which two young mediums, Caroline and Julie Baudin, would place their fingertips on a planchette, a triangular contraption with little wheels and an attached pencil, thus allowing spirits to answer his questions in writing.

It was the spirit "Zéphyr" who assigned him the name Allan Kardec, and, along with other spirits, gave him such a mass of teachings to solve "the controversial problem of humanity's past and future," that Rivail turned them into a book—with additional information channeled by medium Célina Japhet. When the *Le Livre des Esprits* (*The Book of the Spirits*), was published in 1857, it became a best-seller, was translated into multiple languages, and—rare fate for any book—is still in print more than 150 years later.

With easy-to-reference numbered questions and answers, *The Book of the Spirits* purports to be a guide to nothing less than the universe and its laws, the nature of God, the spirit world, and its relations with humanity. The concluding message, channeled from the spirit of Saint Augustine, calls for kindness and benevolence. It is this work that first spelled out the doctrine of Spiritism, as a doctrine based on the specific nature of relations between the physical and spirit worlds, which Kardec distinguishes from Spiritualism—according to him, simply the belief that there is more than physical matter. Spiritism's most notable departure from nineteenth century Anglo-American Spiritualism is its assertion that spirits reincarnate—in life after life, whether on Earth or some other planet—as they evolve into ever greater states of consciousness.

Spiritism was the most modern of modern science, Kardec argued, for, as a scientist might peer through a microscope to perceive the detail in a leaf, so he could employ a medium to hear from the spirit world. Through Ermance Dufaux, a teenaged medium famous for her channeled autobiography of Joan of Arc, a nameless spirit instructed Kardec to publish *La Revue spirite* as soon as possible and using his own money and so he did in 1858. In 1861, Kardec published *Le Livre des Médiums* (*The Book on Mediums*), a how-to and advisory on the dangers of communicating with spirits based on his own and others' experiences, as well as more material channeled from spirits, among them, Erastrus, Channing, and Spirit of Truth. More followed: *The Gospel Explained by Spirits* (1864); *Heaven and Hell* (1865); and *Genesis* (1867). This was the stack of books that young Madero, having finished with *La Revue spirite*, ran to that magazine's offices to purchase. In his own words:

> I did not read [Kardec's] books; I devoured them, for their doctrines were so rational, so beautiful, so new, they seduced me and ever since I consider myself a Spiritist.

In other words, Madero believed he had incarnated on this planet in order to help usher in a golden age, evangelist for the doctrine that was nothing less than, to quote Kardec in *Genesis*, "the pivot on which the human race will turn."

### Foment Between Kardec's Passing and Madero's Arrival on the Metaphysical Scene

So the story that Francisco I. Madero found Spiritism in France is not simple. First, as we have seen, Spiritism itself cannot be fully grasped outside the context of developments in the Burned-Over District, which itself has a deep network of roots in Andrew Jackson Davis and Emanuel Swedenborg's works, and in a tangle of concepts and influences extending from American Spiritualism back to the Renaissance and into blurriest antiquity. Toss in newfangled ideas of evolution; a dash of Comptean Positivism (which Compte's followers would have sniffed at, but let's take a flying pole-vault over that for now); Romantic, Socialist and Gnostic ideas; and Mesmerist notions of invisible bodies and "fluids."

As for Spiritism, its father had many children. In addition to members of uncounted private circles, one early convert in 1861 was Camille Flammarion, a leading astronomer and popular science writer. After reading Kardec's *Le Livre des Esprits*, Flammarion attended a séance in which, he believed, a spirit who called himself Balthazar raised a table to hang in midair. In *Laboratories of Faith*, Monroe quotes from Flammarion's letter to his confessor dated that same year, "I am in intimate relations with spirits who have already lived on Earth, particularly Galileo and Fénelon...." The following year, Flammarion would publish *Les Habitants de l'autre monde, révélations d'autre-tombe*, a book I found in Francisco Madero's personal library.

Kardec's successor was Pierre-Gaëtan Leymarie, a left-leaning tailor and medium Monroe describes as "an exuberant, pugnacious activist." With the blessing of Kardec's widow, Leymarie took over the publishing of Kardec's books and *La Revue spirite*. Unfortunately Leymarie also became a promoter of "spirit photography," the foremost purveyor of which, one Édouard Buguet, soon confessed his methods to the police. After a sensational trial, both Leymarie and Buguet were condemned to a year in prison for *escroquerie*, a species of fraud.

Nearing the turn of the century, as Madero arrives on the scene, the chief personalities in French Spiritism become Léon Denis, the "Apostle of Spiritism," author of *Pourquoi la vie?* and *Après la mort*, and Gabriel Delanne, an engineer and enthusiastic researcher who launched a new journal, *Le Spiritisme*, in 1883, and a book, *Le Spiritisme devant la science*, in 1885. These were Madero's contemporaries. (Indeed, Madero corresponded with Denis and together with his father, Francisco Madero, sponsored the publication of the 1906 Spanish translation of his book as *Después de la muerte*. The translator, who signed himself "un estadista mexicano" was Ignacio Mariscal, one of the most distinguished diplomats, intellectuals and literary translators of nineteenth century Mexico, and who was then serving as Secretary of Foreign Relations.) As Madero begins publishing his pseudonymous articles and the *Manual espírita*, both Denis and Delanne continue to publish on, past Madero's demise, into the third decade of the twentieth century.

A new generation of mediums appeared, books were written and books were translated, people traveled, people talked. In 1879, Spiritualists established their summer camp, Lily Dale Assembly, south of Buffalo, New York—Burned-Over District, to be sure—and this soon became the Mecca for the American Spiritualist community. The late nineteenth century was the heyday of mediums such as the English writing medium William Stainton Moses, and the American Dr. James Martin Peebles, a staggeringly prolific author, friend to Walt Whitman and Ralph Waldo Emerson, and peripatetic Spiritualist lecturer. (Moses's *Enseignment spiritualists*, the French translation of his *Spirit Teachings*, and Peebles' *Seers of the Ages: Embracing Spiritualism Past and Present*, are both in Madero's library.) And many proponents of Spiritualism, long associated with Abolitionism, also took up the banner for Suffragism—notably, Victoria Woodhull, who was the first female candidate for President of the United States in 1872.

Mystics difficult to categorize emerged, such as the French musical historian and playwright Édouard Schuré, who would become a close collaborator of Rudolph Steiner. Steiner, once free of the Theosophists, founded Anthroposophy and the Waldorf Schools. Through Marguerita Albana Mignaty, a Greek medium, Schuré gathered the material for his 1889 opus—still in print—*Les Grands initiés: esquisse de l'histoire secrète des religions*, those "great initiates" being Rama, Krishna, Hermes, Moses, Orpheus, Pythagorus, Plato, and Jesus. This, too, I found in Madero's personal library, and echoes of it ring through his *Manual espírita*.

Now we must pay our visit to Madame Blavatsky, a cigar-smoking Russian noblewoman... whom we find, in 1891, alas, having just expired of the flu in London. So let us wind back the clock to 1875, to glimpse her in Ithaca—heart of the Burned-Over District—ensconced in the book-lined home of a Cornell University professor, busy at work on her first bombshell of a book, *Isis Unveiled*. An intriguing image. Let us frame that, leave it propped on our metaphorical mantel piece, and proceed.

### Madame Blavatsky, Messenger from the Mahatmas

As Madero's grandfather, Don Evaristo, cast his massive shadow over northern Mexico, so Helena Petrovna Blavatsky cast hers over the metaphysically-minded Western civilization of Europe, England, Australia, and the Americas, for she was the monumental figure of modern esotericism. (Not that that those two ever met. I am quite sure that if they had, any crockery in the vicinity would have exploded.)

"The greatest pythoness of the age," as Henry Ridgely Evans called her, was obese and her eyes bulged. She swore like a stevedore, her tobacco was cheap, and the flower pots around her piled up with stubs. Madame Blavatsky had left her husband in Russia, first breaking a candlestick over his head. Before arriving to settle for a spell in New York, she traveled to Central America, all over Europe, several times to Egypt (where, among other exploits, she disguised herself as a Muslim man and studied Coptic magic), and twice trekked into Tibet, where, she said, she attended a secret school led by enlightened sages called "Mahatmas," or "Great White Brothers." After her return to the West, she claimed to remain in telepathic communication with the Mahatmas. Moreover, these sages of astounding longevity could travel anywhere in the universe in their astral bodies. Sometimes she transcribed their messages by "automatic writing" and sometimes their little letters "precipitated" from the ceiling.

Madame Blavatsky exuded a charisma impossible to fathom. Her presence seemed to occasion fires, raps, knocks, tables rising from the floor, and messages in golden ink from the Mahatmas dropping out of thin air. The Irish mystic William Quan Judge recalled "marvels wholly unexplainable on the theory of jugglery," including little orbs creeping over the furniture in her apartment in New York City. Once, as she sat in the parlor, a spoon flew into her hand all the way from the kitchen. In a word, Madame Blavatsky made Cagliostro look like a pipsqueak and Monsieur Kardec, for all his spirit world adventures via teenaged mediums, thoroughly bourgeois.

For Madame Blavatsky, there were higher truths than Christianity and Spiritualism and its Johnny-come-lately offshoot, Spiritism. The Orient, wellspring of Buddhism and Hinduism, was the authentic source of spiritual knowledge.

Now, to take an orbit-worthy leap over novel-length episodes—among them, Blavatsky's meeting with Col. Henry Steel Olcott in the Vermont farmhouse of the Eddy brothers, mediums who brought forth such shades of the dead as a giant Winnebago chief, a squaw with her pet flying squirrel, and a naval officer in full dress with a sword—Blavatsky, Olcott, and William Quan Judge founded the Theosophical Society in New York in 1875. Not a religion, it was an association to promote religious universality, and that included Buddhism and

Hinduism—which, as one might imagine, did not endear them to Christian missionaries and many of the colonial authorities.

Madero never considered himself a Theosophist, but like many outstanding figures we remember today—from inventor Thomas Alva Edison to novelist D.H. Lawrence to the leader of India's independence movement, Mohandas Gandhi—he was influenced by Madame Blavatsky, and, as we shall see in Madero's case especially—and crucially—by the Theosophists' enthusiasm for the Hindu wisdom book, the Bhagavad-Gita.

Blavatsky affirms that her first book, *Isis Unveiled,* published in 1877, was inspired by the Mahatmas. She professes it to be, as the subtitle says, the Master-Key to the Mysteries of Ancient and Modern Science and Theology. A decade later, in 1888, after she and Olcott had stirred up a Buddhist revival in Ceylon and removed the headquarters of the Theosophical Society to Adyar, near Madras in India, Blavatsky published her two volume *The Secret Doctrine,* also still in print, which provides the spiritual history of the cosmos and human life based on the stanzas of the Book of *Dzyan.* The first:

> THE ETERNAL PARENT (SPACE), WRAPPED IN
> HER EVER INVISIBLE ROBES, HAD SLUMBERED
> ONCE AGAIN FOR SEVEN ETERNITIES.

And another, number 40, plucked at random:

> THEN THE THIRD AND FOURTH (RACES)
> BECAME TALL WITH PRIDE. WE ARE THE
> KINGS, IT WAS SAID; WE ARE THE GODS.

No one had heard of the *Dzyan,* nor has any scholar yet found it. Blavatsky claimed that it was part of the ancient commentary esoteric literature of Tibetan Buddhism and that she had memorized the stanzas as given to by her teacher in North India and Tibet, where she first arrived in the 1850s. That she, a European woman traveling solo, made it into Tibet at all might sound preposterous if not for the fact that, among other sightings, one Captain Charles Murray of the Bengal Army encountered her on the Sikkim border.

Leopold Fischer, aka Agehananda Bharati, the Syracuse University anthropologist and Sanskritist, called Blavatsky's magnum opus "a melee of horrendous hogwash." Yet according to Michael Gomes, editor of the abridged version of *The Secret Doctrine*, esoteric scholars have noted similarities of these stanzas to the literature of the Kalachakra, or "Wheel of Time," the ancient Tibetan Buddhist esoteric scripture blending Hindu and Buddhist ideas. And the Kalachakra is a living idea. A quick Google search brought up a lengthy discussion by His Holiness the Dalai Lama on his website and a video tour of the fabulously intricate three-dimensional structure of the Kalachakra Mandala, a visual representation of the teachings made in honor of the Dalai Lama's 2007 visit to Cornell University. With the low-voiced chanting and clanging, it is wonderfully mesmerizing.

What to conclude about Blavatsky's *Dzyan?* I am not planning to get a PhD in Tibetan Buddhist studies (not in this lifetime anyway), but I can stretch so far as to agree with Gomes, who concludes that, "[f]act or fiction, the stanzas [of the *Dzyan*] provide one of the greatest mythos of our time, whose influence on modern esotericism is undeniable."

### Heavy Weather

The Pope continued to rail against Spiritualism and Spiritism and now these Oriental "cults" and "superstitions" and the whole bubbling pot of ever-spicier heterodoxy (add ¾ teaspoon of occult Freemasonry and continue to stir). But never mind the objections of the Church of Rome, the thousands of followers as the Spiritualists and Spiritists and Theosophists may have had, and the cartloads of books and magazines that may have been sold; for many of the less-than-fervently-religious of the

Western world, these philosophies and "spirit" communications and multitudinous bizarre phenomena made too atavistic a pudding to digest.

This, the nineteenth century, was the modern world: rational, material.

But what was modern and what was rational? And what was the true nature and context of the material world? (What did it mean that there were phenomena such as electricity and ultraviolet light, which we can measure but not see with our eyes?)

Allan Kardec was not the only one fascinated by the possibilities of spirit communication who immersed himself in research that he, an important educator of his time, considered scientific. Indeed, Spiritists call their philosophy both a religion and a science.

The exploits of mediums such as the Fox sisters, D.D. Home, the Eddy Brothers, and later in the nineteenth century, prim Leonora Piper (channel for the long-dead "Dr Phinuit" and the mysterious "Imperator"), and wild Eusapia Palladino (whose séances featured billowing curtains, floating mandolins and, popping out of the dark, ectoplasmic hands), spurred the studies of investigators, journalists and a small group of elite scientists. Noted German, Italian, and French scientists, such as Nobel prize-winning physiologist Charles Richet undertook the examination of these anomalous phenomena, but the British Society for Psychical Research, founded in 1882, and the American Society for Psychical Research founded three years later, led the fray. Though their ranks included leading scientists such as chemist William Crookes, naturalist Alfred Russel Wallace, physicist Oliver Lodge, and William James (the Harvard University professor considered the father of psychology), their research almost invariably met not with celebration, nor curiosity on the part of their fellow academics, but ridicule, often to the point of personal slander.

Mediums, scoffed most scientists, were "vulgar tricksters," maestros of inflatable bladders, wire dummies, trick mirrors, and muslin painted with phosphorous to create the shiny extrusions of what Charles Richet termed "ectoplasm." As for the personal information mediums imparted from the so-called spirits of the dead, surely those fraudsters preying on the bereaved had hired children to listen at the keyhole, detectives to steam open letters, oh, and they placed shills in every audience. "Spirit photography" and "slate writing"? Henry Ridgely Evans showed how that was done, illustrations and all, in *Hours with Ghosts or Nineteenth Century Witchcraft*. Rope tricks? Harry Houdini learned a thing or two from the Davenport Brothers.

I have already mentioned that in 1875, Kardec's successor Pierre-Gaëtan Leymarie and photographer Édouard Buguet were jailed for fraud. This was two years after the fall of Louis Napoleon (following the catastrophe of his Mexican adventure, his army had been crushed by the Prussians at Sedan). As Monroe notes in *Laboratories of Faith*, "Leymarie and Buguet failed to comprehend the change in political and social climate that had begun after the tumult of the Commune and intensified with the rise of the Government of Moral Order." To the new and on-their-toes authorities, Spiritism was a dangerously well-organized anti-Catholic cult. Shortly after a large gathering at Kardec's tomb, police officers arrived at Buguet's atelier, compelled him to confess and show them his secret stash of dummies, old photographs, and gauze for his preliminary exposures on which portraits of his customers could be superimposed (thus yielding, for example, the widow of Allan Kardec next to the wraith-like image of her departed husband). Yet Buguet recanted his confession, and at the trial, Leymarie and the parade of his fellow Spiritists, among them lawyers and engineers, continued to insist that spirit photography was real! The prosecutors concluded that Spiritism is evidence of insanity. Furthermore, reported the controller general, "Spiritism and absinthe cruelly ravage democracy."

In 1888, Maggie Fox Kane, one of the Fox sisters of Hydesville, sinking fast into alcoholism and drug addiction, accepted payment from the *New York World* for her confession that the now world-famous show of rappings in her family's cottage back in 1848 had been a hoax; she and her sister Kate, in cahoots, were ventriloquist knucklecrackers. But a year later, to the Spiritualist's *Banner of Light*, Maggie lamented, "would to God I could undo the injustice I did the cause of Spiritualism." She had lied, she said, because a Catholic priest told her that mediumship was the work of the devil and besides, she needed the money, and, moreover, she had been enthralled by an incubus. Maggie would die in 1893, alone in a New York tenement house. Her sister Kate fared no better, also dead in her 50s, of complications of alcoholism. The Spiritualists would rescue the Fox cottage, rebuilding it as a shrine of pilgrimage at Lily Dale, but the Fox sisters' blow to their cause was a grave one.

As for attitudes toward psychical phenomena in the latter half of the nineteenth century and into the early twentieth, both in and outside the academy, behold the crossfire of rotten tomatoes, flaming arrows, grenades:

> "It's absolutely absurd, but it's true!"
> —*Charles Richet, Faculty of Medicine, Paris*

> "Dante's motto must be inscribed over any investigation of Spiritualism and all hope must be abandoned by those who enter on it."
> —*Howard Furness, University of Pennsylvania*

> "Outside our scientific knowledge there exists a Force exercised by intelligence differing from the ordinary intelligence common to mortals."
> —*William Crookes, as President of the British Association for the Advancement of Science*

> "No scientifically-minded psychologist believes in telepathy"
> —*Edward Titchener, Cornell University*

"[M]ental telegraphy is not a jest, but a fact,
and...it is a thing not rare but exceedingly
common."
—*Mark Twain*

"Spiritism and Occultism in particular have
already claimed too many victims, and I imagine that it will become almost the duty of an
alienist to intervene in accordance with public
powers in the effort to achieve the prohibition
of all manifestations of this type."
—*Paul Duhem, a doctor at the sanatorium of
Boulohnesur-Seine (as quoted in Brower)*

As the saying goes, open your mind too wide and your brains
might fall out. But the opposite also holds true: close your
mind too tight, and whatever is in there will fester in the dark.
And in the dark, it's easier to feel afraid—and not so much of
ghosts and, say, astral wildlife, but of what is for most people
that most agonizing of tortures: to be shamed as a fool, or
worse, a lunatic.

Recently, I happened upon an article in the on-line *New
York Times* (Green 6/5/13) about a New Age "space clearer,"
someone who takes a fee to come into a home and brighten
up the energy with chants and tinkling bells and whatnot.
Though I was surprised that such a newspaper would run such
a sympathetic piece, the comments, bashing hammers, could
have come straight out of the 1880s apropos of the Fox sisters:

As P.T. Barnum said, "There's a sucker born
every minute."

I'm ashamed of myself to have read this article
in its entirety!

Total waste of money. Like believing in angels.

Interesting. Is your wallet thinner now?

Our fearless young Coahuilan prince is going to cross paths with some characters, a battle-hardened Porfirian general and a cock-sure American ambassador among them, who would have heartily applauded such contempt. And for them, a world was at stake, and their arsenals included more than sticks and stones.

I think William James took the most balanced stance so as far as the words of nineteenth century scientists speaking on psychic research go, I'll give him the last one: "If you wish to upset the law that all crows are black, you mustn't seek to show that no crows are; it is enough if you prove one single crow to be white." And indeed, while many purveyors of the supernatural have been caught cheating, there are many "white crows," genuinely anomalous phenomena and for anyone who troubles to look, a mass of published documentation about them. Among present-day researchers, Stanford University professor of physics William Tiller, who researches what he calls psychoenergetics, British biologist Rupert Sheldrake who researches his hypothesized "morphic fields," and the late Harvard Medical School's John Mack, best-known for his work with hundreds of patients claiming to have been abducted by aliens, have all been on the butt-end of a reception not unlike that which their nineteenth century colleagues received. This zooms us into the twenty-first century, however, beyond our itinerary. Young Madero is tapping his foot rather loudly, so at last we breeze on—trailing the little flag of a comment that, like his fellow Spiritists, Madero considered research into spirit communication, spirit photography, and other anomalous phenomena both valid and urgent, and by the way, for those wishing to delve deeper into the history of nineteenth century psychical research, a very weird swamp to wade through, a batch of well-researched books are:

Deborah Blum's *Ghost Hunters: William James and the Search for Scientific Proof of Life After Death*;

Janet Oppenheim's *The Other World: Spiritualism and Psychical Research in England, 1850-1914*;

M. Brady Brower's *Unruly Spirits: The Science of Psychic Phenomena in Modern France*;

Sofie Lachapelle's *Investigating the Supernatural: From Spiritism and Occultism to Psychical Research and Metaphysics in France, 1853-1931.*

## Between Public Image and Political Action or, Yucky Chunks of Cognitive Dissonance

So what did Madero do between 1893, when he arrived home in Parras de la Fuente, Coahuila, and 1910, when he risked everything to launch his first presidential campaign and, later that year, the Revolution? As we shall see, his every move was motivated by his Spiritism and even precise messages he believed he received from the dead. Official and mainstream history gloss over or altogether ignore the awkwardness and, for many Mexicans, the sheer creepiness of his Spiritism. The fancy term for this discomfort that causes willful blindness is "cognitive dissonance." For many, it simply does not chime that an educated man could be sane and at the same time believe in tables rising from the floor without human agency or hearing messages from invisible entities. Then as now, someone who claims he hears voices telling him that he has "a great destiny" is more likely to end up in a padded room than the presidential office.

In 2012, I visited a show in Mexico's National Museum of History in Chapultepec Castle, *Francisco I. Madero, entre imagen pública y acción política, 1901-1913.* Its several commodious salons featured posters, letters, photographs, medals, artifacts of all kinds. As far as I recall, only one case displayed a few cartoons circa 1910-1913 of President Madero as a medium—rumored even then—and the only other evidence of Madero's Spiritism I could find was a pair of framed letters, hung in the least advantageous place, the wall behind the entrance. For a long while I watched the incoming stream of tourists and teachers leading gaggles of students. Not a single person paused to look at those letters. If they had, they would have had to squint to read the label indicating that the letters were from Madero's brother Raúl.

Madero actually had two younger brothers named Raúl. One fought by his side in the 1910 Revolution, became governor of the state of Coahuila from 1957 to 1963, and died in Mexico City in 1982. The other died as a toddler. Playing with a reed, he brushed a kerosene lamp off the wall; it fell on him and his clothes caught fire. It was the latter Raúl, a spirit that had apparently matured and become far-seeing on the Other Side, whom Francisco Madero believed he was channeling, writing down his messages—sometimes loving, sometimes chiding—of moral and dietary instruction. (Later, a spirit who called himself José took over with messages of encouragement and direction for his political endeavors.)

By the time I bought my ticket for that show in Chapultepec Castle, I had finished my translation of the *Manual espírita*, having bushwacked through such sticky wickets as the manipulation of magnetic fluids, astral projection, and interplanetary reincarnation (not to mention having dug out obscure verses from the Douay-Rheims version of the Bible, and scratched my head over which of the many translations of the Bhagavad-Gita to consult). In the stop-and-start process of working through my own cognitive dissonance in trying to give this strange little book an introduction, I had amassed a library on Madero, the Mexican Revolution, Spiritism and metaphysics. Thanks to the Ministry of Finance archivist, I also had in my possession a CD with copies of the communications supposedly from his little brother Raúl and the other spirits Madero had scribbled down while in a trance. I was not in a hurry to look at them. Neither had I made the walking-distance trip from my house to the Centro de Estudios de Historia de México CARSO in Chimalistac, where, as historian Manuel Guerra de Luna had urged me to do, I could consult Francisco I. Madero's personal library.

I realize now my procrastination was not laziness; I needed to come at Madero's Spiritism elliptically, to slide in, not crash into a brick wall of easy conclusions. As a translator and a writer, I wanted to treat the author and his book with dignity, and for that I needed time—time to read, time to reflect, time to chip away at my cognitive dissonance. That is to say, I wanted to quit squinting and look at things openly and clearly.

Cognitive dissonance: I certainly was not alone. Before delving into all the esoteric literature, the Swedenborg, Kardec, Madame Blavatsky, et al, I had read Stanley R. Ross's 1955 biography, *Francisco I. Madero: Apostle of Mexican Democracy*, which sums up the nature and influence of Madero's spiritual philosophy on his political career in the space of only a few pages (the *Manual espírita* itself rating a single sentence in a footnote). Highlighter in hand, I worked my way through John Mason Hart's *Revolutionary Mexico: The Coming and Process of the Mexican Revolution*, a tour de force now in its tenth edition, which is even more reticent about Madero's Spiritism. (Though of course, the Mexican Revolution, fought by uncounted thousands of people over several years, had other causes than one man's Spiritism, and Hart's is the best introduction to those.) And though I sincerely salaam the great professor Friedrich Katz, it does strike me as remarkable that in the chapter "Origins, Outbreak, and Initial Phase of the Revolution of 1910" of his *The Secret War in Mexico*, we learn that Madero was "a spiritualist [sic]" with nary a word more in that direction. One popular university press textbook even describes Madero as an atheist!

I polled my Mexican friends, all well-versed in the history of their country. Spiritism? Most drew a blank. *(Is that something to do with Amy Semple McPherson?)* Madame Blavatsky? *(Madame Who?)*

The Revolution forged modern Mexico—I don't know any Mexican who would disagree. The sunless abyss into which had fallen something so basic to understanding the Revolution as the philosophy that prompted and shaped the actions of the man who launched it began to seem ominous to me.

I know what it takes to write a book. It is easy to come up with an idea, but to sit down and write hour after hour, day after day, and then to marshal the fortitude to send it out into the world, is only possible when you have a passion, a coal-fire knowledge that you *have* to do this. And for Madero to have written the *Manual espírita* in the frantic flurry of 1910, the year of his presidential campaign and the Revolution itself? The *Manual espírita*, published in early 1911, and the Revolution declared by Madero's Plan de San Luis Potosí on November 20, 1910, are intimately connected, each the elephant in the room of the other.

It turns out that while I may be the first to translate Madero's *Manual espírita*, I am not the first to write about his Spiritism. Madero did leave testimony for the public, a memoir of a few pages, first published in the *Anales del Museo Nacional de Arqueología, Historia y Etnografía*, in 1922 (good luck finding that—by the way, it is reprinted in his *Epistolario* of 1985 and *Obras Completas*, edited by Alejandro Rosas Robles in 2000). During Madero's presidency, gossip about his Spiritism was rife in Mexico City society and diplomatic circles, and newspapers relished printing caricatures of him as a medium. A typical example of 1911 (reproduced in Tortolero Cervantes), shows a seated Madero, tipping a table toward himself, and looming behind him, a phantom with an insect's antennae and a Turk's curly-toed slippers:

> Why is it that when I evoke the spirits of Richelieu, of Bismarck or Gladstone, so that they may enlighten me in politics, this naughty table gives me Mephistopheles?

> I must give up Spiritism, give up politics, give
> up the table and give up everything, all of it,
> except the little golden chair in which I feel
> so comfortable.

José Juan Tablada's 1910 play, *Madero Chanticler*, which portrayed Madero invoking the spirits, caused some uproar, and in Mexico City high society, jealous at the loss of its preeminence, there was malicious and often absurdly exaggerated gossip about his Spiritism—and about his wife—but anyone with two minutes of experience in Mexican politics would have known to discount that. Even many of his closest supporters disbelieved that Madero was a Spiritist.

José Vasconcelos, a towering figure in twentieth century Mexican intellectual history, an early political collaborator of Madero's and the author of *Estudios indostánicos,* (Hindu Studies) which includes some of Madero's commentary on the Bhagavad-Gita, said (quoted in Tortolero Cervantes):

> I dealt with Madero frequently in the last
> three years of his short life and, in fact, we
> would often discuss philosophical subjects
> and I never heard him take the Spiritist credo
> seriously, nor even mention it.

(I am not the only one to find that a bit of a stretch however, for in his autobiography, *Ulises Criollo*, Vasconcelos tells us that Madero had discussed the Bhagavad-Gita with him and confided that he would like to go India to study philosophy.)

Not until 1960, nearly half a century after Madero's death, with José C. Valadés's *Imaginación y realidad de Francisco I. Madero*, was a brief overview of Madero's Spiritist activities made available in print. Thirteen years later, José Natividad Rosales published a slender paperback of Madero's letters and channellings, aimed at the mass market (the back cover features an advertisement for *La vida erótica y criminal de los Borgia*).

In 1978 (obscurely, for I have yet to find a copy of this edition), Gustavo de Anda reprinted the *Manual espírita*, as did Alejandro Rosas Robles in 2000 in the 10 volume *Obras completas de Francisco Ignacio Madero*, and the state of Quintana Roo in a small edition, *La Revolución espiritual de Madero*, of that same year. Nonetheless, the fact remains that after Madero's assassination in 1913, more than seven decades went by before any major historian addressed Madero's Spiritism in depth and seriousness. That was Enrique Krauze, with *Francisco I. Madero: Místico de la libertad*, published by Mexico's prestigious Fondo de Cultura Económica in 1987. In a relatively brief text lavishly interspersed with photographs, Krauze's book included some of the channelled messages Madero had recorded in his notebook, for example, this one from "José" (my translation):

> You bear an enormous responsibility. You have seen... the precipice your country is about to fall from. A coward you will be if you do not prevent it... You have been elected by your Heavenly Father to accomplish a great mission on earth... It is necessary that, for this divine cause, you sacrifice everything material, everything earthly, and dedicate all your efforts to its realization.

Two years later, when Ignacio Solares brought out his novel, *Madero, el otro,* it caused another sensation, though mainly in urban literary circles, for in reconstructing the inner life of the revolutionary hero, Solares delved into Madero's mystical beliefs, dreams, communications with the Other Side and his belief in his destiny—as, curiously, had been foretold in a séance when he was a teenager.

Not until 2003, ninety years after Madero's death, did we see the first in-depth examination of the Spiritist philosophy behind Madero's political decisions: Yolia Tortolero Cervantes's splendidly researched work based on her doctoral dissertation at El Colegio de México, *El espiritismo seduce a Francisco I. Madero*. More recently, Mexican historians Manuel Guerra de Luna, José Mariano Leyva, Álvaro Matute, Jean Meyer, Alejandro Rosas Robles, Antonio Saborit, José Manuel Villalpando, and others, have written and spoken to this issue. Guerra de Luna, author of the two volume biography of the family, *Los Madero: la saga liberal,* and the prologue to volume VI *Cuadernos espíritas* of the *Obras completas,* also wrote the screenplay for the 2006 documentary directed by Alejandro Fernández Solsona, "1910: La Revolución espírita," which was based on four years of research and filming in venues as distant as Allan Kardec's tomb in Paris, the École des Hautes Études Commerciales, Mexico City's National Palace, and the remote desert ranch and astronomical observatory called Australia where Madero retreated to perfect his psychic powers and confer with the spirits.

As I write these words in 2013, that is about the sum of what we have on Madero's Spiritism. Shining as some of these individual works are—Krauze's, Tortolero Cervantes's, Guerra de Luna's and Rosa's especially—for a figure of the stature of Madero, this seems to me surprisingly little and late.

To be fair, for most Mexicans, Madero's Spiritism is a hot-potato subject. After all, the current version of Spiritism includes examples in Mexico, but more famously in the Philippines and Brazil, where Kardecian Spiritism, melded with Catholic and folk and shamanic traditions, attracts not only local followings, but tourists who fly in from all over the world, many in wheelchairs, on crutches, and suffering from all manner of tumors, pains and paralyses, for healing services including "psychic surgery." In the Philippines, psychic surgeons have been filmed digging into a patient's body with their bare hands, bringing up bloody tumors and gobs of who-knows-what. Brazilian João de Deus, John of God, operating out of his Casa Dom Inacio Loyola in the village of Abadiana, south of Brasilia, is currently the most famous psychic surgeon. His signature technique is to thrust a kitchen knife between his patient's eye and eyelid or, say, up her nose. John of God also operates at a distance. In the summer of 2012, best-selling American self-help guru Wayne Dyer gave an interview to TV show host Oprah Winfrey about his long distance psychic surgery, in which, while he was in Hawaii, from Brazil, through John of God, spirit doctors "cut out" his leukemia. I am not making this up. The interview, I mean. From the video on Oprah's website:

> *Oprah:* So what you mean, you had the surgery?

> *Dyer:* Well, I was skeptical, but you know, when you have leukemia... and someone says...

> *Oprah (to the camera):* Stay with me, people! Because this is as woo woo... I know how, I know how this sounds. It sounds like, woooOOO, it sounds crazy!

I was trying to get my mind around such exotica when I found the books by Andrija Puharich, the Northwestern University-trained medical academic and inventor who drove his once-promising career off a cliff Evel Knievel-style with the publication of *Uri: A Journal of the Mystery of Uri Geller* in 1974. Geller is an Israeli psychic known for his prodigious spoon bending, friendship with the late pop star Michael Jackson, and, in the early 1970s, shepherded by Puharich, demonstrations of psychokinesis and telepathy at the Stanford Research Institute. In *Uri Geller,* Puharich recounted his and Uri's contacts with the disembodied voice of "Spectra," representing the extraterrestrial intelligence "Hoova"; UFO sightings of all sizes, shapes, and colors; time slips; teleporting pen cartridges, camera cases, and people; tape recordings made by invisible entities; and a transcript of communications from the cosmic beings who identified themselves as "The Nine," first channeled in "a deep sonorous voice" by an otherwise soft-spoken Indian mystic from Poona named Dr. Vinod.

> M calling: We are Nine Principles and Forces,
> personalities if you will, working in com-
> plete mutual implication. We are forces, and
> the nature of our work is to accentuate the
> positive, the evolutional, and the teleolog-
> ical aspects of existence... To be simple, we
> accentuate certain directions as will fulfill
> the destiny of creation.

Was Puharich a dupe, a novelist, or barking bonkers? Apart from conspiracy-mongers and the incurably gullible (which usually is to say the same thing), few have dared to consider any other alternative. *In Memories of a Maverick,* however, his ex-wife, H.G.M. Hermans, paints a portrait of a passionately dedicated scientific daredevil, who may have worked for and been hounded by more than one intelligence service.

Puharich had caught my interest because he also researched the Spiritist "psychic surgeons," in the 1960s, Ze Arigo in Brazil, and in Mexico in the 1970s, Bárbara Guerrero, aka Doña Pachita. And many Mexicans of my generation and older are familiar with her.

Pachita was only eight years old in 1907 when she and her adoptive father, an African American ex-slave, joined a circus, he as a roustabout, she, a high-wire acrobat. She began her career as a healer working on circus animals. At 18, she fought alongside Pancho Villa in the Revolution, and as a nurse on the battlefield, dug out bullets with her hunting knife. Called "one of the great shamans of Mexico" by Mexican scientist Jacobo Grinberg-Zylberbaum, Guerrero was the subject of his book, *Pachita.* For her psychic surgeries, powered, she said, by the Aztec king Cuauhtémoc, whom she fondly called "Hermanito," Doña Pachita favored her hunting knife.

According to Hermans, Puharich was losing his hearing from otosclerosis when he allowed Doña Pachita to operate on his ears. He recalled that she plunged her knife, all seven rusty inches of it, straight into his ear drum, and suddenly, he heard a roaring noise like a subway train. He allowed her to do the same on his other ear. She prescribed a daily application of some unspecified drops. The roaring in his ears continued after the surgery, decreasing a little every day for about a week, until it stopped and his hearing was painfully sharp for another two weeks. After one month, he said he had "normal pure tone hearing in both ears." Puharich's descriptions of Doña Pachita's organ transplants, including of a brain, are not for the squeamish.

I find this more fantastic than science fiction but neither have I forgotten that a friend of mine, who I am quite sure would not want his name mentioned, for he is a respected banker, once told me that he had been present at one of Doña Pachita's surgeries. It was real, he said, in the sense that somehow, she could sculpt the clay of reality itself.

It would be interesting to ask Dr. Grinberg-Zylberbaum what he thinks of all this today. But in 1994, as if into thin air, he disappeared.

Doña Pachita, however, is but one chapter of the 20th century story— the story into which we must fit Don Francisco Madero.

### El Niño Fidencio and *Una ventana al mundo invisible*

Anyone who explores heterodox Spiritism in 20th century Mexico comes to the enigma of José Fidencio Sintora Constantino, "El Niño Fidencio," who laughingly predicted his own sudden death in 1938. As a healer, Fidencio is far more famous than Doña Pachita and than his predecessor, Teresa Urrea, the "Santa de Cabora." Throughout northern Mexico and in U.S. Chicano communities in Texas and as far as Chicago and Seattle, it is not uncommon to see, right alongside those to Jesus, San Judas Tadeo (St. Jude Thaddeus), and the Virgin of Guadalupe, candles, pictures, and even elaborate plastic flower-draped altars dedicated to Fidencio. Called niño or "child," because of his high-pitched voice and gentle, playful nature, as a boy, Fidencio was taken underwing by a German-born Spiritist, Don Teodoro von Wernich, who recognized and encouraged his development as a mediumistic healer. As news of Fidencio's healing powers spread, increasing numbers of pilgrims arrived in his remote desert home in Espinazo, Nuevo León, so many that the place became a tent city, with its own post office, and far more substantial than Teresa Urrea's colossal gatherings, or *romerías* of Mayo Indians, Yaquis and mestizos all yearning for her magic touch, that had so disturbed the Porfirian authorities. The apogee of Fidencio's career came in 1928: President Plutarco Elías Calles, seeking healing for a skin ailment, pulled into Espinazo on his private train.

Espinazo was not in my travel plans, but I was able to visit from my armchair with Juan Farré's documentary, "Niño Fidencio: de Roma a Espinazo." Ancient ranch people, their voices slow, eyes rheumy, remembered Fidencio, contradicting each other about the color of his skin. One said the Niño cured President Calles by slathering him in honey. The camera panned slowly over the jars immortalizing the tumors the Niño had extracted using his specially-chosen pieces of broken glass. An old blind woman who had known Fidencio told the story of a boy who had been swimming in the ocean with two friends, and when the two were eaten by a whale, he was so shocked he could no longer speak. In Espinazo, Fidencio put him on a swing, pushing him so high he screamed and was cured. Another old woman said the Niño operated on cataracts using a razor blade. Another remembered that he fed the lepers boiled coyote and vulture, but they all died anyway.

More techniques: El Niño would smack people with an apple or a tejocote. On others he would sic his mountain lion, a declawed pet named Concha. He might climb up onto a swing, holding a paralytic close to his heart, and then, when the swing stopped, the man would walk—said one devotee.

The variety in Fidencio's repertoire seemed endless: plants and herbs and the Charquito, or "little puddle." In a sunny contemporary scene in the Charquito, men who might have been truck drivers (jeans, T-shirts), spread their arms wide and fell backwards; a circle of pilgrims, the water jostling above their knees, held hands, closed their eyes and prayed. Zombie-like men, women, children, hair and faces covered in mud, sloshed through the waist-high murk. Alongside the Charquito, to the pound of drums, Aztec dancers with headdresses of quetzal feathers and rattles on their ankles stomped and whirled. On the ground, a teenager held his elbows and slowly rolled, over and over, his T-shirt becoming yellower and yellower with the powdery dirt.

Fidencio, said another of the old timers, knew he was going to die. But he said, "Don't bury me right away because I am going to rise on the third day." With the news of his death, pilgrims rushed in from all over northern Mexico and parts beyond to witness the miracle. But their "saint" did not revive, or at least, not in the literal way they were expecting.

Some of the fidencistas believed they could now enter a trance and receive his spirit, so that, through them, the Niño could continue his work. These *materias*, or mediums, call themselves *cajitas*, or "little boxes," and they wear white robes trimmed in gold and capes the colors of popsicles. Their modus operandi is to stand close to their patient, a hand on his shoulder, and whisper into his ear words of compassion and instruction in Fidencio's babylike voice. I watched as they, too, shiny capes and all, waded into the Charquito. Someone dumped a bucket of mud over a child's head. More men fell backwards, stiff as planks, splash, into the chocolately soup.

The film's finale was rare footage, a scratchy black-and-white flickering, of Fidencio, from on high, pitching fruit at his followers; then, like a rock star, writhing over a mosh pit of their arms; everywhere arising from that carpet-like tangle of humanity, hands, more hands, hands like hungry spiders on his hair, his hip, his shoulder, his foot.

When imagery such as this is the first thing that comes to mind for many of Mexico's intellectual and political elite when Spiritism is mentioned, perhaps we can understand the desire to suppress or ignore the Spiritist beliefs of a national hero.

Francisco I. Madero was also a healer who ministered to those too poor to pay a doctor, many of whom might have been no different than the grandparents of those old ranch people in the movie about Fidencio. But no, he did not perform "psychic surgery" nor thrash around in a mud pit or chuck apples at anybody; Madero performed hands-on "magnetic" healing, hypnotism, which he apparently learned from French books, and homeopathy, a German doctor's innovation of treating illnesses with remedies of "like with like," tiny white sugar pills infused with extremely diluted substances. But Madero's true calling, as he understood it, was to heal the Mexican body politic.

When Madero finished with his studies in France and boarded his ship to Mexico, neither Fidencio nor Pachita had yet been born. Teresa Urrea, the "Santa de Cabora," heroine to the Tomochitecos, had just fled to Nogales, Arizona. Madero's fellow mystics would prove to be a more educated, more literary-minded type: among them, as already mentioned, Porfirio Díaz's own Secretary of Foreign Relations, Ignacio Mariscal.

And after Madero, a small but adventurous portion of Mexico's intellectual, political and scientific elite was dedicated to communicating with disembodied consciousnesses. I send interested readers to *Una ventana al mundo invisible* (A Window to the Invisible World), a now very rare book published in 1960 which contains the detailed records of dozens of séances held from 1940-1952 and lists of their participants—among them, both in life and as a spirit, Plutarco Elías Calles—for the Instituto Mexicano de Investigaciones Síquicas (Mexican Institute for Psychic Research).

Onward now to Madero's metaphysical odyssey. As you know, it is going to end in a slick of blood.

# THE LONG, LABYRINTHIAN, AND
# BOOK-STREWN ROAD TO AUSTRALIA

## From Paris to Parras

Abandoning the belle époque wonders of the Eiffel Tower, the *théâtrophone*, and Monsieur Leymarie's *biblioteque*, Madero took an academic year at the University of California, Berkeley, to study English and agricultural sciences. Then, in 1893, he arrived home to Parras de la Fuente, a farm town in northern Mexico, one of many oases in the nearly 300,000 square kilometer desert that stretches across the Río Grande into Arizona, New Mexico, and Texas, and south as far as Zacatecas and San Luis Potosí. Translation: Parras de la Fuente, which means "vines of the fountain," was the middle of nowhere. Parras and its environs were populated mainly by desperately poor mestizos, many of them seasonal peons and others in the Madero family's employ. But Parras boasted a sixteenth-century vineyard, an early seventeenth-century church with a churrigueresque altar, a wedding cake of a neoclassical palacio municipal, an electric plant and, thanks to Madero's grandfather, Don Evaristo, a major reservoir. For most, this was a bare-knuckled life in a sky-haunted place. For Francisco Madero and his brothers and sisters, the bubble of isolation from the larger world was easily popped with, say, a train trip to Mexico City.

Madero may have brought home to Parras, and two months later, to his new home in nearby San Pedro de las Colonias, a

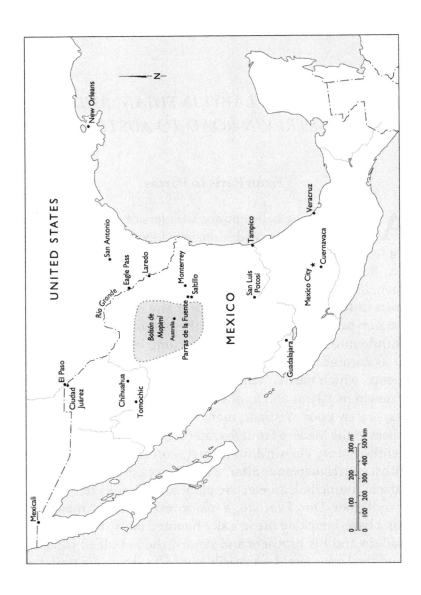

suitcase full of Spiritist literature, but Kardec's ideas had already sunk roots in Mexico, thanks in large part to translations by a Mexican general, Refugio I. González. How General González came upon Kardec's books is lost to the mists, but in *El ocaso de los espíritus,* a history of Mexican Spiritism in the nineteenth century, José Mariano Leyva makes a good argument that González, an officer in the Republican Army fighting the French Imperial Army, may have read Kardec's books while a prisoner of war. Neither is it known whether General González or any other Mexican had seen the first Spanish translation of one of Kardec's works, José María Fernández Colavida's *El libro de los espíritus,* published in Barcelona in 1863-64. (One or the possibly both of these translations must have arrived elsewhere in Latin America. Among the influenced: Cuban national hero José Martí, Nicaraguan poet Rubén Darío, Argentinian writer Leopoldo Lugones, Chilean naval hero Arturo Prat, and Carlos Paz Soldán, founder of Peru's Compañía Nacional Telegráfico.)

In 1872—the year before Madero's birth—General González published Kardec's *L'Évangile selon le spiritisme* (*The Gospels According to Spiritism*) as *El evangelio según el espiritismo.* That same year, under General González's direction, the Sociedad Espírita Central de la República Mexicana began publishing their magazines, *La Ilustración espírita* and *La Luz en México,* for evaluating mediumistic sessions. Spiritist circles cropped up in various cities; according to Leyva, *La Ilustración espírita* listed ten circles in Mexico City, five in Tacubaya (a suburb of Mexico City), three in Guadalajara, one each in Guanajuato, Monterrey, Tampico, Matamoros, Saltillo, and San Luís Potosí, in addition to five others in 1875. With names such as La Caridad (Charity), Jesucristo, Amar a Dios (To Love God), and Humildad y Fe (Humility and Faith), they proclaimed their Kardecian concern with Christian morals. In this landmark year when Madame Blavatsky, Col. Olcott and William Quan Judge founded the Theosophical Society, and Pierre-Gaëtan Leymarie and Édouard Buguet went to jail for the *escroquerie* of "spirit photography," the Liceo Hidalgo, a high school in

Mexico City, held a series of public debates between Spiritists and Positivists. As quoted in Tortolero Cervantes, a newspaper described the first day as a gathering of

> assorted ladies from the Spiritist Society, a crowd of students from the National Preparatory School, fervent defenders of the positivist theories of Stuart Mill and Auguste Compte, a large number of Spiritists and, finally, a phalange of poets, most of them spiritualists.

For those rusty on their nineteenth century philosophers, Compte (1798-1857) was considered the first philosopher of science in the modern sense. Until the first World War, he was enormously influential, not only in France, the rest of Western Europe, and the United States, but also in India, Turkey, and Latin America, primarily among educated elites avid to help their countries progress in education, democracy, and industry. One key Comptean idea was that morality need have nothing to do with the supernatural; any rational assertion could be scientifically tested or subjected to mathematical proof; therefore, Spiritism, and along with it the whole of metaphysics, could be swept into the dustbin of anachronisms.

On the first day of the debates, when a young Spiritist asserted that it was possible to demonstrate that his religion was a science, he might as well have jumped into a shark tank. Justo Sierra, one of the Porfiriato's preeminent jurists and educators, summed up the entire event as "so much useless noise."

But if Spiritism flowered in Mexico in the early 1870s, it began to wilt after those infamous debates. Its most zealous champion, General González, died in 1892. The idea, increasingly popular among alienists, that Spiritist beliefs in themselves were evidence of madness must have put a shiver down the back of anyone who might be tempted to entertain them (and another shiver to imagine the conditions inside the typical lunatic asylum). Moreover, by the 1890s, Porfirio Díaz had reconciled with the Vatican. Both Díaz and the Church, if for different reasons, considered esoteric ideas magnets for trouble—witness Teresa Urrea and Tomóchic. Long at odds over money, land, and power, the Mexican state and the Church had suffered their greatest rift to date during the French Intervention of the 1860s. While the Vatican had never come to an agreement with Louis Napoleon's puppet, Maximilian von Habsburg, haggling until the very end over its privileges and the return of its properties confiscated by the Republic, the Pope had given his blessing to the French invasion of Mexico and to Maximilian personally when he and his consort, Carlota, visited Rome *en route* to Mexico in 1864. One might imagine that Porfirio Díaz, whose star began its rise with his exploits in that conflict, might remain unyielding toward the French and their allies. Knowing his career's end, exile in Paris, we forget what a canny and flexible politician Don Porfirio could be. But by the 1890s Don Porfirio's hair was turning white (and, so it seemed, his complexion), and in his ostrich feather-topped tricorn, epaulettes, and barrel-chest bespangled with medals, this former Oaxacan mule-skinner was beginning to look as he was acting, rather Louis Napoleonesque.

But back to Coahuila. In 1893 Madero might have been described as a dabbler in Spiritism, a young man with fine sentiments and noble intentions, attuned to *le dernier mot* in modernity as he perceived it, and drawn, as so many are, to the glamor of psychic adventure—perhaps feeling very special and brave to join a secret circle in a darkened room and to place one's fingertips upon the planchette, or witness a tilting table, ghostly raps, and mediums channeling the wise words and prophecies of invisible beings on the Other Side. (The more swashbuckling types also claimed to travel by astral projection, à la Madame Blavatsky's Mahatmas. Some who remembered Teresa Urrea, for example, told the historian William Curry Holden that, in what seemed like a supervivid dreams, she flew with them to the Mexican pyramids and the ocean.)

Surely Madero had not forgotten that séance in the home
of a friend, while on a visit home from Paris between school
terms, asking the spirit directing the planchette to foretell
their futures. His: President of Mexico. But when he returned
home to Parras for good, it did not seem that he would amount
to much of a politician; he was brilliant at the family business.
Given his own hacienda, San Pedro de las Colonias, to manage,
he did so with seriousness and gusto. He bought new machin-
ery, tried out new seeds, and helped manage his father's lands
and businesses. His grandfather, Don Evaristo, had introduced
cotton-growing to the lower Nazas River region, also known
as the Laguna. Young Madero traveled throughout the area,
working to improve yields on family lands, and encouraging
his brothers to settle there. According to his biographer, Stanley R. Ross, "Madero merits recognition as a pioneer of the
Laguna region which became one of the most productive areas
of Mexico." If there were an entrepreneurial gene, Francisco
Madero did not lack it: Among his many other businesses, all in
motion by the end of the century: a soap factory, an ice factory,
and a goat-breeding operation, in addition to irrigation works
and the project of an astronomical observatory on one of his
ranches, the remote Australia.

Traveling to small towns and farms in provincial Mexico,
Madero encountered heartbreaking poverty, and many sick
people without the means to pay for a doctor, let alone a veteri-
narian for their animals. And of course, no matter how wealthy
a person might be, there were ailments that no doctor, for
any fee, knew how to cure. Madero found a helpful tool in
homeopathy, which he learned in 1896—this the beginning
of what would be many more dedicated efforts, well beyond
garden-variety *noblesse oblige*, to help his fellow Mexicans.

True, he had been given every opportunity, every privilege, and he treated his workers with unusual beneficence, but
Madero was so successful that he accumulated a stupendous
fortune for the time—Ross estimates "a personal capital in
excess of a quarter of a million dollars"—and a connoissieur's

wine cellar to go along with it. There was a friend of his sisters from their time at San Francisco's College of Notre Dame, Sara Pérez, whom he courted, but cavalierly, he broke that off. After all, she was two-and-a-half years older than he, and she lived on her family's hacienda outside Querétaro, what must have been a less than convenient distance for courting.

At the turn of the century, however, the winds of his fate gained force.

### Keep Your Brain Vibrating!

In the town of San Pedro, Madero joined a Spiritist circle with a deceptively low-profile name: the Círculo de Estudios Psi-cológicos (Psychological Studies Circle). The idea was to develop the members' mediumistic abilities. In Paris, encouraged by members of his Spiritist circle there, and following the instructions in Kardec's *Le Livre des Médiums,* Madero had attempted "automatic writing," what he terms *escritura mecánica,* allowing a spirit to control his handwriting, but he had no luck. Now, with greater seriousness, he tried again. One day, while practicing during a vigil at the bedside of an uncle, his hand jerked and then seemed to take on a life of its own. In another session, his hand wrote:

> Love God above all things and your neighbor
> as yourself.

Soon Madero was regularly channeling messages from his brother, Raúl, the one who had died when his clothes caught fire in 1887. The scribbles, which Madero's Spiritist circle helped him decipher, offered moral instruction. One from early 1900, apparently intended for the circle, said they should "take care in speaking of other people and only do so to celebrate their qualities or defend someone whose reputation is being justly or unjustly attacked."

In 1902 Madero's mother, Doña Mercedes, contracted typhoid fever. It must have been terrifying not only for Francisco but everyone in that large extended family to see her in the agonies of fever and blindingly painful headaches that often ended in death. Francisco gave his mother homeopathic remedies, and thanks also to dietary counsel channeled from the spirit Raúl, she survived.

A now more serious-minded Francisco Madero, closing in on the end of his third decade, and transformed, in his words, from "a young libertine, useless to society, to an honorable family man, concerned with the good of his country," determined to go back to Sara Pérez, if she would have him. One wonders what had happened when he broke with her earlier, and what her Catholic family would have thought of his whole-hearted embrace of such exotica as homeopathy and Spiritism. Her father, a "wall of ice," as Francisco described him, did not attend their wedding in January 1903, when Sara was 32 and he 30, in Mexico City. By Mexican society's standards of the time, they were both well past the normal age for a first marriage.

Back in Coahuila, the newlyweds made their home on the main plaza of San Pedro. By this time, Madero had given up drinking and given away all the wines in his cellar, quit smoking, become a vegetarian, and, while still active as a businessman, dedicated himself to charitable work as instructed by the spirits, and further developing his mediumistic powers. Together he and Sara cared for orphans, provided scholarships, and operated a soup kitchen. By 1909 they were feeding several hundred people a day.

In the early years of the new century, especially after his marriage, Madero was also devouring books, as I learned when, finally, in late 2012, crowbarring out a last chunk of resistance, I ambled over to Chimalistac to look at his personal library, preserved in the Centro de Estudios de Historia de México CARSO.

One cannot know for certain which books Madero read word for word, which were gifts never glanced at a second time, or, in the case of those lacking his dated *ex-libris*, which were purchased by or given to Sara after his death. And, according to María del Carmen Collado Herrera and Laura Pérez Rosales's biography of his widow, some of the books were lost in 1914 when Huertista soldiers went rampaging through the Laguna, burning Madero family houses, ranches, offices, and stores of cotton found in their house in San Pedro. But as Samuel Johnson said, "A man will turn over a library to make a book," and many of these surviving works served as sources for his *Manual espírita*. And any library, however incomplete, offers insight into the mind of its owner.

Alas, I was unable to take in the whole of it on the shelves. The archivist brought the books out, an armful at a time, to my table in the reading room.

Who owned the collection of "Little Leather" books? Small enough to stash in a purse and bound in various colors of dyed suede: *Uses of Great Men* by Ralph Waldo Emerson, *Hamlet* and *Julius Caesar* by William Shakespeare, *Speeches and Letters of George Washington*, and (I had to smile) George Bernard Shaw's *Socialism for Millionaires*. There were quite a number of these to shuffle through. *Poems* by Robert Burns, Dante's *Inferno: The Divine Comedy*, Dickens' *A Christmas Carol*, and incongruously, *Mother Goose Rhymes*. I did not see any markings in the Little Leather books; they seemed to me (book snob that I am) the sort of pay-by-subscription collection aimed at aspirational types.

More and handsomer books came out in French. These struck me as the impersonal furnishings for a "gentlemen's library," exacting no more notice from their owner than the bookends themselves. (Though perhaps I am wrong about that. I own a pristine copy of *War and Peace,* and by Jove, I did read it.) With a sigh or ten, I went through a great number of red leather-bound tomes such as *Oeuvres de Chateaubriand; Oeuvres de Descartes; de Seneque; Tacité; Virgile,* and so on. Many of the books' frontispieces had an *ex-libris*, but hardly the bespoke bookplate one might expect: just an oval stamp with date, such as a shopkeeper might affix to a receipt. *Oue-vres Completes de Séneque* and *de Tacité* were from Paris 1905 and stamped *Francisco Y. Madero, Mar 16, 1908, San Pedro Coahuila, Méx.*

But things got interesting with the 1908 edition of Édouard Schuré's *Les Grandes initiés: esquisse de l'histoire secrète des religions*, originally published in Paris in 1889. The title page featured the names of the "great initiates":

Rama — Krishna — Hermès — Moise —
Orphée — Pythagore —Platon — Jésus

And the epigraph:

*L'Ame est la clef de l'Universe*
(The soul is the key to the universe).

Pretty high-octane stuff for cotton-farming Coahuila. And I did note, as I imagine any beady-eyed cleric would, that Jesus was named last. As I leafed through the pages looking for marginalia and, alas, not finding any, out fell a visiting card from one María A. de Larralde Martes. (I alerted the achivist; she said to put loose cards and such back where I found them, so I did).

Unsurprisingly, there were several works in French by Kardec, as well as many by later Spiritists such as Léon Denis' *Pourquoi la vie?*, J.-E. Gillet's *L'Amour et le mariage selon le spiritisme*, Louis Jacolliot's *Le Spiritisme dans le monde,* and Flammarion's *La Pluralité des mondes habités* (these inhabited worlds would include the moon, Mars, Saturn, et al.) There was an elegantly bound collection of *La Revue spirite.* Neither was I surprised to find several bound volumes of *La Ilustración espírita.* Tomo I, of 1868, included "Apuntes biográficos de Daniel Home, médium"—that is, biographic notes on our old friend the levitating chandelier duster, D.D.

An Anglo-American influence was clearly seen in French translations such as the English medium William Stainton

Moses's *Enseignments spiritualistes*, that is, *Spirit Teachings*, considered the Bible of the Anglo-American Spiritualists; and there was a French biography of the American medium, a favorite of William James, *Madame Piper* by M. Sage.

But Madero also read in English. His *ex-libris* stamped 1908 appears in works such as J.M. Peebles's *Seers of the Ages: Embracing Spiritualism Past and Present; The Encyclopedia of Death and Life in the Spirit World;* and *Art Magic or, Mundane, Sub-Mundane and Super-Mundane Spiritism*, the Chicago publisher of which urged the reader to:

> KEEP YOUR BRAIN VIBRATING!
> You can always do so by reading
> THE PROGRESSIVE THINKER.
> There is nothing that will so perfectly keep
> your brain in a healthy condition as to think
> well and wisely. Hence you should not only
> read The Progressive Thinker, but the var-
> ious Occult Premium Books it offers. They
> will quicken your brain vibrations, and enable
> you to maintain a position in society as a
> well-informed person.

What surprised me, however, was the large number of Spanish translations of English and French Spiritist and Theosophical works, most but not all out of Barcelona, for example, the little prayer book, *Devocionario espiritista;* Gabriel Delanne's *El fenómeno espiritista: testimonio de los sabios* of 1893; Kardec's posthumous works channeled by mediums, in the *edición económica* 1888; the two volume *La vida de ultra-tumba* by medium Rufina Noeggerath, aka "Bonne Maman"; Theosophist Annie Besant's *El Poder del pensamiento* (*Thought Power*) and *Karma*, into which was tucked a Nippon Trading Co. card.

Then came a copy of the Bhagavad Gita, the 1887 Boston translation from the Sanskrit by Mohini M. Chatterji, who

introduced it as "an attempt to present to the English-speaking people the pearl of price from the ocean of Brahmanical
Scriptures." (Chatterji was a Theosophist from Calcutta, and
a staunch defender of Madame Blavatsky and her mysterious
Mahatmas, one of whom, "Koot-hoomi," or "Kuthumi," Chatterji claimed to have met in Madras, India, when the latter was
passing through on his way to China.)

Another Bhagavad-Gita, with notes by Annie Besant was a
Spanish translation by Federico Climent Ferrer published by
the Biblioteca Orientalista in Barcelona in 1908. A red sticker
from the bookseller on the lower right of the cover, bright as
if it had been pasted there yesterday, read:

> San Felipe Jesús 572
> J. Ballesca y Cª Sucrs.
> 5 de Mayo
> México

Another Spanish copy of the Bhagavad-Gita, translated by J.
Roviralta Borrell, carried Madero's *ex-libris* stamped October 16,
1909, and in contrast to his other books, all nearly impeccable,
almost every page was filled with scribbles in his handwriting.
The first, on the flyleaf (my translation):

> It would be good to do an edition of the Bhaga-
> vad-Gita that could be titled Teachings of
> the Bhagavad-Gita or The Bhagavad-Gita in
> Western Language, writing in the same way
> Allan Kardec wrote The Gospels According
> Spiritism, that is to say, to organize the most
> important essays of the Bhagavad-Gita into
> different chapters about [?] and Reincarna-
> tion of the Soul, Existence of God [?] moral,
> etc., etc.

And the translator's dedication to Madame Blavatsky:

> Extraordinary woman, so unjustly slandered
> but deserving of universal admiration; illus-
> trious writer in whose books I have found
> vivifying rays of light for which I have
> searched but not found elsewhere

Who was this passionate seeker, J. Roviralta Borrell? A chase after the answer took me down the rabbit hole into the smoky parlors of the Spanish and Catalan Theosophists: the aristocratic Francesc Montoliu (1861-1892), and José Xifré Hamel (1855-1920), a wealthy banker and industrialist, close friend of Madame Blavatsky, and one of the founders of Barcelona's Biblioteca Orientalista. I learned that Federico Climent Ferrer had also translated several Theosophical works, including Blavatsky's *The Secret Doctrine*. Josep Roviralta Borrell, it turns out, was a Catalan doctor and Theosophist, translator of many works in addition to the Bhagavad-Gita, including Shakespeare's *Hamlet* and Goethe's *Faust*, and author of the 1902 *Boires Baixes* (Low Mists), a Catalan play so modernist it was unperformable.

But back to the remains of Madero's library.

On one visit, for some hours I was kept busy looking through histories, G. Maspero's *Histoire ancienne des peuples de l'oriente* (quoted in the *Manual espírita*); Donead's *Histoire contemporaine de la Prusse*; Gustave Le Bon's *La Revolution française et la psychologie des revolutions*—goodness, quite a number of books about the French Revolution.

And the Roman Empire. In Madero's 1907 copy of *Vie des romains ilustres*, I found a visiting card from one Carlos M. Esquerro, and in his 1908 edition (*ex-libris* 1909) of *Grandeza y decadencia de Roma*, Vol II *Julio César*, I found two cards, one from Mathilda Fellinger de Knapp, and another minor mystery:

Sabina González
Desea á Ud. Un Feliz Año Nuevo
San Pedro Coah, enero 1 de 1909

(Wishes you a Happy New Year
San Pedro Coahuila, January 1, 1909)

Then came *Ciencia oculta de la medicina* by Franz Hartmann, a translation from the English, *Occult Science in Medicine.* A German Theosophist and translator of the Bhagavad-Gita, Hartmann had been at Adyar, India, with Madame Blavatsky. The 1902 edition of *L'Occultisme en le Spiritualisme,* by Gérard Encausse, offered chapters on the astral body, the esoteric history of the white race, and the secret histories of the lost continents Atlantis and Lemuria. Encausse, I knew from my reading, was a medical doctor and hypnotist otherwise known as "Papus," the most famous Theosophist-turned-Occultist of his time, friend to the Spiritists and mystic to the Tzar of Russia (very down on Rasputin)—just to offer a grossly abbreviated description of this most energetic and charismatic Parisian personality. And with the 1905 French translation—stamped with Madero's *ex-libris* of May 17, 1907—*La mort l'au delà, la vie dans l'au delà* (Death and Life Beyond) from the German by Baron Carl du Prel, one of the several researchers who took part in Charles Richet's celebrated experiments with medium Eusapia Palladino; it occurred to me, very late in the game, that I was pawing through one of the most important, perhaps the most important among turn-of-the century libraries of esoterica in the Americas.

Diagrams from the Qabalah, Jewish esoteric thought, appeared in Ely Star's *Les mystères de l'être,* and exotic Himalayan adventures in A. Van Der Naillen's *Dans le sanctuaire;* a book on yoga by Swami Vivekananda; and then, a tower of titles evidencing Madero's interest in hypnotism, among them:

*Médiumnité hypnotique* by M.M.F. Rossi-Pagnoni and Dr. Moroni

*Hypnotisme et magnétisme: somnabulisme, suggestion et telépathie influence personelle (cours pratique)* by Jean Filiatre

*Le Sommeil naturel et l'hypnose* by M. Sage

*Rapports du magnétisme et du spiritisme* by Rouxel

*El Hipnotismo* by César Lombroso (this author a leading Italian criminologist-turned-paranormal researcher, one of the first to study medium Eusapia Palladino)

One book apparently did not belong to Madero: *Las últimas treinta vidas de Alcione,* Federico Climet Terrer's 1912 Barcelona translation of Annie Besant and C.W. Leadbeater's *Lives of Alcyone,* because it was inscribed to *Sara Pérez Vd. de Madero* (Sara Pérez, Widow of Madero).

Now, as we see in Madero's own library Spiritist and Theosophical ideas so overlapped and intertwined, though at times at odds, it behooves us to venture a little way down another rabbit hole for the answer to the question, Who, pray tell, was Alcyone?

### Alcyone (and Other Lives) in the 20th Century: Jiddu Krishnamurti, Felix A. Sommerfeld, and Dr. Arnold Krumm-Heller, aka Maestro Huiracocha

There are myriad answers to this question, who was Alcyone?
Greek: A star-nymph, daughter of Atlas and lover of Poseidon;
Astronomical: The brightest star in the Pleiades;

Literal: Jiddu Krishnamurti, a sickly Brahmin boy;

Theosophist: As revealed by the Mahatmas, the human vehicle for the Lord Maitreya, the Christ, the World Teacher.

It was C.W. Leadbeater who had discovered the adolescent Krishnamurti playing on a beach in 1909, identifying him as said vehicle by clairvoyant means. Alas, no story of the Theosophical Society gets told without the taint of Leadbeater's, shall we say, intimate involvement with other young boys. In 1906, after vociferous complaints from parents, Leadbeater was obliged to resign from the society. By 1909, however, his fellow Initiate before the Mahatmas and expert on the Bhagavad-Gita, Annie Besant, had taken the reins of the Theosophical Society and engineered Leadbeater's readmission. In the society's headquarters in Adyar, Besant and Leadbeater together arranged Krishnamurti's care and education. Almost immediately, Leadbeater, by psychic means known only to himself, began researching the "Akashic" or astral records on the lives of "Alcyone," that is, the previous incarnations of Krishnamurti in mind-numbing permutations reaching back to 22,662 B.C. in which Annie Besant appeared under the code-name "Heracles," Leadbeater as "Sirius," and various other Theosophists under various other code names taken from Greek mythology. In her memoir, *To Be Young,* Mary Lutyens, daughter of the Theosphical Society's benefactress Lady Emily Lutyens and a childhood friend and biographer of Krishnamurti, recalled of the *Lives of Alcyone,* "a great deal of heart-burning and snobbery."

> 'Are you in the Lives?' Became the question
> most constantly asked by one Theosophist of
> another, and, if so, 'How closely related have
> you been to Alcyone?'

At night, by means of their astral bodies, Leadbeater took Krishnamurti to study with "Master Kuthumi," that "Great White Brother" first introduced to this world by Madame Blavatsky, and in the morning, in his octagonal office, Leadbeater obliged Krishnamurti, whose English and writing skills were what one would expect of a little boy whose first language was Telegu, to record what he could remember of those lessons. Flash forward two decades to 1929, when that little boy had grown into the world-traveling, English-educated World Teacher, the venerated head of Leadbeater and Besant's creation, the 43,000-member Order of the Star in the East, and he took the stage at Erde Castle in Holland before 3,000 members and with a solemn salaam dissolved that order. Krishnamurti did not deny being whatever they conceived him to be; he said:

> I maintain that Truth is a pathless land, and you cannot approach it by any path whatsoever, by any religion, by any sect... I do not care if you believe I am the World Teacher or not... I do not want you to follow me... You have been accustomed to being told how far you have advanced, what is your spiritual status. How childish! Who but yourself can tell you if you are incorruptible?... You can form other organizations and expect someone else. With that I am not concerned, nor with creating new cages, new decorations for those cages. My only concern is to set men absolutely, unconditionally, free.

That signaled the decline (though not the disappearance) of the Theosophical Society, as well as Annie Besant's health. But fantastically, Krishnamurti's career, unleashed from official disciples, continued to flourish. Like Teresa Urrea and the Niño Fidencio, Krishnamurti had a serene and childlike quality and an ability to draw and mesmerize crowds, but unlike them, Krishnmurti exuded an urbane polish. He wrote some 30 books articulating a philosophy of freedom that appealed to such diverse figures as physicist David Bohm, writer Aldous Huxley, Indira Gandhi, and the Dalai Lama.

On YouTube, I found an old film of the white-haired Krishnamurti holding forth in a tent in Ojai, California, and what
struck me was not anything he said—he sounded halting and
vapid to my ears—but the faces of the hundreds of people sitting in folding chairs and on the lawn before him, eyes shining,
jaws slack. I could not help but think of Niño Fidencio—and
the strange power I had seen in Francisco Madero in the films
and photographs of his political rallies.

If I were to write a novel about someone like Jiddu Krishnamurti, this sad-eyed and androgynous-looking person who
seemed to have dreamwalked out of a Frances Hodgson Bur-
nett-meets-Rudyard-Kipling-on-mushrooms fantasia, I don't
think anyone would believe a word of it. And yet, it nudged
a corner of my mind that, though I never crossed paths with
Krishnamurti, for many years, we inhabited the same state:
California. I was probably in kindergarten when Krishnamurti
was holding forth to those crowds in Ojai that I watched on
YouTube. I was in eighth grade in Palo Alto when Krishnamurti
gave four talks in nearby San Francisco, as Lutyens recalls,
in "a hall holding over 3,000 people which was packed each
time," and I was in high school in 1976 when Krishmaurti
gave yet another series of talks in Ojai, the last one to more
than 5,000 people. I'd had no idea that in 1979 he met with
Indira Gandhi in India, that he went to London, Paris, Rome,
and so many other places where large and adoring crowds
always awaited him. Neither did I know that from 1965 to
1984, Krishnamurti and David Bohm, a leading theoretical
quantum physicist and professor at the University of London,
conducted an exploration of consciousness in 30 dialogues,
some of which were recorded.

Where and when did Krishnamurti die? I had to look it up:
Ojai, California, 1986. The same year I married, in California,
and moved to Mexico City.

1909, the year Krishnamurti was whisked off that beach by a
modern Merlin, was the same year that, following the dictates
of the spirits, Francisco Madero launched his first presidential

campaign and so ripped apart and began to reweave the very fabric of Mexico itself.

Francisco Madero, too, spent some time in California. Apart from studying in Berkeley, he, his brother Gustavo, and his sisters strolled among the giant redwoods near Santa Cruz and visited Monterey, where they followed the scenic coastline's "Seventeen Mile Drive," and then went inland to the even more spectacular scenery at Yosemite—all places I visited with my family as a child.

Francisco I. Madero sometimes seems a marble bust on a herm, a piece of history, yet if he had lived to say, 92, I would have been old enough to remember meeting him (though I cannot imagine under what circumstances with no Mexican connections yet in suburban California of the 60s). But I did, after all, meet his great niece, my husband's Tía Susana. Oh, how I love to explore these labyrinths. Another example—hang on, there's a Minotaur:

When she was in her eighties, my long-widowed high school German teacher married Ralph Smith, the last four-star general of World War II, then in his nineties. General and Mrs. Smith, for reasons too detailed to go into here, became friends of my family, and my father, an historian of World War II, became especially close to General Smith. A football-player sized man, even in old age, General Smith was hard of hearing, but so clear-sighted, he kept his license and drove his own car until he was 101 years old. One evening when I was visiting my sister, who lived near my parents, I felt a sudden intuition to go out-side and stand on the curb. I did so, and not a minute later, I waved down my father, who happened to be driving General Smith home to his apartment. General Smith rolled down the passenger window and put his hand out. I shook it and said something like, good to see you, but he couldn't hear me. He didn't let go of my hand for a long moment. I understand now, for he died at 104 shortly afterwards, he was saying a final goodbye. He had served with General "Black Jack" Pershing when, in a later episode in the Mexican Revolution, they went after Pancho Villa with airplanes. I regret immensely that I never asked him about that. I never asked his wife, my teacher, about her translating Hermann Göring during the Nuremburg Trials, either.

What I mean to say with this little digression is that what we call history is but a nano-slice of an intricate complexity, and it's not that I am special for knowing a certain general or a great niece, or having had a teacher who translated the Nazis' post-Hitler Grand Poobah in the greatest war crimes trial of the twentieth century, but that all of us, however tenuously, are connected to everyone else, every humble person, every famous and rich and powerful person, every criminal, every saint. And each incident in each life enfolds layer upon layer of meaning and mystery, each diffusing through the realms of time itself. Do we, denizens of the twenty-first century, not understand World War I differently, knowing as we do that Adolph Hitler's cruel politics were forged in that cauldron? And do we not see Maximilian von Habsburg differently than those of his own time, because we know that Maximilian, little as he may have had in common with another century's Führer, was also an Austrian? And here let me toss in this eye-crossing factoid: General Refugio I. González, that translator of Kardec and tireless promoter of Mexican Spiritist circles, had served as deputy prosecutor in Maximilian's trial of 1867, which found him guilty of war crimes and condemned him to execution by firing squad.

And one further fantastic fact that came to light in 2012 with Heribert von Feilitzsch's *In Plain Sight: Felix Sommerfeld, Spymaster in Mexico, 1908 to 1914,* based on meticulous international archival research in Mexico, Germany, and Washington, D.C.: Madero's secret service chief, Sommerfeld, and his personal doctor, fellow mason and Spiritist, the Occultist Dr. Arnoldo Krumm-Heller, were both German spies.

The human brain has its limits. How else but with brutal simplification can we begin to take in Niagaras of detail, hubs and continents of webs of connections, and shape some sort of narrative? But brutal simplification is brutal, and when a mutilated, or shall we say, surgically enhanced story is told and retold without question, it becomes a kind of lie. The story of the Revolution of 1910 which knowingly leaves out Madero's Spiritism and the influence of the Theosophists and others in turn-of-the-century American and European esoteric spheres is that kind of lie.

As for his opinions on the Theosophists themselves, it seems Madero said little and he was careful to whom he said it. On September 7, 1907 to a fellow Spiritist, on the publication of another Spiritist's article which criticized Theosophy:

> But doesn't it seem it would have been better not to address this issue and so not injure the feelings of some of the members of the Board? ... I believe the only enemy we should take seriously is materialism. The other religions, with more or less zeal, try to encourage good works, and right there, that's everything we the true Spiritists are about. It's the same with Theosophy: the only thing they say in plain language that can be understood is that they recommend we improve ourselves by our own efforts; the rest of what they say are dogmatic and unintelligible digressions and as such, almost no one can comprehend them. Intelligent people quickly discover how absurd they are.

Madero did some reading after that. On January 28, 1908, to another fellow Spiritist:

> I have read the works of the leading Theosophists and in them I have found one doctrine in particular that seems to me more admissible and that is the doctrine of involution and

evolution: involution is the act of Creation,
God unmanifested, manifesting in the material... I have always believed that Theosophy
and Spiritism must eventually arrive at the
same thing, for they have the same foundations, that is, the soul's unending progress by
means of evolution and the conviction that
each is responsible for his acts and only by
his acts will he owe his progress.

Four years earlier, in 1904, Henry Ridgely Evans, Madero's
brother Mason, also of the 33rd degree (the highest, awarded for
service to humanity or the fraternity), and an expert on magic
and psychic phenomena, wrote in *The Monist* that Blavatsky's
Mahatma stories were "as improbable as those invented by the
mythical Baron Münchhausen," yet in nearly the same breath
he acknowledged "the honest and earnest work" of many of
the members of the Theosophical Society, especially in Washington, "where the prime movers of Theosophy are composed
of ladies and gentlemen of intelligence." This rejecting, yet
carefully diplomatic stance, is strikingly similar to Madero's.
I doubt that Evans and Madero ever met, but—and even more
striking to me—Evans was a childhood friend of Agustín de
Iturbide y Green. (In his 1927 *Adventures in Magic*, apropos of a
wild scene involving a magic lantern, both boys, some supersti-
tious mammies, and the daughter of the Japanese ambassador,
Evans added, "Poor fellow, he was a prince, but he did not plume
himself because of that fact.")

In 1908, in the Second Spiritist Congress held in Mexico
City, Madero may have received a fresh infusion of the latest
in European esoterica from Dr. Arnoldo Krumm-Heller, aka
Maestro Huiracocha, German spy, Brother Mason, devotee of
Blavatsky, indigenous healing and magic aficionado, homeo-
pathist, and student of Franz Hartmann (the medical doctor
and Theosophist mentioned earlier) and of none other than
Papus, the renowned Occultist and medical doctor of Paris.

I cannot say what Madero thought of it, but one of Dr. Krumm-Heller's books, published in 1912 and inscribed to him by the author, is in his library: *No fornicarás* (Thou Shalt Not Fornicate), an early treatise on what would become Dr. Krumm-Heller's specialty: sexual magic. The opening epigraph:

> *Las pasiones humanas son piedras de molino;*
> *será grano, el que no se convierta á tiempo*
> *en molinero.*

> [Human passions are millstones; he who does
> not become a miller in time will be grain.]

According to von Feilitzsch, Krumm-Heller became Madero's personal physician in early 1911, and probably reported to Sommerfeld who, in turn, reported to both Gustavo Madero and the German embassy. Archival documents reveal that contrary to what many historians believe, German Ambassador Paul von Hintze worked behind U.S. Ambassador Wilson's back through Sommerfeld in support of Madero's government. But what kind of person was this double agent Sommerfeld? In an e-mail (I quote by permission) of August 14, 2013, von Feilitzsch told me:

> With respect to Madero's Spiritism, Sommerfeld not only knew all about it. I am convinced that he was a kindred soul. I have scoured the earth for a book Sommerfeld wrote around 1918, likely under a pen name. I cannot find it. This might be the only possible source for a glimpse into this man's deepest convictions and emotional structure. Sommerfeld became so close to Madero at the exact time, when Madero must have been under the most emotional pressure. Madero hated bloodshed and violence and exactly that he set off when the

revolution started. In his innermost circle
were Sommerfeld, Krumm-Heller, his wife
Sara, and Gustavo, which is documented.
... (Sommerfeld was [Sara's] bodyguard in
Mexico City and the last address I have for
Sommerfeld reads: c/o Sara Madero, Mexico
City. This was in 1930). Just like Krumm-
Heller and Madero, Sommerfeld did not drink,
gamble or smoke. In that time and considering the background of Sommerfeld as a
mining engineer in the "Wild West," this is a
very unlikely coincidence. In his interviews
with the American authorities, he said that
Madero was "the purest man I ever met in
my life. When I spoke to him, he took my
breath away—the child's faith of this man in
humanity." (Justice 9-16-12) In his appearance
before the Fall Committee in 1912 he testified:
"President Madero is the best friend I have
in this world..." Senator Smith "...you became
interested in him?" Sommerfeld: "Yes, we
became very close friends." And so on. I defi-
nitely hear undertones of esoteric connection.
Sommerfeld was very private, rarely allowed
a picture taken, and certainly never talked
about his faith or personal life to anyone. As
someone very rational he kept his distance to
others and never described any other relationship in these highly emotional terms. Until I
can put my hands on his personal papers or
his book, these are only indications but still
worth thinking about.

Not even von Feilitzsch knows when and how Sommerfeld
left this world. Always careful to stay in the background, in late
middle age Sommerfeld seems to have melted into fog—but

perhaps by the time you read this, von Feilitzsch will have uncovered more. Sommerfeld could not have had an easy time had he remained in Nazi Germany into the 1930s, for he was Jewish.

Krumm-Heller, on the other hand, had a flair for showmanship. A photograph that might have been taken around the time he was in Mexico shows a head shaved bald as an egg, large ears and deep-set eyes in a theatrically lit face smudged with shadows, as if he were an actor posing for the role of villain (but he betrays a sparkling humor). The powerful Occultist, the thaumaturge! In another photo Krumm-Heller poses in his white robes of the Gnostic Church, hooded, deadly serious, a gigantic crucifix embroidered across his chest. In his later years, he grew his snowy beard into a most unusual and fluffy fan shape.

After Madero's murder, General Victoriano Huerta had Krumm-Heller arrested—but he was freed when the German embassy intervened. Krumm-Heller then went on to work for Venustiano Carranza in the counter-revolution against Huerta and served as General Obregón's chief of artillery. Later, Krumm-Heller busied himself founding the Fraternitas Rosicruciana Antigua (FRA) and working for the Red Cross. In Germany in the 1930s, according to Krumm-Heller's son Parsival in Sabazius's biography, someone circulated a pamphlet accusing him of being a Jewish-Masonic conspirator, and the SS confiscated his library. He died in Marburg in 1949, only four years after the end of World War II.

There is much more to say about these and other German spies' escapades in and out of Mexico, but I leave those chock-full-of-enigmas stories to others; for my purposes, establishing the context of Madero's *Spiritist Manual*, what blinks like a lighthouse on a moonless night is the nexus of Krumm-Heller, someone so close to Madero, with such celebrities of the heterodox esoteric scene as Papus, Rudolph Steiner, whom he apparently met in the 1920s in Germany, and the English poet and Occultist Aleister Crowley, aka Baphomet, author of the

Gnostic mass, the purportedly channeled *Book of the Law*, member of the Hermetic Order of the Golden Dawn, notorious drug addict, and confrère in the Ordo Templi Orientis. Add to all that the fact that Krumm-Heller was a student of indigenous healing traditions in Mexico, Chile, and Peru, and active in movements as diverse as Gnosticism, Martinism (a French revival of Hermetic tradition), Masonry, Rosicrucianism, Spiritism, and Theosophy. That's a large number of "isms," to be sure, and Krumm-Heller left an even larger number of books, one of which, though revised and published in 1929 as *El Tatwámetro o las vibraciones del éter* (The Tatwameter or, Etheric Vibrations), inspired by Theosophical and Hindu teachings, he wrote in 1911 while he was working for Madero in Mexico. In 1910, he published what surely came to the attention of at least some portion of Mexico City's esoterically-minded community, *El zodiaco de los incas en comparación de los aztecas* (The Inca and Aztec Zodiacs Compared). His *Conferencias esotéricas*, (Esoteric Lectures), which addressed the evolution of the human races and the planet, healing, and breathing exercises for longevity, was published in Mexico in 1913, so it seems more likely than not that Madero, his own patient and fellow Spiritist, would have seen it. Furthermore, though Krumm-Heller did not publish *Del Incienso a la osmoterapia* (From Incense to Osmotherapy, osmotherapy being an early form of aromatherapy) until 1934, in Mexico he was already carrying around vials of perfume as a remedy for men injured on the battlefields. According to Mexican cultural historian Ricardo Pérez Montfort, Dr. Krumm-Heller had his clinic on Mexico City's Calle Empedradillo near the Monte de Piedad. This would have been close enough to trot over to the National Palace upon a phone call.

It is a fanciful scene to conjure: President Madero, fatigued after an overlong meeting with recalcitrant legislators and too heavy a lunch of cheese enchiladas, has already taken his own homeopathic remedy, a half dozen little white pills. Let's say it's nearing Christmas. The afternoon is fading. Out the window of the Presidential office, to the north, the towers of the Cathedral, great speleothems, are turning the color of ashes. In the plaza below, the ocean-like Zócalo, the newshawkers, the ladies on their way home from shopping, the messenger boys, the beggars, they stand, sit, or trundle by all chubby in their jackets, serapes, rebozos. And then suddenly, like a lament: the tolling for vespers.

There's a sofa, and to the side, an armchair; a spindly-legged coffee table between them. (Don Porfirio's leftover French furniture.) Any furniture in a room this cavernous seems undersized.

But first, the patient has to come out from behind that mammoth desk.

Now, like old friends, they settle in. Dr. Krumm-Heller's bag lands on the floor between them like a cat.

Dr. Krumm-Heller prescribes a series of deep, pranic breaths.

"In! ... four, three, two, one... and out!" Dr. Krumm-Heller times them on his pocket watch.

The series finished, Dr. Krumm-Heller holds both his palms out, fluttering his fingertips, feeling the air around his patient, as if palpitating the shell of an invisible enveloping egg.

"The vibrations are better, Señor Presidente, yes!"

More exercises. They are replenishing the President's pulmonary chakra—both vocalizing the vowel, *"Ahahahahahah,"* when, behind them, the door creaks open; his secretary scoots in with the scribbled message that Don Gustavo, urgently, would like to speak with the President.

"Tell him to wait," the President says, refolding the scrap of paper. Once the secretary has pulled the door behind him, the President doesn't seem sure what to do with the piece of paper. He tosses it on the far side of the sofa. He grabs it back. He stuffs it in his vest pocket. Out the window, a trio of pigeons lights on the railing of the balcony; in the twilight, bobbing, they look somehow sinister.

Dr. Krumm-Heller, his hand disappearing into the maw of his bag, says, as if it were a question, "A little osmotherapy would not be contraindicated."

He uncorks a vial and, as he waves it under his patient's nose, the room, this magic lamp-lit room from which men and women from every corner of the Republic expect every day miracles, fills with the moist graveyard smell of mushrooms, mint, and rosemary.

## Doña Sara

Very slowly, in several visits over several months, I combed through Madero's library. In the intervening days and weeks, trying to make sense of what I found, I made many scrambles down many rabbit holes, as it were, some empty but for a dead beetle or two, some draped in velvet and thick with cough-inducing incense. I had seen a good portion of his library when the archivist brought out the black leather-bound book with his initials, F.I.M., embossed in gold on the lower right corner. This was "Bhîma's" *Manual espírita*, the same I had seen so long ago, but that one cheaply bound in thin paper, in the Ministry of Finance. And so I held this finest monogrammed century-old book, the object of all these years of reading and research and reflection, in my hands. Slowly, I opened it. The front– and backboards were papered in a William-Morris-style pattern of moss-green leaves. The inscription was to Sara Pérez de Madero.

That same afternoon in the archive, I came across Adrien Majewksi's *Médiumnité guerrissante par l'application des fluides électrique, magnétique et humain* (Healing Mediumship by Application of Electric, Magnetic and Human Fluids); as I thumbed through it, I found, tucked in tight, an envelope with the typed address, Doña Sara Pérez de Madero, Zacatecas 90, México, D.F. The post office had stamped it 4 JUN 16. That is, June 4, 1916: A little more than three years after she had been made a widow. By this time she had returned to Mexico City from her exile in New York and New Jersey to this house in the Porfirian neighborhood built over Aztec floating gardens and nineteenth century circus grounds.

She had no children; she lived alone.

And now, summer of 1916, the hero's widow a mere bystander, the Revolution grinds on. General Victoriano Huerta, the traitor, is already overthrown, dead of cirrhosis of the liver and buried in El Paso, Texas. U.S. Ambassador Henry Lane Wilson—whom Huerta had asked, *should Madero be sent to the lunatic asylum?*, and who had answered, after all his outrageous meddling, after Huerta's troops had tortured and killed Madero's brother Gustavo, *whatever Huerta thought right and best for Mexico*—has been recalled in disgrace. The U.S. Navy has already retreated from its occupation of Veracruz, and now General "Black Jack" Pershing's troops—including my dad's old friend, Ralph Smith—are chasing Pancho Villa, like a dog after its tail, around the desert. Maximilian von Habsburg's nephew, the Archduke Franz Ferdinand, has been assassinated in Sarajevo, now the Germans intrigue for an advantage, fighting on every front of World War I, and fighting among themselves over increasingly byzantine strategies regarding Mexico.

Emiliano Zapata, the campesino leader of Morelos, is still alive and fighting, as is his nemesis, the also soon-to-be-assassinated President Venustiano Carranza, whose Constitutionalist Army overthrew Huerta. The cities are plagued by strikes, the countryside by banditry. The peso buys less each day.

June is the rainy season in Mexico City. The trees turn lush and the air—back then—would have smelled sweet, even on the grayest of afternoons. Even in the midst of political chaos, the city goes on.

Imagine: From the roof next door, where a maid is pulling down laundry, a dog barks. In the street beyond Doña Sara's window, umbrellas bounce by, and cars and horse-drawn wagons spray their wakes onto the sidewalk. Doña Sara, surrounded by her books, sits on her sofa, her letter-opener poised...

I drew out the envelope's contents. A postcard of President Madero on horseback and a photo, sepia with age: a middle-aged man, seated in profile, whom I did not recognize; behind him and to the left, unnaturally, as if pasted in from another photograph, a blurry image that, for the shape of the face and beard, could have been Madero; a hazy woman to the right; and, floating mid-air front and center, the large white blob of a baby.

A spirit photograph.

Who sent it to her? (I found no return address, no letter.) Who slipped it into Majewski's *Médiumnité guerrissante?* A cataloger? Another researcher? Was it Sara Pérez de Madero herself?

(Another rabbit hole: Majewski. One could write a book about him, but I'll suffice to note that a Google search brought up the news that three of his photographs of hands emitting "magnetic fluid," photographs reproduced in Majewski's book, were sold by Sotheby's at auction in New York City in December 2012 for 18,500 dollars.)

Back to Doña Sara. You don't have to live in Mexico long before you begin to see her. In the iconic photographs from the Revolution—and the Revolution is celebrated more often than Christmas, it seems—she is grimly smiling with her mouth closed, yet easy-eyed and with the placid forehead of a madonna. By 1911, we see her as First Lady in a high-necked blouse and extravagant hat, the fashion of the time; and also in an incongruously heavy-looking coat as she follows behind President Madero—he lifting his bright fedora—as he strides through a crowd (note the huge cone of a campesino's sombrero and raised sword). In Enrique Krauze's biography of Madero we see the couple in twin bergères, framed by lace curtains, their elegantly shod feet upon an Oriental carpet: President Madero in a pale suit and tie, Señora Madero in a sailor-collared frock and Edwardian bouffant. And then 1913, shot from below (the photographer must have been crouching): the young widow's swollen, grief-ravaged face.

But in Collado Herrera and Pérez Rosales's 2010 biography, there are two more photos of Doña Sara I had never seen before. Perhaps taken in the late 1930s or 40s: a halo of white hair, laughing eyes, a big, surprisingly toothy smile: she's patting a cat. And, a decade or two later, perhaps shortly before her death in 1952: in a chair, dressed in a dark skirt, dark sweater, and large crucifix, and with a wise, weary, whisper of a smile, Doña Sara looks straight into the camera—that magic portal to us.

It must have been so strange for her, a girl from a small town near Querétaro, to have been swirled into the vortex of her husband's political career, fueled as it was by Spiritism and that text so beloved by the Theosophists, the Bhagavad-Gita—certainly not reading assigned in late nineteenth century Catholic girls' schools!

The Bhagavad-Gita or "The Lord's Song" is a chapter added in about 200 BC to the possibly even more ancient Mahabharata, jewel of Sanskrit literature, a scripture of yoga, and the world's longest epic. Lord Krishna, the blue-skinned eighth incarnation of the god Vishnu, appears on a battlefield and reveals to the warrior Arjuna the true nature of reality, morality, and the need for calmness and courage. It was introduced to the West in an English translation in the late 18th century; French, German, and other languages quickly followed. Annie Besant, who retranslated it into English, called it a "priceless teaching;" Henry David Thoreau, poet of *Walden Pond*, considered it his textbook. Introduced to it by English Theosophists, Mohandas Gandhi considered it his "infalliable guide to conduct," and reread it while in prison in South Africa in 1908. Madero found it of such inspiration that he kept it with him during the Revolution and later, while in office as President of Mexico in 1912 and early 1913, he published his commentary as a series of articles "by an adept" in *Helios*, a Spiritist magazine, concluding that,

> [T]he Bhagavad-Gita encompasses glorious conceptions and it is far indeed from recommending those superstitious practices so in fashion with the majority of religions, including those professed by civilized peoples and, according to which certain religious practices are given more importance than fulfilling one's duty, overlooking that, in fulfilling

one's duty, one better aligns with a vaster
and greater plan for humanity's progress and
well-being.

What did Sara think of her husband's passion for the Bhagavad-Gita? It might seem a koan of a question but for the fact
that she was a warrior herself. She was there, right beside him,
throughout her husband's first presidential campaign of 1910,
and his arrest and imprisonment in San Luis Potosí by Porfirio Diaz's henchmen, who stole that election in the crudest
way. She helped him escape across the border to Texas, she
helped him launch the Revolution of 1910—he even asked her
to sell her jewels to help pay for it—and then, she was there
by his side campaigning all over again to win the Presidential
election of 1911. She was never braver than that terrible day of
February 20, 1913, with downtown Mexico City under seige and
strewn with bodies, her husband and his vice president held
prisoner. Just the day before, her brother in-law, Gustavo, had
been beaten, blinded with a bayonet, and finally shot to death
by a gang of Huerta's jeering soldiers, and Huerta himself was
now triumphant in power thanks to negotiations hosted by
the U.S. ambassador in the U.S. legation. She led her mother-
in-law and two sisters-in-law to that legation and addressed
herself directly to Ambassador Wilson, who she said she found
drunk. As Doña Sara recalled, several times Mrs. Wilson had
to tug at her husband's jacket to prompt him to change his
language. In *Los últimos días del Presidente Madero* (The Last
Days of President Madero), the Cuban ambassador, Manuel
Márquez Sterling, who would help the Madero family escape
to the United States via Havana, having heard it from Doña
Sara, renders the scene (my translation):

> *The Ambassador:* Your husband did not know
> how to govern. He never asked for nor would
> listen to my advice...I do not think he will be
> killed, but I would not be surprised if Pino

Suárez were to be sacrificed on the scaffold, forever extinguishing his virtues...

*Señora Madero:* Oh, that would be impossible! My husband would prefer to die with him...

*Ambassador Wilson:* Nevertheless Pino Suárez has done him nothing but harm... He's a worthless man...

*Señora Madero:* Pino Suárez, sir, has a beautiful heart, he is a patriot, a good father, a loving husband...

As the brusque conversation continued, Mr. Wilson offered not one kind, gentle, nor consoling word... What, he ask for the freedom of Madero, interest himself in the fate of Pino Suárez? Huerta could do whatever he thought best!... The Ambassador was unmoved.

*Señora Madero:* Other ambassadors, your colleagues, are trying to avoid a catastrophe. The ones from Chile, Brazil, Cuba...

*Mr. Wilson* (smiling cruelly and hammering out each word): They... have... no.... influence.

It must have seemed to Doña Sara, her heart in an agony of grief and terror, her mother-in-law and sister-in-law beside her, in blackest mourning for Gustavo, that she had confronted Satan himself.

Márquez Sterling, arriving for his own appointment with the ambassador, met the Madero women, Sara in tears, in the foyer. He escorted them to their car, directing their driver to the Cuban Legation. He then went back inside and found

Wilson smilingly cool as if nothing untoward, nothing at all, had happened.

From Wilson's photographic portrait, a quick sketch of this late-on-the-stage character who would have made our good John Bigelow squirm in his grave:

His big chin crowned by an animal-sized mustache; his receding hair, parted in the middle and arranged into wings oiled and combed into exquisite submission. Head cocked, arms crossed, he wears a double-breasted jacket, starched collar, and an expression that says, "Mine, that's the answer." Those smirking eyes are sharp enough to nail a sparrow. Henry Lane Wilson, a Hoosier lawyer who had lost his money in the panic of 1893 but whose political connections with the McKinley administration levered him into a first ambassadorship in Chile, may not have worn a Stetson, but he was a diplomatic cowboy, who went a-roaming on the Mexican range by his lonesome, packing a crappy little pistol that Madero's enemies mistook, alas, for an army's worth of howitzers.

"Poor Mexico," as Porfirio Díaz so famously said, "so far from God and so close to the United States." (I had never forgotten my dismay to read John Bigelow's diary of his visit to Mexico in the early 1880s, wherein he confided that the then U.S. ambassador, "a large and pleasant looking man," an ex-judge from Louisiana, "betrayed his diplomatic experience... by saying that when he came there they told him he ought to call on people of the city whom he wished to know but he said to himself, if they wish to know me, let them come to me." The U.S. ambassador to Mexico then casually called Matías Romero "a nigger.")

And, no, Ambassador Wilson did not think it necessary to send Señora Madero's telegram to President Taft. She insisted. It made no difference. Two nights later, Madero and Pino Suárez were killed by the *Ley Fuga*, that is, executed quick and dirty, Porfirian-style. Doña Sara would not have received her husband's body if not for the intercession of the Cuban ambassador.

But what Ambassador Márquez Sterling either was not told or chose to leave out of his memoir is the little exchange between Ambassador Wilson and Señora Madero just before that business about Vice President Pino Suárez. As she told the American journalist Robert Hammond Murray and later attested to the American Vice-Consul (my translation from the Spanish in Collado Herrera and Pérez Rosales' biography):

> The ambassador told me: "I will be frank with you, señora. Your husband's fall is due to the fact that he never wanted to consult me... You know, señora, that your husband had very peculiar ideas." I answered him: "Mr. Ambassador, my husband does not have peculiar ideas, but high ideals..."

"Peculiar ideas": two small words encapsulating a thunderstorm of visceral disgust.

Wilson knew of Madero's Spiritism. In his memoirs, *Diplomatic Episodes in Mexico, Belgium, and Chile*, Wilson repeatedly disparages Madero as "a dreamer of dreams," "more of a mountebank than a messiah," "the dreamer of Coahuila who essayed the role of a Moses," "a person of unsound intellect, of imperfect education and vision," with a "disordered intellect," "disorganized brain," "dangerous form of lunacy," and so on.

Henry Lane Wilson may have been a lush and a heartless blowhard, but his hostility toward "peculiar ideas" fell lockstep in line with those of most educated men of his day and certainly with Mexico's "*científicos*," those Porfirian-era followers of Compte, exemplified by Finance Minister José Yves Limantour. Material men in a material world: oil, mining, breweries, railroads! The afterlife? Concern with such insubstantialities was for old ladies—or, say, for Freemasons of the more esoteric stripe.

Indeed, the Freemasons set up a howl of protest at the murder of Brother Madero, the Scottish Rite's *New Age* editorial of March 1913 calling it "the foulest and blackest crime of the age." When President Woodrow Wilson (no relation) took office that same year, he refused to recognize Huerta's outlaw government. To Ambassador Wilson's indignation—for he thought he had done a swell job protecting American interests, considered General Huerta "an able, adroit [and] courageous man" and Mexico "an ignorant nation," unfit for democracy—he was dismissed, to spend the rest of his life suing for libel and otherwise attempting to defend the indefensible.

But again I venture too far ahead of the story. Let's boomerang back to when Victoriano Huerta was just another Porfirian officer whack-a-moling another campesino uprising and Henry Lane Wilson just another junior ambassador *en route* from Santiago de Chile to Brussels: 1904, the year after Sara and Francisco's marriage, and the year the words her young husband believed came from another realm propelled him onto the battlefield of the Porfirian political arena.

### 1904–1907: First Messages for Arjuna

Out in the desert, it's like being on the open sea; the sky becomes your world. You see the weather before even it knows what it wants to do. Time relaxes under the infinity of sun, and the sun is an oppression—everything, agave, ocotillo, canyon wall, grudging obeisance by its shadow. It is so quiet that apart from the tiny flies and black bees and the rare chirp of a cactus wren or *gwhee-gwha* of quail what you hear is the whine of your own blood in your ears. At night, coyotes sing to the stars and the stars, they are watching. It's one of the thin places, as the Irish call them, where the veil between this world and the invisible, so they say, is easily traversed—though it looks nothing like the mist-drifted Burren, but rather the Negev desert, where at twilight one might fancy a djinni crouching behind every outcropping. In the night, on both sides of the border around the western bend of the Rio Grande, and into

Coahuila, little colored orbs, blinking and dancing along the mesas, have been reported since the times of the Apaches. I have seen them. They cannot be cars nor planes, for they slide and bounce far too high and fast, and sometimes—I have seen this, too—they split like balls of mercury, or at their whim, it seems, pull apart like strings of taffy. (What are they? Who knows. But so many people, prickly with hostility, refuse to even hear about the lights. Hmm, isn't that interesting?)

Australia was the name of Madero's ranch that lay like an islet in this sea of silence, two hard days by horseback from his home in San Pedro de las Colonias. It was a working ranch, with a crew to harvest guayule, a native shrub processed for its latex. And this was no minor enterprise: about half of all U.S. rubber imports came from guayule, and Mexican guayule was so profitable that such heavyweights as John D. Rockefeller and Daniel Guggenheim invested some 30 million dollars in the Madero family's competition, the Continental-Mexican Rubber Company. Madero also used Australia as his personal retreat. Here, on a hill high enough to provide a Moses-like survey of wind-swept cinnamon-and-lavender distances, he constructed his stone observatory.

Ah, the juxtaposition: earthly profit, starry wonder.

And speaking of earthly profit, in 1904, Don Evaristo, pater-familias of the ever-expanding and ever-wealthier Madero clan, was, like Don Porfirio himself, nearing his 80th. Born in the decade after Mexico had won its independence from Spain, Don Evaristo had witnessed, in his long life, the revolving-door madness of Antonio López de Santa Anna, Napoleon of the West, President of Mexico on eleven occasions, who once named himself Serene Highness and commanded a state funeral for his leg—which had been blown off by a French cannon in the Pastry War of 1838, then disinterred from his hacienda to be placed in a specially-built Mexico City shrine. Don Evaristo had also lived through the secession of Texas in 1836 and the U.S. invasion of 1846-48, when the Stars and Stripes flew over Mexico City's National Palace, after which Mexico lost nearly half its territory—today's states of California, Colorado, Nevada, Utah, and Wyoming, as well as parts of Arizona and New Mexico (and, to add to the booty, Santa Anna's prosthetic leg, still on display in the Illinois State Military Museum). With the Gadsden Purchase of 1853, the rest of what are now Arizona and New Mexico went to the United States, and Santa Anna, who had authorized it, promptly embezzled the 10 million dollar proceeds. Even with Santa Anna finally yanked off the stage, Mexico had not yet taken its full dose of humiliation: after another round of civil war, its infrastructure in shambles and treasury hopelessly indebted to European banks and bond holders, it was pummeled by the 1861 invasion of the French Imperial Army, then subjected to Maximilian von Habsburg's mirage of a reign, and then, with the restoration of the Republic in 1867, another tumultuous period of weak governments. In the north, none could stop the ravages of the Apaches and Comanches and general banditry. Don Evaristo's century was, as Krauze titled his book, the *Siglo de caudillos*, the century of strongmen, and the strongest of all, "master and hero of modern Mexico," as one American journalist would describe him, was Porfirio Díaz, who took power after his 1876 coup d'état against President Sebastián Lerdo de Tejada, successor to Benito Juárez, who had died in office in 1872.

If the kaleidoscope of nineteenth century Mexican history makes you dizzy, you are not alone (and you haven't heard the half of it).

The take home point: until Porfirio Díaz, Mexico was a bloody mess of civil war and foreign invasion.

How did Don Evaristo accumulate such a fortune in such a century? As Manuel Guerra de Luna details in *Los Madero: La saga liberal*, after inheriting lands in Texas, Don Evaristo made the bulk of it in two periods: the early 1860s, when he traded in various goods across the Mexico-Texas border, most notably Confederate cotton handily relabeled for export as Mexican to avoid the Union blockade; and then during the *pax porfiriana*, when Don Porfirio's harsh but foreign investor-friendly rule allowed for improvements in rural security and a nation-wide network of railroads.

Under Porfirio Díaz, "Mexico became safe for the right people," as historian Stanley Ross put it.

Having served as governor of Coahuila in the early 1880s, Don Evaristo had lost his appetite for politics. But his enormous business empire, extending as far as Yucatan, ranging from textiles to guayule to cotton, ranching, mining, banking and more, depended upon the favor and protection of high-placed friends in Mexico City. Porfirio Díaz's rein was never monolithic; even the most autocratic government has *camarillas*, men clustering around a given underling, expressing a certain view of how the world should work and what their personal advantage might be. The go-to friend for Don Evaristo was no small player: José Yves Limantour, that arch-*científico* who had been serving as Porfirio Díaz's Minister of Finance since 1893. No story of the fall of Porfirio Díaz is complete without several appearances by this magnificently wealthy, whippet-thin, and most sophisticated of Mexico City's silk top-hatted figures—who, it so happens, owned tens of thousands of acres surrounding Tomóchic, which in last years of the Porfiriato, he would sell for the then staggering sum of over half a million dollars to the Cargill Lumber Company. We will hear more about Limantour.

But consider Limantour's Mexico City: for all its ragged beggars, donkeys and carts, and the spectacle of campesinos, with whistles and stick, driving their turkey flocks to market, it was a city of palaces, charming hotels, theaters, fine restaurants, and a Jockey Club. We must remember, for it explains so much, that unlike, say, Villa or Zapata, the Maderos were men who had both the means and the social savvy to segue from a dusty guayule ranch to meet, on a Thursday, with such as Limantour.

Many a time I have ridden the cage-like private elevator up to that handsome wood-paneled lair in Mexico's National Palace. One corner of this building belongs to the President, the other, directly overlooking the Cathedral, to the Minister of Finance. I wonder whether Limantour, for all his years there, ever got used to the place. One enters from the noisy, crowd-filled Zócalo past a gauntlet of armed men into a maze of cold, dark patios. The stone staircase to the Minister of Finance's office, a freestanding marvel of engineering, dates from the time of Maximilian. (The empress Carlota, doubtfully, asked how sturdy it was. The legend says a troop of soldiers, three abreast, were marched up to demonstrate.) Interminable hall-ways, floors slanting from earthquakes past, stone lintels carved with animal faces, evoke the ghosts of viceroys, scurrying mes-sengers, plume-hatted ambassadors. Before Maximilian, the palace served as a jail and had fallen into such dereliction that it became infested with fleas; under Maximilian, it was the venue for balls with Viennese waltzes and pink champagne; under the restored Republic, its ground floor was reborn as the austerely tidy home of President Benito Juárez and his family. Extravagantly refurbished *à la française* under Porfirio Díaz, its Oriental carpets and antique sofas exude a musty smell, and one suspects they always have. Underneath the foundations lie the broken-dragon ruins of Moctezuma's palace. Moctezuma, whose golden sandals did not touch the ground, whose seers had forewarned him that "our cities will be laid to waste, we and our children and our vassals will be annihilated."

Yes, it is haunted.

And you will remember, the National Palace was where in 1913, President Madero and his vice president were impris-oned for several days, and from there, hustled away to their executions.

Don Evaristo never claimed to be clairvoyant, but from the first moment his grandson stepped into the political area, in 1904, he must have had a terrible foreboding. In 1905 it was his influence that saved Francisco from arrest after his Benito Juárez Democratic Club very publically protested the usual ballot-stuffing in Coahuila's gubernatorial election. (According to Madero's biographer Ross, Sara had to bar the door to their house to the police, who were after the editors of the club's

magazine *El Demócrata* and satirical paper *El Mosco* (The Fly).
The editors clambered over the wall and hid in a wagon under
a pile of straw; eventually, they made it to the United States.)

We know from Don Evaristo's letters that, as his grandson
began to move toward his first presidential campaign, the patriarch became increasingly worried for his family and businesses
and embarrassed before his friend, Limantour. But not all the
Maderos were immune to Francisco's magnetic visions of power.
To the Revolution itself, Francisco brought along his wife, his
father and mother, his brothers Gustavo, Raúl, and others, as
well as various cousins and uncles—so many indeed, that as
President, when he kept Gustavo as his right-hand man and
appointed family members to his cabinet (Ernesto Madero to
Finance and Rafael Hernández to Justice), he would be roundly
accused of nepotism. But only a few, if any, joined his camp
purely in sympathy with his Spiritism. For most, Gustavo especially, it was some combination of personal loyalty, shared
political ideals, patriotism, an alignment with the David most
likely to topple the Porfirian Goliath, a chance for adventure
and a chance for power. As we know, many of Madero's followers, even decades after his death, never imagined that his beliefs
were anything but a typical Mexican gentleman's Catholicism;
active as he was in Spiritist circles, Madero wrote his Spiritist
articles under pseudonyms, requested discretion of his cor-
respondents, and otherwise remained, coyly, and sometimes
very lumpily, behind the curtains.

*We are not our physical body; we are spirits, and as such we
are immortal and we are destined, lifetime by lifetime, not by
any ritual intermediated by clerics, but by freely chosen good
works, to evolve into ever higher levels of consciousness and
so return to God.* This was the message Madero believed that
he had descended onto this earth to deliver, to raise the consciousness of his brother Mexicans and humanity, and he would
do it, with help from the invisible world, by political action.
Like the warrior Arjuna of the Bhagavad-Gita, with faith in his
immortality and the cosmic justness of his cause, he marshaled

the courage to fight. The fight: a real vote and no re-election; in other words, the end of tyranny, for democracy to reign in Mexico—and, ultimately, for the religion and science of Spiritism to supplant the Catholic Church.

It might have seemed a mad dream, but in the space of four years, from 1904 to 1908, ever attentive to the instructions from the spirits, Madero advanced by prodigious bounds, from provincial political novice to formulating his presidential campaign, from fledgling medium to visionary mystic, author of several Spiritist articles (under the pen name "Arjuna"), Maecenas of the Spiritist magazines *La Cruz astral, El Siglo espírita*, and *Helios*, and lynchpin of two Spiritist congresses, held in Mexico City in 1906 and 1908. If Spiritism had declined in the years after the death of its peripatetic evangelist, General Refugio I. González, Madero played a leading role in reviving it and giving it wings.

Madero was already publishing books as well: the previously mentioned Spanish 1906 translation by Ignacio Mariscal of *Après la mort* by Léon Denis (co-sponsored with his father, Francisco Madero), and his own elegantly designed and privately printed folio of 1907, *Estudio sobre la conveniencia de la construcción de una presa en el Cañón de Fernández, para almacenar las aguas del Río Nazas* (a study for the project of a dam)—and sent copies of the latter to both President Díaz and Secretary Limantour.

Madero's activism in two realms, political and Spiritist, were inseparable. As Enrique Krauze put it, Madero's "politics does not displace Spiritism; it is born of it." And as we shall see, Madero approached them in tandem, and with similar modus operandi—that of Kardec's Mexican translator, General González, which worked as well for Spiritist circles as it did for political cells: first, communicate a set of ideas, preferably backed by a widely-circulated book; invite the audience to organize themselves into groups that meet regularly; knit them together with a newspaper or magazine; and convoke a national congress.

The spirit of his dead brother, Raúl, was the first to encourage him in his public endeavors, as Madero had shakily transcribed in late 1903:

> [The man of higher consciousness] aspires to helping his fellow citizens, with whatever useful project, working toward some higher good to will raise society's moral level, which will bring it up from oppression, from slavery, and fanaticism.

After the failure of the gubernatorial campaign he backed in Coahuila in 1905, Madero recognized that the greatest chance for change, the shining prize—the Presidency of the Republic—would come in 1909, with the campaign for the election in 1910. In the meantime, Madero kept up his wide-ranging and constant letter writing, carefully nurturing allies. He sent both money and advice to political agitators and prisoners, among them, the Flores Magón brothers, Enrique and Ricardo, who were leaders of the Liberal Party, union organizers, anarchists schooled in the Russian literature of Bakunin and Kropotkin, and publishers of *Regeneración*—although, disapproving of their confrontational tactics, Madero withdrew that support after 1906. It was not the time for revolution, in his judgment, but peaceful struggle within the confines of the law for fair and open elections in 1910.

Neither had Madero joined his fellow Spiritist Lauro Aguirre in calling for armed insurrection, though he shared many of Aguirre's ideas about the spirit world and social justice—and his indignation over Díaz's decision to smash Tomóchic. In his first book Madero mentions *Tomóchic*, a popular novel of 1893 by Heriberto Frías, an army lieutenant and eyewitness to the atrocities, but I do not know whether Madero saw Aguirre's screed of the same title, published from his exile in El Paso in 1901; I did not find it in the remains of Madero's library. In *Ringside Seat to the Revolution*, David Dorado Romo describes

Aguirre's *Tomóchic* as "a metaphysical-revolutionary book,"
which puts forward Teresa Urrea "with her extraordinary light-
ness of being," as Mexico's best hope to attain a higher level of
consciousness—as Romo puts it,"Revolution [as] a collective
form of astral projection." No doubt Aguirre had been influenced by the Spiritists' fascination with the patron saint of
France, Joan of Arc, that peasant girl of the fifteenth century
who heard angels' voices commanding her to save her people
from the English. Incredibly, Joan was given troops to lead;
dressed in armor, she led them on a white horse, and they were
saved. But then, for refusing to recognize the authority of the
Church—"I answer to God alone," Joan told the Inquisitors—she
was burned at the stake.

Teresa Urrea, remarkable as her many alleged talents may
have been, was no Joan of Arc, much as Aguirre and some of
her followers wanted to see her this way. Well, maybe a mini-
Joan of Arc. According to Romo, back in 1896, five years after
the rebellion in Tomóchic, a few dozen mainly Yaqui Indians
shouting, "Viva la Santa de Cabora!" attacked the customs
house in Nogales, Sonora; a few days later, 19 rebels attacked
Ojinaga, at the Texas border in the remote "Big Bend"; and a
month after that, fifty Teresistas tried to take Palomas, on the
border with Columbus, New Mexico. Small stakes, all suicidal.
And anyway, it seems Aguirre's reference to the Maid of Orleans
may have sailed past most of the Santa de Cabora's followers.
According to Vanderwood, they also called Teresa "the mother
of Moctezuma" and "the long-dreamed of Mexican Messiah."

To look at Teresa's portrait, her languid expression reminis-
cent of Jiddu Krishnamurti's, her hair done up, the little star
earrings, a sleeping puppy in the crook of her arm, one might
easily assume that she had nothing to do with such violence,
that the much older Aguirre, with whom she purportedly wrote
and published a newspaper, acted in her name, and on her
father's authority. Her great-nephew, the novelist Luis Alberto
Urrea, spins vivid tales of her shamanic and romantic life on the
run from Don Porfirio's assassins, while historian David Dorado

Romo argues that Teresa may have had more of a hand in these bloody rebellions than has been previously suspected—but as far as the 1910 Revolution goes, it's neither here nor there, for by 1904, a new Messiah had stepped forth, at least in his own mind, and Teresa had become a different creature. At the turn of the century, she had taken a hefty fee from a promoter to display her healing powers, touring from New York to Los Angeles (shades of the Fox sisters and P.T. Barnum), and this seemed to have dimmed her powers. She lived for a while in Los Angeles. In 1906 she died of tuberculosis in her bedroom in Clifton, Arizona.

As for Lauro Aguirre, whose grainy photograph in the *El Paso Times* shows a brittle fierceness and wild hair, his fellow revolutionists took him for a crackpot. Romo quotes Ricardo Flores Magón to his brother Enrique: "He's an old, innocent Christ, a bit unbalanced, but incorruptible... we shouldn't trust him with any secrets."

Nonetheless, by 1905, the possibility for revolution began inching closer to reality. Now past his seventy-fifth year, Porfirio Díaz was becoming stiffer, stuffier, increasingly ham-handed. Portraits of him echo those of the Emperor Franz Joseph in the same period: noble, snowy-haired, distant (we can imagine them being ignored by the clerks in every post office). How he had changed over the decades, and how Mexico had changed! According to John Mason Hart, by the turn of the century, in addition to British, French, German, and other European investments in Mexico, fully fifty percent of all U.S. foreign investments were in Mexico. Foreigners controlled every major Mexican industry from banking to communications to mining, as well as the clattering web of railroads that now criss-crossed the country. From his first years in office, and avidly upon his return in the early 1880s, Porfirio Díaz's government welcomed foreign investment, and the investors, who coveted Mexico's wealth of natural resources and piteously low labor costs, obligingly put Porfirio's men in their pockets—that is, they paid them to sit as nonparticipating members of their boards and for "consulting." As Agustín de Iturbide y Green had foreseen back in 1894, the entire Díaz operation was ultimately unsustainable; what held it together was "money and murder"—and one day the money would run out.

As the regime tottered into the twentieth century, the Mexican middle and lower middle classes, and many members of the provincial elites, the latter now having to compete with Guggenheims, Rockefellers and Stillmans, were increasingly squeezed and sidelined. (To take one example of many, the Maderos themselves had a long-running legal dispute over water from the Nazas River, diverted away from their cotton-growing estates to irrigate lands owned by an American and British company.) Campesinos, who had suffered successive crop failures and lost so much of their ancestral land to the hemp, lumber, sugar and other commodity plantations owned by Porfirian cronies and unimaginably huge U.S. trusts, were becoming restless. According to Hart, by 1910, 90 percent of the campesino population had no land at all.

The fractures, at first hairline, began to gape open in 1905 when, in part due to Mexico's over-borrowing and the United States' decision to restrict silver purchases, the silver-backed peso underwent a sharp devaluation. This hit Mexicans' purchasing power like a gut punch—and made their land all the more attractive to buyers with dollars. With food prices up and wages sinking, Limantour's fiscally conservative response compounded the pain and the urgency with which urban workers, like their counterparts abroad, began organizing and agitating for better wages and conditions.

Limantour, for all his power and *savoir faire*, could not repress the winds and tides of international finance. After the San Francisco earthquake of 1906, which put U.S. insurance companies under tremendous pressure, dollar interest rates rose, further cramping his ability to finance the Mexican government. Then, in the spring of that year, the Mexican workers at Cananea, an American-owned copper mine in Sonora, erupted in a strike—thanks in part to the now staggering wage differentials between

American and Mexican workers and the organizing efforts of the Flores Magón brothers and *Regeneración*. Hired police fired on unarmed strikers, killing twenty-three. Afterwards, Mexican soldiers and rural police did their brutal mop-up. Muckrakers took notice. John Kenneth Turner wrote of Cananea in his sensational *Barbarous Mexico*, a book often called the *Uncle Tom's Cabin* of the Mexican Revolution:

> Miners were taken from the jail and hanged. Miners were taken to the cemetery, made to dig their own graves and were shot. Several hundred of them were marched away to Hermosillo, where they were impressed into the Mexican army. Others were sent away to the penal colony on the islands of Tres Marías. Finally, others were sentenced to long terms in prison.

Even more scandalous for Mexican public opinion was that, in his panic, the Mexican governor had allowed a party of armed Arizona Rangers in to help guard the company's property.

In January of the following year, near Orizaba, an industrial town between Mexico City and Veracruz, the army fired on strikers and their children at the European-owned Río Blanco Textile Mills. No one knows how many were killed; estimates range from 100 to several hundred. Turner:

> Volley after volley was discharged into the crowd at close range. There was no resistance whatsoever. The people were shot down in the streets with no regard for age or sex, many women and children being among the slain. They were pursued to their homes, dragged from their hiding places and shot to death. Some fled to the hills, where they were hunted for days and shot on sight.

One begins to appreciate the terrible risk Francisco Madero was taking even to be in communication with the Flores Magóns and giving financial support to Paulino Martínez, jailed for merely commenting on the strike in his Mexico City newspaper.

In 1907, it seemed that Agustín de Iturbide y Green's long-ago prophecy of "impending collapse" was at last coming true. The Mexican economy was still reeling from the 1905 crisis, and the north was afflicted by droughts when prices for Mexican sugar collapsed. Then, in the fall of 1907, for six terrifying weeks, New York City and other American banks were attacked by runs. Frantic depositors jostled in lines and crowds that spilled into the streets. It was like a fire without a fire station; there was no monetary authority to inject emergency liquidity; the Federal Reserve Bank would not be created for another six years. J.P. Morgan, "the Jupiter of Wall Street," came to the rescue with loans—for the big boys. Dozens of other banks failed (according to Hart, 20 percent of Texas banks alone). Now Limantour was finding it increasingly painful to finance Mexican debt. Tax revenues fell. Corn had to be imported.

In April of that year, the spirit Raúl receded as Madero began to receive messages from a new spirit, a kind of Saint Ignatius of Loyola, zealous and demanding, who claimed to have been a Mexican in previous incarnations and signed himself "José."

> My love for you is immense and my greatest
> pleasure is to talk with you, but in order to do
> so easily, it is indispensable that with bound-
> less energy you do as I say.

José prescribed frequent and fervent prayer, constant work, impeccable self-control, giving frequent healings, and reading uplifting books with utmost concentration—all to raise his vibrations and so be able to receive the communications that would help him formulate his plan, a vital part of which

would be writing the book that would become his platform,
*La sucesión presidencial en 1910* (The Presidential Succession
in 1910).

Porfirio Díaz's term would end in 1910, the year he would
be eighty. Would he run for yet another term? And if anything
should happen to him, a stroke for instance? He did have a
son, "Porfirito," a colonel in his mid-thirties, too green to be
taken seriously. (His nephew, Félix Díaz, who would get up a
rebellion against Madero, was not yet on anyone's radar.) There
was Limantour, leader of the *científicos*, but he seemed unlikely
to gain the support of the military or general public. General
Bernardo Reyes, Governor of Nuevo León, briefly emerged as a
popular favorite, but he lost his nerve, if he ever had any, and
accepted a mission to "study military tactics" in Europe. Ramón
Corral, the incumbent Vice President, was a long-time insider
but in poor health. (The Revolution would find Corral in Paris,
close to death from pancreatic cancer.) In sum, various names
floated in the air, none of them with weight.

Meanwhile, though Madero had not yet begun to neglect
his businesses as seriously as he would after 1908, already the
list of his extracurricular activities would make a Hercules
hyperventilate: channeling the spirits, performing healing
with magnetic passes (which excited some comment when he
performed them on a drunk who'd passed out in the street),
prescribing homeopathic remedies, running his and Sara's
soup kitchen and a school for his worker's children, the Club
Democrático Benito Juárez and its publications *El Demócrata*
and *El Mosco*, his work for the Spiritist Congresses, incessant letter-writing to all corners of Mexico and abroad—from
Limantour himself (about the project for a dam) to a businessman in Del Rio, Texas, to his little brothers at school in Culver,
Indiana, to León Denis, *"Cher maitre et frère en croyance…"* It
must have seemed to his wife Sara that he had become a blur,
three different men in eleven places at once. And though he
would travel much more after 1908, even now, whether by mule,
by car, or by train, Madero went toing and froing so much that

it would be difficult to characterize him but by a list (read in random order, oft-repeated): Scribbling letters and notes at his desk on the porch of his house in San Pedro de las Colonias (bougainvillea blossoms littering the tiles); in tails and top-hat, dashing from a Mexico City restaurant (one imagines Sara, skirt in hand, heels clicking, behind); at a noisy family dinner in Parras de la Fuente, the obedient eldest grandson kissing Don Evaristo's hand; in boots and a straw hat, inspecting the fields with his foreman; in tweeds, on a cold winter's night in Australia, adjusting his telescope, the better to identify Polaris, Mars or, say, the craters of the moon.

It was in the silence of Australia that the spirits could come through louder than anywhere else. They would urge him to go there. They would have much more to say. And whether in Australia or his house in San Pedro, Madero was listening, pen in hand.

## The Struggle That Is About to Begin

And then, if there were a banana peel of destiny, apparently Don Porfirio smoked it. Perhaps the old dictator was suffering from the effects of arterial sclerosis; perhaps, never free of his retinue of sycophants, he had come to believe in some Potemkin Republic where slave labor, outrageous land grabs, jails filled with political prisoners, and the most lascivious corruption did not exist; or perhaps, for the interview was arranged by his ambassador to the United States, Don Porfirio was simply over-anxious to reassure U.S. opinion about Mexico's prospects, and naïvely assumed that no one in Mexico would notice something published in English. Nonetheless, his cabinet, including his *éminence grise*, Limantour, were agog to read the interview by James Creelman in the March 1908 issue of *Pearson's Magazine*, which was widely disseminated in Spanish translation, as early as March 3 in *El Imparcial*, then *The Mexican Herald* and *El Tiempo*.

Often cited but rarely read today in its entirety, Creelman's is an extraordinary article, a bubble bath of drool. The author, a well-known yellow journalist, gazes upon "the greatest man of the continent," "the nation-maker," "master and hero of modern Mexico," "the slender, erect form, the strong, soldierly head and commanding, but sensitive, countenance with an interest beyond words to express," and "dark brown eyes that search your soul"—and, Whoa Nelly, that was just the first page.

The oft-quoted dynamite fuse fizzes 12 pages in:

> "I welcome an opposition party in the Mexican republic," [Don Porfirio] said. "If it appears, I will regard it as a blessing, not as an evil. And of it can develop power, not to exploit, but to govern, I will stand by it, support it, advise it and forget myself in the successful inauguration of complete democratic government of the country.

> "It is enough for me that I have seen Mexico rise among the peaceful and useful nations. I have no desire to continue in the Presidency. This nation is ready for her ultimate life of freedom."

Within days, Madero was writing to his political allies about the Creelman interview, "the great sensational question in the Republic." On March 9, to a friend in Saltillo:

> although we should not put much faith in the Strongman's offer... we should start thinking about the matter, both what political position we should take and who we might decide on as a candidate. . .

That same month, the Second Spiritist Congress, of which Madero was a key organizer and sponsor, would meet in Mexico City. On March 15, the morning he was to board his train, he transcribed this message from the spirit José:

> Today you go to the great capital of the Republic. You are going to fulfill your duty. You will not be alone in this noble task; we will be with you and most of the Congress. Have faith. Every day try to concentrate with greater calm, to pray with more feeling, so that you will attract more divine energies, energies which will give you the strength to fulfill your mission.

And just a few days later, the Second Spiritist Congress having concluded:

> Now that you have time, dedicate yourself more often to meditation, to prayer, and when you feel you have greater calm, formulate the plan you must follow...

On April 2:

> As I have told you many times, try to take advantage of being alone now, so that you may undertake a more intense intellectual work.
>
> Do not forget to do, and often, your emanations and prayers... so that you may guarantee your definitive triumph in a short time.
>
> You see how your steps have obeyed... your preconceived plan. You see how you are going with the flow of things, or better said, by the power of what you yourself have developed, in a given direction, and there is no human power that can stop you.

It seems Madero had begun to formulate his ideas about challenging Porfirio Díaz. On April 8, José said:

> You have loosed the arrow! You would be mad to try to stop it. The only thing you can do now is prepare yourself as well as you can to await the consequences. What you need is to protect yourself with all your powers, with all your energy ...
>
> The great battle is drawing close. If you triumph, it will be the victory of highest fruits, it will be the beginning of a series of triumphs and then yes, I can assure you emphatically that you will be sure of a definitive triumph, of realizing all your ideals and with dignity you will fulfill the mission you have taken on and for which we have based so many hopes, the evolution of this part of humanity.

By May, José was congratulating Madero for having raised his vibrations with prayer, clean eating, clean living, rising early and foregoing his afternoon siesta; now he could be rewarded with greater powers. In the meantime:

> Flee from everything that wastes time, try to keep yourself constantly busy... May God shower you with his blessed rays so that you may strength yourself and give yourself greater vigor for the struggle that is about to begin.

The problem was that to challenge Porfirio Díaz was to poke a not-yet-toothless tiger. Madero and his family members could be arrested or assassinated. The haciendas and other businesses and relationships that Don Evaristo and his sons and grandsons had built at great effort over many decades could be damaged or lost. Francisco would have to be firm with his father; for the higher good, he was going to proceed with what he needed to do for the presidential election in 1910. Perhaps he knew he could never get Don Evaristo's blessing, but he wanted his father's. His father, after all, was a fellow Spiritist. He would not get it for many months, but on June 22, the spirit Raúl popped back in to reassure him:

> When you settle this matter you will feel like an aviator when, all of a sudden, he feels the ties that have bound him to earth break, and rapidly he rises to the heights of peace and serenity, of calm, of happiness, and from these heights you will be able to better contemplate the smallness of earthly matters and you will value them as they should be justly valued and you will see more clearly the road you must follow to its end, shining with glory and happiness.

On July 18, José counseled him that he needed to raise his vibrations further, that he should spend some ten days in Australia, where,

> in greatest calm, and surrounded by such favorable conditions, you can do your work, which will have an immense resonance. Everything you note in movement in this sense only better prepares the ground for when your book appears.

José was referring not to the *Manual espírita*, but the book that would precede it, *La sucesión presidencial en 1910*. It was intended to launch a fair, open, and entirely legal presidential campaign, but in hindsight we see that in fact, it launched the beginning of Mexico's twentieth century, its defining moment as a modern nation. Yes, the Mexican Revolution was launched not by a grenade or a bullet or a cannonball but by a book. And as Madero was writing it on the porch of his house in San Pedro, Coahuila, he received multiple messages from José, such as, on August 13:

> Very dear little brother: Keep doing your auto-magnetization experiments... Once again I recommend that you zealously dedicate yourself to finishing "Mexico Through the Centuries," so that you may start your book as soon as possible. You see what a mistake you have made in putting off this reading, for now your time is very limited and who knows when you can go to Australia to finish writing your book...the truth is, there is no comparison with the advantages you would have in Australia...

August 29 (still in San Pedro):

> My dear brother, you are on a very good road... Very soon you will feel the surprising results of this regimen of life. With this and with zealous prayer... you will be completely invulnerable and you will triumph with greatest brilliance in the struggle that is approaching...

September 10:

> you can take out a typewriter when you finish so that as you write on the typewriter you can give it a thorough revision... when it is finished you will send it to be printed.

September 19:

> If you can, start right away with organiz-
> ing your notes so that they can go into their
> respective chapters, but do not yet start writ-
> ing the chapters because it might hurt your
> eyes to do so much work... Keep doing your
> daily inspirations, emanations and prayers,
> the latter as zealously as you can. As for com-
> municating with us, you should do so every
> time you have any doubt...

September 20:

> Tomorrow start writing the introduction, but
> always, before stating your work, first invoke
> the help of the Highest, eat a little less for
> breakfast than usual, and pray with zeal...

October 2:

> in some two weeks you will have finished your
> work and you will be able to begin to clean it
> up and send it to the printer... You still have
> to do the most important part, you still need
> to make a big effort to finish it...onward...

October 18:

> We have closed the parenthesis. Onward now.
> I believe that today you will be in excellent
> condition to write this chapter...

October 27:

> You must look away from the material world
> and turn your eyes toward the spiritual world,

toward your noble ideals, higher, toward the mission you have embraced and that will raise you up so high, that will give you such dignity. To begin, the best thing would be to spend all of today on preparing your work. For now, I believe the best would be for you to correct what you have written by working on the type-writer and go back over the manuscript up to the end of the [part on] militarism...

October 30:

You turn thirty-five today! Very dear little brother: Your divine Creator has put on your shoulders a heavy cross. May you never lack the strength to carry it...Your destiny is glori-ous...You have been selected by your Heavenly Father to fulfill a great mission on earth... We have given you great revelations. Take advan-tage of them. Fulfill your duty. March onward, always, always onward.

November 1:

Very dear brother: Now you can start to work with ardor. Dedicate all of today to work-ing out the plan for the chapters... I tell you that our efforts are having admirable results throughout the Republic and everywhere there is a certain ferment, a certain anxiety, which your book will calm, direct, and your previous efforts will definitively channel. Each day we clearly see the brilliant triumph that will crown your efforts... [General Díaz] is committing stupidity after stupidity and we are making powerful suggestions in his

mind so that he will not be an obstacle to
reestablishing liberty in Mexico. We can now
have a very large influence on him because
he no longer has the vigor he once did, and
his energy has declined considerably at the
same time that the passions that motivated
him have softened with the years...

November 5:

you have worked on [your book] splendidly...
Until very soon, my very dear brother.

The signature on this letter, however, was *Francisco I. Madero.*

On November 16, a new spirit came in, addressing Madero
fondly but more formally:

Very dear brother...I will begin by very cor-
dially congratulating you on your triumphs
over yourself, which have put you in the condition to successfully begin the colossal work
of reestablishing Freedom in Mexico.

It is an arduous enterprise, but you are up
to it and you will happily reach the summit.

Your triumph will be very brilliant and it
will have incalculable consequences for our
beloved Mexico...

The work that follows will be of great
importance but the truth is that everything
rests upon the powerful impression your book
will cause. We have already told you that it
will greatly upset General Díaz, he will fall
into a true panic and his panic will paralyze
him or divert all his strength.

You must understand that before you came

into this world, we agreed to undertake this
mission and to give you all you would need
to succeed.

Toward this end we have been working and
preparing everything, and now that the spirits
are ready, all we need is the powerful electric
current your book will produce...

You must fight a man who is clever, false,
hypocritical. You already know the antithe-
sis with which you must answer him: against
cleverness, loyalty; against falseness, sincerity; against hypocrisy, frankness.

May you have an unshakable faith in the
justice of your cause, in the confidence that
you will fulfill your sacred duty and that the
powers that gather around you will help your
enterprise and will permit you to give your
country immense services. When you call me,
I will return with pleasure, for I am part of
a group of spirits that surrounds you, helps
you, guides you so that you may successfully
crown the work you have begun.

May our Heavenly Father shine upon your
head His treasures of love and goodness.

B. J.

Who was B. J.? Madero did not say in his notes, but it seems
more probable than not, and his grandfather very disparag-
ingly mentioned it in a letter to Limantour, so I am inclined
to agree with the first Mexican historians to write about the
channelings, Rosales and Krauze, that Madero believed it to
be Benito Juárez.

And José? Maybe Madero thought this was José María Morelos, "the slave of the nation," a priest and popular leader of
Mexico's first revolution for independence, who was executed

by a Spanish firing squad in 1815. Maybe. In Mexican history, Josés are legion.

What these spirits actually were, whether of Mexican heroes, disembodied poseurs from the astral realm, parts of Madero's own psyche, or fantasy, or something else, is another question.

### The Last Revolution?

It may not have qualified for any literary prizes, nor overly impressed professors of history or political philosophy, but as a work of propaganda and call to action, Madero's *La sucesión presidencial en 1910* did its job brilliantly. It opens with a trumpet call of a dedication:

> To the heroes of our nation;
> To independent journalists;
> To good Mexicans.

Madero's lengthy prologue, explaining his motives for writing the book, ends thus—and listen to the music of a natural and powerful public speaker:

> In spite of all these great difficulties and dangers an independent writer in Mexico faces, I have not hesitated in undertaking this arduous enterprise... I have always endeavored to work with impartiality and patriotism, and with this I will have fulfilled my duty, which is always relative to one's degree of advancement, of example, of morality, and no one is obliged to give more than they have. As to facing the above mentioned-dangers, when my friends have tried, with energy, to dissuade me from my enterprise, I have always answered with the same dilemma: "If it is not

true that the danger is so great, then we have
some liberty which we can enjoy and work for
the betterment of our country in trying to
form a National Independent Party; or, if the
danger is such that we have no liberty at all,
that our Constitution is a joke, our institutions tread upon, the government's oppression
unbearable; and in those extreme cases when
liberty is in danger; institutions threatened;
when the inheritance our fathers left us,
whose conquest cost them rivers of blood,
has been stolen; it is not the moment to go
around with ruinous anxieties, servile fear,
this is the time to throw oneself into the fight
with resolve, without counting the number
or estimating the power of the enemy, this is
the way our fathers conquered so gloriously,
and we must follow their noble example in
order to save our institutions from the ship-
wreck of tyranny's terrible waves, which aim
to take them prisoner and drown them in the
bottomless abyss of oblivion.

He signed this, *San Pedro, Coahuila, October 1908.* Below
appears a picture of spread wings with a central disc flanked by
two cobras, an image connoisseurs of Egyptian history and his
brother Freemasons might appreciate: Horus Behdety. Horus,
god of Kings, his father's avenger, who soared to the sky as a
winged disc.

In Madero's rendition of Mexican history, which takes up a
good portion of the book, José María Morelos and Benito Juárez,
standing for the principles of Liberty, Democracy, and Law, are
the heroes; Santa Anna and his fellow militarists down to Porfirio Díaz, the villains. He exposes the insidious nature of Díaz's
tyranny, and most damningly, quotes Díaz's own call for revolution against President Benito Juárez in 1871, which ended thus:

> May patriots, sincere supporters of the Constitution, men of duty, lend their support to the cause of electoral freedom, and the country will be saved from its most costly interests. May public officials, recognizing that their powers are limited, honorably return trust in the law to the people who have elected them and strict adherence to the Constitution will be a true guarantee of peace. May no citizen impose himself and remain in perpetuity in power, and this will be the last revolution.

> PORFIRIO DIAZ

That attempt failed, but five years later, with President Lerdo de Tejada in office, Díaz launched his Plan de Tuxtepec, and the coup d'état succeeded.

Díaz, winning crooked election after crooked election, had dominated Mexico for over 30 years. And how had he done this? Agustín de Iturbide y Green called the method "money and murder"; Madero calls it "bread or stick," that is, rewards to friends and terror to enemies, and the latter included the notorious *Ley Fuga*.

> Such brief procedures very quickly cleaned out the bandits, but with such good results that they continued to apply this same procedure to all malcontents and lovers of liberty who, in their limited sphere, protested against the arbitrary rule of local strongmen. How many infamies were hidden at the crossroads of the highways! How many forgotten martyrs sacrificed for their love of liberty!

Madero recounts the destruction of Tomóchic; the enslavement of the Yaqui Indians, who were rounded up, separated from their families, and shipped south to be worked to death on plantations; and the murderous crackdowns on workers in Cananea and Orizaba.

Madero then calls upon his fellow Mexicans to build a true democracy, and toward that end, immediately form a party, the Partido Antireeleccionista (Anti-Re-electionist Party), based on the principles of a fair vote and no re-election. He spells out the precise steps: in local areas, sympathizers could form clubs; these clubs could elect a board in Mexico City, which would then form a national party and set rules for electing delegates to a national convention, and the national convention would elect the party's candidate for the presidency. In this nearly 300-page book, he does not once suggest himself. But of course, this was precisely the idea.

But *La sucesión presidencial en 1910* was not published in 1908. Madero wanted his father's blessing, and his father, already facing serious financial difficulties, and the complete intransigence of the family's patriarch, Don Evaristo, would not give it.

## Querido papacito

Francisco Madero knew perfectly well what was at stake, and with respect and affection, always addressing him *Querido papacito*, Dear Daddy, he wrote to his father at length several times, explaining the urgency of his project. Finally, with *La sucesión presidencial en 1910* already printed and awaiting distribution in the printer's warehouse, on January 20, 1909, he drew back the curtain, as it were, and threw down the gauntlet:

> Although you may be a convinced Spiritist, you have never studied it in more depth in order to discover the mysterious laws it reveals to us, or that we can discover through it. So: it is good that you know that among the spirits

who populate space there is a group that is intensely concerned with the evolution of humanity, for its progress, and every time there is an important event in any part of the world, a large number of them incarnate in order to bring humanity forward, to save this or that people from the yoke of tyranny, of fanaticism, and to give them liberty, which is the most powerful means by which people can progress.

Now Mexico is menaced by a great danger, for if we leave things as they are, absolute power will perpetuate itself in our country; corruption will become even greater, and instead of our country being able to fulfill the designs of providence, serving as mother to generations of virtuous men, it will have to succumb, victim of its sons' weakness and corruption.

This is the idea that my book demonstrates with irrefutable arguments. I want everyone to open their eyes, may those good hearted men who are still here make a powerful effort, and all of them and I in their company, throw ourselves with resolve into the battle to save the Nation, to fulfill our mission, for undoubtedly, ever since we were together in space, we foresaw this battle and we have incarnated with the object of starting it and sustaining it.

Everything is ready now... Dear Daddy: do me the favor of addressing yourself to God who is in heaven, and evoke your mother Rafaelita's help, that you may receive illumination, that you may comprehend the terrible thing you will do to not allow me the freedom to fulfill my mission that providence has given me...

> Consider your decision very carefully: no
> matter what, I will throw myself into the fight,
> for previous commitments make it inevita-
> ble. Tomorrow I go to Torreón to a political
> meeting, we are going to send an announce-
> ment all around the state in order to start
> the campaign...
>
> It will be impossible to not publish [the
> book], and to publish it late, we will lose all
> the advantages that would have resulted...
>
> Send me your blessing. Daddy, remember
> that we come into this world to fight. Let us
> fulfill our destiny with valor!

Two days later, on his return from Torreón, *La sucesión pres-idencial en 1910* already sent out to hundreds of people, Madero received the telegram with his father's blessing and he cried tears of happiness.

> Now at last I no longer have the least doubt
> that Providence guides my steps and visibly
> protects me, for in receiving your blessing I
> see its hand clearly...

He would take his family with him! He did not realize it then, but this meant some of them would die, his father and mother's house would be burned, their lands taken, they would live through days of joy but many more of terror and horror and grief. And his fame would make Don Evaristo's a pale provincial shadow. Today President Francisco I. Madero's bones rest in Mexico City's Art Deco cross between the Arc de Triomphe and a pagoda on steroids: the Monument to the Revolution.

## Australia

There is an apocryphal story that, after writing *La sucesión presidencial en 1910*, Madero spent forty days and nights on his desert ranch, Australia, communing with the spirits. We know he went back and forth to Australia, but the journey required four days on horseback and he wrote too many letters and notes from San Pedro and elsewhere to make that Biblical number of days add up.

But it is wonderful to imagine.

On this last night of 1908, the moon, waxing gibbous, would have been enough to prompt shadows, such as: The stone observatory's down the hill. On the mesa: pearly pools of silken light beneath which mice and jackrabbits and scorpions crouch like djinns, awake and listening in their dens. Cabeza de Vaca, the conquistador who got lost, naked and shivering, unmoored in such immensity but for twinkling Polaris, may have staggered across this very mesa of guayule, whips of ocotillo, torture cushions of biznaga. And in the days of Cabeza de Vaca, the grizzly bear still roamed, a creature so fearsome the Indians would not call it by its name. In such silence, every footstep hits the earth like a giant's, every breath is an ocean's breaking surf. A star trills to earth. And the earth, with everything and everyone, hurtles through eternity, precise in its nested geometry of orbits.

*The time is accomplished, and the kingdom of God is at hand.*

On this last night of 1908, Madero received the message from the spirit José that he would write a second book, one "which will cause an even greater impression." This would be his *Manual espírita*.

Under the name of a Hindu warrior, he would publish it in the winter of 1911, in the midst of fighting the Revolution. He dated its dedication 1909, but he would write it in 1910, the year of that star with the quetzal's tail.

In the spring of 1910, Halley's comet appeared close to the horizon in the early hours of the morning. Children were trundled out in their blankets into gardens and streets and told to remember what they'd seen, for as young as they were, they would not likely see it again. In Paris the patisseries filled their vitrines with special comet petit fours. In New York, hotels offered comet parties on their roof-tops. In the countryside and all over Mexico many prayed, "God save us." Newspapers fanned fears with stories about its wake of poisonous gasses. It was a goddess; it was an omen; it was just a rock of ice blazing in its ancient, mindless ellipse. By summer it was gone. And by August, that book whose author thought it would change the world was a sheaf of papers ready for the printer.

# A BEAM OF LIGHT, A LOADED GUN

## Two Books

When we talk about a "successful book," usually what we mean is one that has a brand-name publisher, enjoys prime shelf space in bookstores, and earns its author buckets of royalties. In other words, we talk about it as a commodity—or, if we're a mite more sophisticated, a hybrid commodity / work of art / scholarship. I say "we" because I am writing and I presume you are reading this in a time and place where books are no longer banned by the government, their authors no longer casually imprisoned—or worse. Lulled by endless streams of made-for-the-movies thrillers and romances, we forget that, as Ray Bradbury put it, "A book is a loaded gun."

Francisco I. Madero intended his *Manual espírita* to be a beam of light, to heal Mexico and the world with his consoling concepts of the nature and meaning of life. However, it is a book that stands on the shoulders of his first book that was, indeed, a loaded gun: *La sucesión presidencial en 1910*, published in the winter of 1909 when Don Porfirio Díaz, the dictator who had stolen the presidency in a coup d'état and ruled Mexico on and off for over thirty years, was about to celebrate his eightieth birthday and, as Mexico's so-called "necessary man," take for himself a seventh term.

Madero had no interest in the capitalist concept of a book's success; he wanted *La sucesión presidencial en 1910* in people's hands, and as fast as possible, and for that he did not need bookstores, he needed a jump-start on Don Porfirio's police. He paid for the printing himself (a first edition of 3,000, and later more) and, as he noted in a letter:

> [T]he first precaution I took was to hand out 800 copies to members of the press and intellectuals throughout Mexico, so when the Government got wind of the book's circulation, it would be too late to stop it. . .

Enterprising, daring, and sophisticated he may have been, but because we are of his future, we cannot see Francisco I. Madero without also seeing his death. From that grim night of February 22, 1913, its shadow seeps back into his presidency of a mere fifteen months; his campaigns, both political and military; the writing of *La sucesión presidencial en 1910* and, what interests us here, his second book, his *Manual espírita*.

A loaded gun, alas, can spray fire in unexpected directions. And then, too, there are the real guns.

## Pandemonium

I spend most of my days alone at my desk, far from Mexico's political fray. But in the seven years I spent writing my novel, which is to say, not only reading and researching in the archives, but with my imagination, spelunking into the nooks and crannies of various characters' points of views— including the Emperor of Mexico's—I had come to understand, more deeply than I had suspected possible, the surprisingly painful realities and conundrums of political power. Despite one's title, how little of it one has at times: the gulf between reality and perception, and the crucial importance of managing perception. On the other hand, in certain circumstances, how much of it—at the snap of one's fingers, appalling, vertigo-inducing amounts of it. The mad, German shepherd-drive of some of those seeking one's favor (my God, where do these people come from?); the oftentimes dangerous naiveté of one's family, friends, and subordinates; the enemies, some decent people fighting for a different flag, but some with all the ethics of rabid raccoons. The idolizers, the paranoid, the gossipers, the hecklers. Then there are the journalists, like an army of sprites, friendly, hateful, helpful, honest, expert, inept. One always opens the newspaper with one's heart clenched. Finally, crucially, I began to understand the necessity, the privilege, the merciless cage, and the possible death-trap, of having always to go everywhere with a team of armed bodyguards.

Just when I had shaped my novel into an advanced draft, President Felipe Calderón named my husband to his cabinet, and though in another century and very different form of government, I learned that what I had so meticulously imagined about the nature of power on a personal level was precisely true.

Of course, the Ministry of Finance is small potatoes compared to the Presidency. And, compared to what it is as I write, the Mexican Presidency in the wake of the 1910 Revolution, never mind who would presume to occupy it, was a very shaky institution.

At only thirty-eight years old, Francisco Madero leapt to the presidency with such velocity he had not had the chance to parse out the nature of that power. He had not learned to consistently distinguish among, never mind elaborate a taxonomy and a roster, of all those high-flying German shepherds, rabid racoons, and sprites—and too, the dedicated civil servants and military officers, the honest men, and the genuine friends. We read his story now, more than a century after his body crumpled to the ground, and it is obvious: of all his many decisions—many of genius, wisdom and bravery, some questionable, some very poor—it was the one he took on February 17, 1913, which proved deadly. President Madero withheld his trust from the person who truly loved him, who, perhaps more than anyone, had made his rise to power possible, and was trying desperately to save his government. Instead, President Madero trusted General Victoriano Huerta.

I am speaking of Madero's brother Gustavo, little more than one year younger, with whom he had spent almost every day of his childhood and who was with him in Maryland, Paris, and Berkeley. Gustavo was taller and had a chubbier face; he combed his blondish hair straight up and back in a pompadour and wore owlish spectacles. His left eye, after a childhood accident with a ball, was glass, but it never proved a handicap. He was a scrappy, hair-trigger fighter (if we believe the Jesuit headmaster of his school in Saltillo). By his early thirties, married to a first cousin, and father of several children, Gustavo had become an incessant traveler, an investor in textile factories, mining companies, a salt-making operation, cotton, guayule, ranching, and railroad cars—the exemplary grandson of Don Evaristo. Early on, sharing his political ideals though apparently not his ardent Spiritism, Gustavo helped his older brother with his Club Democrático Benito Juárez. When he read *La sucesión presidencial en 1910*, Gustavo helped distribute it and, to prepare for his brother's presidential campaign, he started forming clubs. Gustavo donated money, raised money, and later—after Francisco's imprisonment during the presidential election of 1910, his escape and declaration of the Revolution on November 20, 1910—Gustavo became the Revolution's representative, its financial agent and arms procurer. His travels then ranged as far as New York City, Washington, San Antonio and El Paso, Texas—where he slipped across the border to join, at various times, and finally for the decisive Battle of Juárez, his brother, Pancho Villa, Venustiano Carranza, Abraham González, Pascual Orozco, Costa Rican Spiritist poet Rogelio Fernández Güell, Giuseppe Garibaldi II, German agent Felix Sommerfeld, a passel of gringo machine gunners, Mexican patriots, and the rest of the motley crew that was their army.

It was a small army filled in with foreign mercenaries. Gustavo Madero had managed to finance it by an act of political acrobatics, and with the aid of the best Washington, D.C.

lobbyist money could buy: Sherburne G. Hopkins. But these
facts cannot eclipse the largest: the outpouring of celebration for the revolution's victory over Díaz in 1911 showed it
had achieved genuine, nationwide support. Typical, if more
eloquent than most, is the report of Edward I. Bell, a journalist
in Mexico City (*The Political Shame of Mexico*):

> Not in the history of the modern world has
> such an exhibition of idolatry been given as
> that of Mexico's lower orders for Madero as he
> traveled from his home in Parras, in the state
> of Coahuila, to Mexico's capital. His train was
> four days making the seven hundred miles
> journey. Starting on the third of June, 1911,
> nine days after de la Barra had been made
> provisional president, he did not reach Mexico
> City until the seventh, after a triumphal prog-
> ress to the ceaseless shout of "Viva Madero!"
> By day and by night this ceaseless chorus
> rolled from the throats of multitudes gath-
> ered along the track at the crossings, at water
> tanks, at bridges, at culverts, at trestles, and
> in all the towns and cities to do him honor.
>
> It was more than honor this primitive
> people bestowed upon Madero; it was wor-
> ship. From great distances the peons came to
> greet him, to listen to his voice, to look upon
> his face, to touch the hem of his garment. He
> was heralded as a savior of his people; not a
> human, but as a god. The date of this journey
> was unknown, even to Madero himself until
> three days before his departure from the home
> of the Madero clan. Yet all across northern
> and central Mexico the word was carried by
> letter, by telegraph, by grapevine; and those
> who were not bedridden arose and made their

way at the best possible speed to the nearest point on the railway along which the Deliverer was to come.

Those who had money traveled by train from distant points, but immense numbers who had no money came on foot, on burros, on mules, on horses, and in ramshackle carts from as far as two hundred miles, by forced marches, praying that they might arrive in time. They came in rags and bare of foot. They brought their baby children in zerapes [*sic*] swung upon their backs. The aged came with bent shoulders and quaking limbs. The lame and halt came hobbling with cane and crutch. Over mountain trails, across cactus-strewn wastes, the strong carrying the weak, children of tender years, like suckling calves toddling beside their mothers—in every manner by which a primitive people of all conditions of age and action could move about, the poor of Mexico's northern and central states made their way from their customary abiding places to a point on the railroad through which Madero, the peon Messiah, the conqueror of the great Díaz, would pass.

And as his train arrived in Mexico City:

[T]here were fully three hundred thousand visitors added to the city's normal four hundred thousand, and the entry of Madero on the 7th of June was greeted with a testimonial of popular rejoicing beyond anything in the city's history... The streets and plazas were jammed with people without police or military guard. Foreigners of all nations mixed

freely with the natives. Exemplary good nature
and good order marked the day. A new order
of affairs had taken possession of Mexico. The
people were "on honor" and they bore their
dignity well.

And now, as Francisco freely campaigned for and won the
new election for the presidency in 1911, Gustavo remained at his
side, a minister without portfolio, but for all practical purposes,
the President's right-hand man.

Francisco Madero took office in November 6, 1911. By late
1912, things were falling apart.

In the densely populated sugar cane-growing region
of Morelos south of Mexico City, Madero's one-time ally,
Emiliano Zapata and his thousands of followers, impatient
for land reform, had erupted in a rebellion that quickly spread
to neighboring states. In the north, General Bernardo Reyes,
returned from Europe, rebelled and was arrested at the end of
1911; more rebellions broke out in Chihuahua, Oaxaca, Tamau-
lipas. There were disturbances in Yucatan, Tabasco, Campeche.
The press—right, left, center, and gutter—now unleashed and
left unmuzzled by a president who would "prefer to sink with
the law than sustain myself without," turned rabid. Gustavo
Madero was lacerated in the press. President Madero himself
was a cartoonist's dream with his bald head and short legs.
And with the whiff of his Spiritism, vegetarianism, regard for
homeopathy? Oh, ecstasies of satire!

In October 1911, Don Porfirio's nephew, Félix Díaz, a former
inspector of police, had led the Veracruz garrison in revolt; he
expected the army to support him, but it did not. Díaz was
arrested and condemned to death. Against the advice of many,
including his brother Gustavo, Madero commuted his sentence
to imprisonment.

Meanwhile, lawlessness reigned in the countryside.
American and European businessmen complained to their
ambassadors. Ambassador Wilson, who had early on observed

to his Secretary of State that President Madero was "dealing with a most difficult situation and embarrassed by the difficulty of reconciling his peculiar creed [!] and the program of the revolution with the prevalent condition and the stern necessities of the hour," now fulminated to Washington and anyone who would listen, and with such disrespect, that Madero requested he be replaced.

Ambassador Wilson must have known that by this time "Bhîma's" *Manual espírita* was in circulation. At the author's expense, 5,000 copies had been printed—for Mexico at that time, a more than substantial print run.

Somehow—as a snail-paced writer myself, I stand in awe—Madero had written the *Manual espírita* in 1910. In that frenetic year, he campaigned across Mexico for the presidency, was jailed just before the election, escaped to Texas, and then declared the Revolution. Though he dated its dedication 1909, Madero finished writing the *Manual espírita* in August 1910, just about the time he hopped on a train heading north to Texas, disguised as a railroad worker, to escape Porfirio Díaz's police.

Hold that image of late summer 1910: Don Francisco in grease-stained overalls, kerchief, and cap. There is no photograph, so we have to imagine one—taken, say, in the baggage compartment. He's sitting on a mail-bag, one elbow on a knee, the other leg (note that hole in the knee of the trousers) stretched long. The flash catches a gung-ho smile.

Arjuna, Bhîma.

Our author's train chugs north to Texas, its smoke trailing, fabulous ostrich plume, into the sweep of the desert.

Night falls, gorgeous with stars.

Behind him are *La sucesión presidencial en 1910*, the stolen election of 1910, the *Manual espírita* in manuscript.

Before him: the Revolution, the publication of the *Manual espírita*, his second presidential campaign, the National Palace, and the end, Gustavo's murder and then his own.

In the bell-jar of his exile in the United States (lifted only momentarily on November 20, the first attempt at revolution),

Madero will further study the Bhagavad-Gita in the New Orleans Public Library, Sara will await him in San Antonio, and his father and Gustavo will negotiate with Limantour in New York and Washington, and bring arms down to the border. In such a tension-fraught time, so far from home and family in that alien land, what sustains him? In what portions faith, audacity, love?

He wrote frequently to Sara, "my adored wife," always addressing her with the code name "Juana P. de Montiel." Close to Christmas 1910, probably from New Orleans:

> [R]eceive the immense love of your husband
> who thanks God for having given him such a
> good and such a brave little woman, just like
> my dear little mother. With the prayers from
> both of you, who are saints, and with those of
> my sisters who are on the same path, and with
> those of so many unhappy souls who only find
> consolation in God and direct themselves to
> Him, asking help for our cause, undoubtedly
> this will help and we shall triumph.

*Manual espírita* came off the presses in the winter of 1911, in the midst of the fighting. Several months later—the Revolution victorious (so it seemed), and Madero President Elect—the October 1911 issue of *Helios*, a Spiritist magazine financed by Madero, launched the *Manual espírita* with excerpts, an advertisement ("a grand edition at very low prices so that the principles of our exalted philosophy may be widely known"), a formal photographic portrait of President Elect Madero with his father, and this disclaimer of authorship, presumably by *Helios'* editor, Rogelio Fernández Güell:

> Madero's triumph has been the triumph of
> reason and faith against injustice and pessi-
> mism in their governing system, the dreamers'

sublime recovery against the so-called practical men: the apotheosis of the ideal, the glorification of the spirit in its titanic struggle against materialism.

After not exercising their rights for more than thirty years, the Mexican people have elected the leader of the recent liberating revolution, Francisco I. Madero, as head of their Republic.

With the triumph of the revolution, he could have occupied the presidency immediately, however, he preferred to allow the Nation's most free will to show itself in the elections, and the Mexican people, with their unanimous vote in the recent elections, consecrated his prestigious role.

During the past four months, this has been the topic of discussion: Francisco I. Madero as politician, as revolutionary leader, peace-bringer, etc. His enemies, who claimed he was unfit to govern, have praised his moral character, his moderation and temperance, and even the clergy have supported his candidacy, the candidacy of a liberal, a Spiritist, a Mason. His philosophical ideas have been mentioned, and cartoonists have shown him consulting tables or conjuring spirits. To defame him, they have attributed to him the famous *Manual espírita* by Bhima, which was reproduced in part in *El Porvenir* [The Future], the publication of the inner Reyista party. Nonetheless these vain rumors have not influenced the people. The only thing they have achieved is to bring attention to our incomparable philosophy.

But we know from Madero's letters preserved in his archive in the Ministry of Finance that he did write the *Manual espírita*; he was Bhîma, that pseudonym, like Arjuna, taken from the Bhagavad-Gita. In a letter dated September 26, 1909, to the President of the Permanent Board of the Second Spiritist Congress:

> it comes signed with an X. I ask you to please not reveal it to anyone, as you know how in the current political situation it would injure me enormously

To Antonio Becerra y Castro, who also appears on the masthead of *Helios* and was the book's editor: "keep it as secret as possible that I am the author." Specifically, Madero requested that Becerra y Castro only reveal it to two other members of the Permanent Board of the Second Spiritist Congress, Carlos Herrera y López and Alberto Aragón. (Not Krumm-Heller. Hmm, interesting.)

In *Helios*, as we see, Madero was trying to have it both ways: to evangelize yet dodge the political costs.

In August 1912, the Freemasons sponsored a series of speeches in Mexico City by the celebrated Spanish Freethinker, Spiritist and Feminist, Bélen de Sárraga, and *Helios* and Gustavo Madero's newspaper, *Nueva Era*, covered it with enthusiasm. In the midst of this, more than a hundred well-to-do ladies presented themselves at Chapultepec Castle, the Presidential Residence, to convey their outrage at this radical foreign woman's attacks on Mexican womanhood, and they were further outraged when President Madero answered that, "our laws do not permit me to take away Señora Bélen's right to free speech."

Mexico, I remind you, is a handkerchief. Rumors had been flying, now there were angry flocks of them. Anyone who would summon the dead, fiddle with the intermediating role of the Church, never mind discussing "astral projection" and (smelling salts, please!) "interplanetary reincarnation," may as well have put a match to kerosene. The Catholic clergy and Catholic party and its press had a muddled understanding of what his Spiritism was about, at times calling him a freethinker or even an atheist. Whatever, they wanted Madero out.

The old guard, grumbling loudly, wanted back in, and they didn't have a pip of patience for this claptrap of a "fair vote." One oft-repeated story in those circles: a campesina watching Madero's triumphal entry to Mexico City asked her neighbor, "Who is this Democracy they keep talking about?" Her neighbor answered, "I am not sure, but I think she's the one riding next to Señora Madero."

Regarding the rumors of President Madero's Spiritism, his own grandfather, Don Evaristo, had given ammunition to the old guard when he wrote to Limantour back in early 1911:

> If you add to all this, my good friend, all our headaches which have been caused by these blasted political questions, in which high-level government figures wish to make us revolutionaries, or at the least supporters of the revolution, only because the visionary, my grandson Francisco, has decided, as says [the seventeenth century] Father Ripalda's catechism, we should redeem our sins; and all of this apparently by revelations from the spirits of Juárez or I don't know who...

Don Evaristo might not have been so quick to call Limantour "my good friend" had he known what little respect he would be shown in his memoir. But that memoir, the dryly titled *Apuntes sobre mi vida pública* (Notes on My Public Life), which had no sympathy for the revolution every Mexican government after Huerta's has celebrated with a national holiday, did not come out until 1965.

The army and its powerful general Victoriano Huerta, veteran of years of smashing campesino uprisings, turned out to be a lynchpin in sustaining and, in the end, destroying Madero's government. Apparently, if anything bothered General Huerta's conscience, he grabbed it by the throat and drowned it in drink. He was famous for his drinking jags; he would die in El Paso, Texas in early 1916 of cirrhosis of the liver.

It was General Huerta who had escorted Don Porfirio and his family to their ship in Veracruz. Huerta who, on the orders of interim President de la Barra in 1911, and much to Madero's disgust, swept into Zapatista territory, burning villages and executing prisoners. Huerta who, now on orders of President Madero quashed the Orozquista rebellion in the north in 1912. Huerta, who ordered Pancho Villa's execution for stealing a horse; Huerta who, grudgingly, obeyed when President Madero ordered that Villa be sent to prison instead.

And let's not forget General Manuel Mondragón, lean and mean, a gunslinger out of central casting with those sludgy eyebrows. An artillery expert and machine-gun designer, General Mondragón had been Porfirio Díaz's weapons procurer and he was indignant that, thanks to Madero's head of secret service, Felix Sommerfeld, the bulk of that lucrative business had been taken from his French friends and given to the Germans. ("His feverish eyes hide a fierce inner fire," noted the poet José Juan Tablada. "What can this fire be but burning ambition for power, control, and despotism?")

Oh, there are many pieces to this ugly puzzle. There were brave, good, loyal officers, too. Throughout the nineteenth century and well into the twentieth, the Mexican military was a mosaic of both loyal and mercurial sensibilities and, as every emperor, every dictator, and every president including Francisco I. Madero knew or rudely found out, it was impossible to govern without it.

Madero's rude awakening came with a telephone call to the presidential residence, Chapultepec Castle.

In the still-dark Sunday morning of February 9, 1913, General Mondragón led troops of cadets and officers up from their barracks in Tlalpan, a suburb in the south of Mexico City, to the Prisión Militar de Santiago Tlatelolco, where they freed General Bernardo Reyes. In the ensuing riot, the prison was set on fire and more than a hundred men killed. Part of this force, joined by a second detachment of troops and artillery marching from Tacubaya, proceeded to the federal penitentiary Lecumberri where they shot the commander and freed Félix Díaz (after waiting for him to finish shaving).

The plan was for General Reyes along with Félix Díaz, General Mondragón, and the hundreds of troops behind them, to storm the National Palace. Before noon General Reyes would be President of Mexico.

But Gustavo Madero, lightning fast, got there first.

## From Chapultepec Castle to the National Palace

Mexico City's center fans out from Tenochtitlan, the long-ago island in a lake where the wandering Aztecs, as prophesied, encountered their destiny to find an eagle, perched on a cactus, eating a snake. Centuries later, over the rubble of their palaces and pyramids, the Spaniards built the vast plaza known as the Zócalo, the Palace, and the Cathedral.

About two and half miles to the southwest rises the basalt mountain crowned by Chapultepec Castle. If one can endure the stiff winds and winter chill, the vistas from its terraces are breathtaking, though nowadays, crowded round with skyscrapers and the air more often a soupy-gray, one can only imagine those long-ago skies, endless fields, snow-capped volcanoes, and shining lakes.

> "Don't you think," Maximilian says, turning suddenly, his hands still clenched behind his back, "that this castle should be called Miravalle, as my castle in Trieste is called Miramar?"

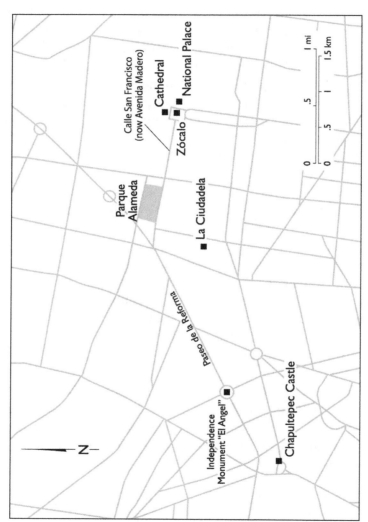

Map of the important sites of the Decena Trágica or Ten Tragic Days.

He actually said that, according to his secretary, José Luis Blasio. I lifted this line from Blasio's dishy memoir, *Maximiliano íntimo*—for my money, politically incorrect as it may be, a treasure on par with Bernal Díaz del Castillo's *The True History of the Conquest of New Spain.*

Like Maximilian and Don Porfirio before him, President Madero lived in the castle. He was often seen riding in the surrounding Bosque de Chapultepec, and commuting on the Paseo de la Reforma to and from his office in the National Palace. Modeled on the Champs-Élysées, Mexico City's most beautiful boulevard had been inaugurated by Maximilian back in the 1860s as the Paseo de la Emperatriz. Over the decades it had become luxuriant with palm-trees and Porfirian-era monuments, among them, the Roman-style victory column topped with a golden angel to commemorate Independence; the 1887 monument to Cuauhtémoc, last king of the Aztecs; and an 1877 statue of Christopher Columbus.

Flash forward to that Sunday, February 9, 1913. Picture a winter's dawn about to break over this high-altitude city full of pretentions, full of ghosts.

Gustavo Madero may have received a phone call or knock on the door; certainly from his house nearby on the Calle Londres, he heard the rumble of the rebel troops and their artillery advancing up the Paseo de la Reforma. However it happened, the President's brother dashed to the National Palace. He was arrested briefly, then freed—when two hundred thirty-two rebel cadets were in turn arrested by the loyal Military Commander of the Plaza de la Constitución [Zócalo], General Lauro Villar. Gustavo Madero rallied the troops in a Shakespearean performance of bluff peppered with comedy, and ordered machine guns placed on the roof.

By the time the column headed by General Reyes and Félix Díaz arrived at the National Palace, Gustavo Madero, General Villar, and the Minister of War (still in his bathrobe, by some accounts), were ready, as was the array of loyal troops bristling with arms all along the roof and the windows.

General Villar ordered the advancing General Reyes to halt. Reyes refused, shouting to his men the order to fire. Within five minutes, the machine guns had mowed down Reyes and some four hundred soldiers and bystanders, not counting hundreds more injured. Márquez Sterling:

> The faithful, startled while hearing mass in the Cathedral, fled in terror; in the surrounding gardens there were cadavers of children, old people and women; in neighboring doorways, horrifying piles of human cannon fodder; and the bullets had gone through store windows and bronze statues. Among the bodies laid out, one by one, were a young girl with her rosary over her arm; a bootblack with his brush in his hands; the newspaper seller, the firewood delivery boy, all drowned in the pools of the hecatomb. The rebel cadets emptied their guns from the towers of the sacred temple, like a rain of lead and death.

Those snipers in the Cathedral's towers would hold out for many more days; the bulk of the rebels led by Mondragón and Félix Díaz now battled a retreat to the Ciudadela, a fortress about mid-way back to Chapultepec Castle. Bullets peppered storefronts, riderless horses galloped wild down the streets. Someone tossed a grenade.

*Be not bewildered, be thou not afraid.*

At 8 a.m., informed that the National Palace was now held by loyal troops and General Villar wounded, President Madero mounted his stallion. The cadets of the Military College— Mexico's West Point—had been summoned and now President Madero mustered all his passion, all his talents to address them. From Martín Luis Guzmán's *Febrero 1913*:

He said, "An uprising has occurred in which the Officers School, dragged along by officers who do not merit their uniform, have thrown the honor of the youth of the army to the dirt. This mistake can only be rectified by the other part of the young officers, and for this I put myself in the hands of this college, whose devotion to discipline and duty have never failed. I invite you to accompany me, as a column of honor, to the doors of the Palace"...

Brief, eloquent in its dignity and contained emotion, Señor Madero's speech caused the two companies of cadets to listen as a single body. The director, Victor Hernández Covarrubias, answered with words of praise for the college, whose reputation alone defined it, and of thanks for the Head of State who, understanding this, would not doubt that the cadets would shield him with their loyalty. Then, directing himself to them, and raising his voice, he summed up everything Señor Madero had said, and what he himself had answered, as:

"Long live the President of the Republic!"

Terse and solemn, as if with a single voice, the cadets answered:

"Viva!"

President Madero, cadets, and presidential guard, a Mexican flag proudly waving high, then came down the hill from Chapultepec Castle. All the way up the Paseo de la Reforma, as he was joined by more guards, more supporters and cabinet members—and, arriving by hired car, the recently retired General Huerta—Madero sat high above the throng, shouting encouragement, waving his hat.

As they arrived at the Avenida Juárez, the leg from the Paseo de la Reforma into the center, they could hear fire coming from the Zócalo. A bullet zinged toward the President, killing a policeman standing nearby. For a moment, Madero and his inner circle slipped into the Daguerre Photo Shop. But unlike the mere humans who would protect him, Madero had no fear of bullets. Soon he appeared on the shop's balcony to reassure the crowd that milled below. There is an iconic photo of this moment—look for it in every picture book of the Revolution. Madero beams down, confident, slope-shouldered, relaxed. Just behind him, walrusian in an overcoat, is General Huerta.

The Apostle with Judas.

In another moment, Madero was back on his stallion, trotting into the shop-lined Calle de San Francisco—today the Avenida Madero. The crowds had thickened. There is a photograph of this, too: high above the sea of hats, Madero raises his, its shadow leaving his face dark but for a scimitar of light on his bald pate. The buildings rise close and dark behind him on both sides. The one on the left, baroque with trim, appears to be the Palacio de Iturbide. He's riding through a canyon. Soldiers surround him, and men in high-collars and neckties.

The next photo shows Madero, still on that stallion, his hat swung up high, its pale lining a little disc, the towers of the Cathedral a baroquely mountainous backdrop. Here the crowd is all men, faces bright in a sun still low in the sky. Many appear to be clapping and running. In the lower left corner of the frame, someone raises his hat to Madero. It is mesmerizing to look into these faces, captured in a moment of such power in Mexican memory. President Madero, hardy, happy—as if this early Sunday morning when his head might get blown off at any moment were just another, albeit especially invigorating, rally on the campaign trail. Other faces are squinting, scared, confused, thrilled.

Márquez Sterling:

> Madero then, his hat in his hand, speaking to the crowd, as if shooting out from a wellspring of men, spurs his horse toward the patios of the Palace.

## "You Are in the Arms of Victoriano Huerta"

So began the first of Mexico's Ten Tragic Days, La Decena Trágica, when a Porfirian cabal who disdained disorder unleashed chaos in monstrous form. A brittle and arrogant U.S. ambassador, without authority, egged them on—making General Huerta believe, wrongly, that his usurper government would be recognized and had he not taken power, the United States would have invaded to restore order. It is a calamity told and retold in Mexico in more books, documentaries, movies, and conferences and museums than a bibliography could list. And so many photographs, each one more horrible than the last. For me there are two that best sum up these days.

First: a trio of horses, still saddled, lie dead on their sides in the middle of the street, to the side, a flag crumpled like a rag. All around, workmen mill in lumpy jackets; a boy in a campesino's white tunic stands feet apart as if stunned; an office worker wears finer clothing; a nun carries a basket on her arm. All wonder at the dead horses, at each other, at this bizarre, sunny day.

Second: Amid the trees of the Parque Alameda, three bystanders have been cut down: one fallen on top of the other, like sacks of grain; the third victim's hand rests gracefully upon his chest, his hips twisted as if in a dance pose. He wears shined brogues. His sock is scrunched down, exposing a pale stretch of leg. His hat, a fedora, sits to the side of his head, as if gently placed there, an oval beside an oval, sharing their black puddle. Better not to describe the face.

The Ten Tragic Days was—no exaggeration—a battle for Mexico's soul. It was not just one group of power hungry men against another, not order versus disorder, but in its essence, a struggle between "might makes right" and those who would have power apportioned and exercised by free men and women through democratic process under the law.

Freedom. As Isidro Favela, a young Maderista Congressman who went on to become one of Mexico's most distinguished elder statesmen, put it with the benefit of all the wisdom he had accumulated up to 1962, "a people without freedom is missing its soul."

We don't know the name or occupation or anything else about that man in the shined brogues who died in the Alameda (probably instantly, guessing from the way he fell). We can assume he was Mexican and old enough to vote. To the conspirators in this battle, his vote meant nothing, lest it be the gesture of a puppet in their show. To the Maderistas and the defenders of the Republic, imperfect as they may have been— and who knows, perhaps it was one of their bullets—his vote was sacred.

Sacred. This word takes us a long way toward Ithaca in the odyssey of trying to understand Francisco I. Madero.

The battles raged on, the rebels from the Ciudadela and the Cathedral towers, the loyal troops still holding the National Palace. There were lulls, some so long that people went back to their daily business—then the streets filled again with sudden killing explosions of fire. Whistles of bullets, *pep, pep, pep*. The shops all closed, and people, especially the poor and those unable to leave or send for deliveries, began to run out of food. (Some of the restaurants remained open, however, and from his own pocket, Gustavo Madero paid for thousands of sandwiches a day for the troops.) Early on, troops loyal to Madero arrived from Cuernavaca. Then more troops loyal to Madero arrived from Querétaro. In the American legation, Ambassador Wilson coped with hundreds of American citizens and other foreigners crowding in for days without food or sanitation. This, together with, perhaps, too much brandy fueling his grinding contempt, prompted him to call for President Madero and Vice President Pino Suárez's resignations.

What was deeply strange over the next nine days was that so much of the city was being destroyed with both civilians and infantry cut to ribbons, while the obvious targets, the Ciudadela in particular, took little fire. Journalist Edward I. Bell:

Huerta batteries were shifted from point to point in residence and business sections to the north, northeast and northwest of the [Ciudadela]. From none of these points was the building visible. Solids blocks of houses intervened on every range. Díaz placed batteries near his headquarters, and always at points from which neither the Palace nor the opposing batteries were in view.

For several hours each day, there was firing by both parties. Buildings were damaged or demolished, inoffensive persons were killed in their own homes, incautious noncombatants in the streets were shot down. Projectiles of various kinds were fired through streets in which no enemy had appeared. Machine guns discharged thousands of bullets without having any target except some mere unfortunate who might happen to be in range, the purpose of the fusillade being to excite terror and advertise anarchy.

Isolated guns were set up by apparently responsible squads, and fired over and over again in whatever position the pieces happened to assume after the recoil of the previous shot.

And during ten days of this terrorizing riot of blood the [Ciudadela] was struck but once and the [National Palace] but twice!

Huerta's brutal farce. Cuban Ambassador Márquez Sterling:

By this time Providence had abandoned Madero. And a diaphanous sky, its happy blue smile in contrast to the sadness, fear, and pain here on earth, pulls down its shades

for a full and satisfied moon that illuminates
Moctezuma's darkened capital. Some auto-
mobile crosses furtively, protecting itself
with friendly flags of the Red Cross or the
conventional white flag that is not always an
envoy of peace. On the corners near the Ciudadela, one could find squads of soldiers or
rural police prone on the asphalt, preparing
to fire, or resting on the hard bed of the side-
walks, with their rifles and machine guns at
the ready. Around the plazas, every once in
a rare while, a living person who would slide
along, glued to the walls...

The streets became littered with more bodies than could be
retrieved. These were piled up like so much firewood, doused
with petroleum, and burned. There are photos of this, too. And
the infamous one of the dog at the gutter, nosing the foot of a
smoldering cadaver, its clenched fist already blackened to an
inedible crisp.

When exactly did General Victoriano Huerta turn coat?

It might have been weeks before the uprising. Or, it might
have been that first day when he allowed (how else could it
have happened?) supplies to get through to the rebels holed
up in the Ciudadela. It might have been the following Sunday,
February 16, during an armistice, when a loyal officer informed
Madero that he had seen eighty carts of provisions rolling
into the Ciudadela. Confronted, Huerta argued that those
carts were filled with women and liquor, a wise move, so the
rebels would be induced to remain in place, and mop-up operations accordingly easier. It boggles the mind that President
Madero found such an argument convincing, but he and Pino
Suárez and Huerta proceeded to discuss strategy, and at the
conclusion of their meeting, General Huerta put his hands
on the President's shoulders and said, "You are in the arms of
Victoriano Huerta."

I am not sure I believe that story. It smells to me like the one about Maximilian having an affair with the gardener's daughter in Cuernavaca or, say, George Washington chopping down the cherry tree. But if true? Never mind the addled inner compass of one who refers to himself in third person; to touch the physical person of a Head of State is a gross breach of protocol. General Victoriano Huerta would have known that.

Multiple sources concur: on the night of Tuesday, February 11, Huerta had met with Félix Díaz in a house on Calle Nápoles.

Stories and theories abound concerning how and precisely what Gustavo Madero discovered about Huerta's treason. Journalist Edward Bell, who evidently had Gustavo himself as a source, claimed a list of conspirators that included Huerta's name, a question mark beside it, came into Gustavo's hands as early as February 4, by happenstance from a colonel, grateful to Gustavo for a personal loan, whose own name was on the list. Gustavo immediately took the list to the President.

> The list, so he assured Gustavo, had been prepared for sale, and Gustavo had bought it. To base any stern procedure upon such evidence would be to make the Government ridiculous, and invite endless complications... The whole thing was preposterous, and Gustavo might be better employed than in listening to such tales from men who wanted to exchange them for money. Mondragón was a malcontent and a plotter, as everybody knew. But what of it?

Heribert von Feilitzsch, whose archival research is the most recent and thorough as I write these lines, guesses that it may have been Felix Sommerfeld, head of President Madero's secret service, who alerted Gustavo that Huerta had turned. Sommerfeld himself could have been told by the German ambassador von Hintze—who heard it from Ambassador Wilson.

However it happened, on February 16, convinced of Huerta's treachery, Gustavo wasted no time. Strip the story to its bones, a leering skull of a poem:

> Gustavo drew his pistol and took Huerta prisoner.
> > *Huerta protested his innocence.*
> The President called for Huerta, that he might defend himself.
> > *Huerta protested his loyalty.*
> The President gave him 24 hours to prove it.
> > *Huerta asked for his pistol.*
> The President obliged Gustavo to return it to Huerta.
> The President chided his brother for his rashness.

But a novel would linger on the scene. It would tell you about the queasy feeling in the President's quarters in the Palace, the unwashed coffee and tea cups and water glasses and overflowing wastepaper baskets, and the way, when General Huerta angrily protested in that voice gruff from years of commanding in the field, the President's eyes shifted. It would mention the beads of sweat that appeared on their foreheads and the backs of their necks, even though they were all wearing woolen jackets and a moment before, the President had been rubbing his hands to warm his fingers.

It was two in the morning. The city silent. The windows curtained.

A clairvoyant could have gone further, to describe the clash of thought-forms floating in the electrified ether above them: Gustavo's a rainbow of valiant sincerity; Huerta's shrapnel-loaded blast of vitiated red; President Madero's an architectural complexity, rotating slowly at first, then suddenly spinning itself into a cocoon as gray as granite.

President Madero had given up automatic writing in 1908, confident that he could receive "inspiration," that is, the spirits' communications directly, telepathically.

The spirits were silent. Or maybe, President Madero was no longer listening.

*What if,* President Madero must have thought, *General Huerta were innocent? Huerta had many times shown his loyalty when he obeyed unpleasant orders. Huerta showed important, very public solidarity when it mattered most—marched by my side and then stood with me, the President of this Republic, at the window of the Daguerre Photo Shop. If I were to believe Gustavo and he were wrong, what shameful ingratitude... Dire karma! And then we could lose the support of the army. We could lose everything. Gustavo, always grabbing, racing, the calf in the china shop. It is so annoying when he presumes to instruct me.*

And in that same electrified ether, the relationship between the two grandsons of Don Evaristo, so close in age, so different in temperament, would appear as a sculptural excrescence intricately layered and studded, like limestone, with fossils of love and comradeship and rivalries and resentments and jealousies, tiny trilobites.

(A proper biography would have the breathing space to go into all the detail of Gustavo's private life—a deeply unhappy spouse—and his political career, so brief, so rocket-bright, but in precipitous decline already. On so many issues, Gustavo had wanted to take a harder line than his brother was comfortable with, and as the government's *éminence grise*, Gustavo made a fat target for the press, unleashed now, to bite and chew without mercy. Gustavo and his wife and children were already packing their bags for Japan. President Madero had decided to appoint his brother Mexico's ambassador to the Empire of the Rising Sun, a land rich with commercial and geopolitical opportunities to be sure, but about as close to the action in the National Palace as, say, Halley's comet, wherever it was in the galaxy by this time. A farewell dinner for Gustavo, with the President, Vice President, and ministers of the cabinet, had been held on February 3. According to his biographer, Hernández y Lazo, Gustavo already had his tickets to sail on the *Tenyo Naru* out of San Francisco on March 1.)

Quick: Decide!

*Rouge ou noir!*

The next day, February 18, during a meeting at the Gambrinus Restaurant, Huerta stepped out to make a phone call. That was when Gustavo was arrested, tied up, and stuffed into the coat closet. According to von Feilitzsch, Sommerfeld testified that he telephoned to warn President Madero to leave the Palace, "that something was wrong. I didn't know what." But Madero did not move fast enough. He was still in the Palace at 1:30 p.m. when Huerta's men burst in and arrested him and Vice President Pino Suárez.

That night, his last on this earth, Gustavo was driven to the Ciudadela.

As for Francisco Madero, on February 19, Huerta turned to Ambassador Wilson. Should he "send the ex-President out of the country or place him in a lunatic asylum?"

Ambassador Wilson replied that Huerta "ought to do that which was best for the country."

After Madero's murder, in his 1914 *The Political Shame of Mexico*, Edward I. Bell, no admirer of Wilson or Huerta, tossed this off:

> Doubtless whatever portion of sincerity might be discovered in the charge that Madero was insane sprang from the story of his hearkening to the dead—which is amusing, in superstitious Mexico.

### Caveat Emptor

It is tempting to judge President Madero as "a dreamer of dreams," just the way Ambassador Wilson so callously dismissed him. As even his great admirer, Isidro Favela put it, Madero was a Don Quixote with "the fury for freedom." Others who loved him said Madero was "made of wood for the cross."

We, blessed with hindsight, know it was a grievous mistake to have disbelieved his brother about the conspiracy and

General Huerta's betrayal. But who in their life has not, at least once, refused to see something that is obvious, yet at the time, unthinkable? We all have our cherished assumptions, our desperate needs.

We all live in glass houses, so let us put down our stones.

It was overambitious for Madero to attempt to promote Spiritism when his fledging government needed all the respect and every friend it could find. But who has not, once in their life, in heart-leaping enthusiasm, overreached and provoked a hostile reaction all out of bounds?

Not everyone hears voices, but a surprising number of people, who do not otherwise present as schizophrenics, do. Suppose you did, and suppose the voices told you to buy a lottery ticket and you did and you won—you won such a pot, by God, never mind shopping at the mall, you could buy Las Vegas! Wouldn't you feel rather eager and not a little obliged to keep listening, and inclined to do what the voices wanted?

And how grounded a decision-maker would you be if you had been met at every train stop from your hometown to your nation's capital, as if you were a god, blue and beautiful as Lord Krishna, descended to earth? It would probably take a while for the helium to leak back out.

Madero may have been an unusual politician, not least in his idealism, his Spiritism, and passion for the Bhagavad-Gita, but consider this: If few people have the wits, the guts, and the luck to grasp the reins of power, as he so brilliantly did, fewer still know how to ride that steed well, to traverse the daily maelstrom of freakish challenges and myriad temptations in such way that, when one dismounts, one can look back with clear eyes and feel proud. Fewer still know how to survive the ride and go on to live another life, free of the blight of its loss. Not Victoriano Huerta. Not even Porfirio Díaz.

"I feel wounded," Don Porfirio told his ex-Minister of Foreign Relations, after his resignation. "Part of the country rose up in arms to bring me down and the rest just stood there with their arms crossed. Both owe me for a portion of things." This quote is in *El exilio*, a family memoir by his great great grandson, Carlos Tello Díaz. It seems that despite his hurt feelings, Don Porfirio had as good a life as money could buy in France—and on vacation. There is fun photo of him astride a little donkey, the ladies of his party on camels, in front of the Sphinx and the Pyramid of Cheops. But I digress.

If Francisco Madero had taken Gustavo's counsel and kept Huerta under arrest, what then?

Madero might have served out his term, and then retired— he had campaigned on no re-election, after all—to dedicate himself to evangelizing for Spiritism and the Bhagavad-Gita. Maybe he would have taken that trip to India to study philosophy. Or maybe, budding media moghul that he was with his newspapers and magazines, he would gotten into that newfangled thing, the talkies. (Now there's a novel! Though I cannot quite picture Doña Sara poolside in Hollywood with Dolores del Río... one spring day, on a whim, Don Francisco at the wheel of their Studebaker, tearing around the curves on the coastal highway, to Ojai for a dialogue with Krishnamurti...)

With so many enemies, Madero might have fallen anyway. Any head of state is a target at any time. And however one defines it—civil war, foreign intervention, insurrection, coup d'état—what revolution has not provoked a counter-revolution? And a counter-revolution to that, and then another, rippling out through the years, the decades. Revolutions take a while to settle down—and, subtle as their effects may be, in a way, they never do.

Many Mexicans will tell you that Agustin de Iturbide, who won Mexico's Independence from Spain, was a ridiculous person because he set himself up as emperor (a crown! a golden throne!) and then he couldn't govern— to make a long story short, Iturbide ended up before a firing squad in 1824. But they forget that, whatever Iturbide's personal virtues or shortcomings, at that time, sufficient political support for a republic did not exist nor did the means to pay the army after the economic catastrophe of a decade of war.

If you cannot pay your army, you're toast—as Maximilian von Habsburg found out when Louis Napoleon, under financial pressure and thumb-twisting from the United States (remember John Bigelow?), withdrew his troops from Mexico.

In Vienna, in Maximilian von Habsburg's archive, there is a letter from Pedro de Montezuma, a Mexican railroad engineer then working in Portugal, and (it's true) the "sole legitimate descendant of the Aztec emperor." It is dated February 17, 1864, nearly a year after the French had occupied Mexico City and much of the rest of the country, and just shy of two months before Maximilian would depart for Mexico.

> French cannon have cowed some into submission; once tranquility reigns, however, there will rise up all of a sudden a terrible counter-revolution. Your Highness, permit me to say that as a Mexican I truly love my country and I hope that my countrymen can achieve the goals they so desire... but Your Highness has been too precipitous in accepting the offer of the Mexican throne. Before abandoning your country, where you are happy and respected, to go to a completely unknown country, Your Highness should consider very carefully that ever since 1812, neither by hook nor crook has there been a functioning government; those in power, ambitious and unprincipled strongmen who are not in the least interested in their peoples' well-being, have done nothing but promote endless civil wars. Without hesitation I can say that those who today form the regency are of the most impious stripe and among them, in fact most of them, are proven depraved evildoers, usurpers, they rob the Treasury, they rob even the Holy Church. They will attack the rights of both Mexicans

and foreigners, insulting foreign flags and representatives in the grossest way... and they
will supplant Your Highness perhaps after a
tragic end.

We can imagine Maximilian in his library in Trieste, this
very letter in his hand. Perhaps, after reading it, a twinge in
the pit of his stomach, he looked out the window at the Bay of
Grignano, dull under a winter's sky. Then, pulling at his beard,
he read it again.

What did Maximilian think of this letter? We only know that
around the time he probably received it he tried to back out of
going to Mexico, but when his honor and that of the House of
Habsburg were called into question by Louis Napoleon, and by
his own wife, Carlota, very reluctantly, he gave in.

Francisco Madero received his *caveat emptor* from his grandfather, Don Evaristo, dated November 22, 1909, and it was
addressed to him with far less respect for his dignity. By this
time, with *La sucesión presidencial en 1910* as its platform, he
had built the Partido Antireeleccionista and was gearing up for
what would be a nationwide campaign for the presidency. When
Porfirio Díaz had not replied to his letter protesting the arrest
of several journalists and party activists, Francisco wrote to the
Minister of Finance, his grandfather's old friend Limantour,
protesting at length and adding, "We sincerely believe that the
coming reelection of General Díaz is not in the country's best
interest." As a courtesy to his grandfather, Francisco had sent
him a copy of the letter. Don Evaristo, opening with, *My very
dear son*, and closing with, *An affectionate hug for you and Sara
from your papa who loves you very much*, replied:

If [Limantour] does not show your letter to
the President, it will be a dereliction of duty
on his part and if he does, it will be worse
for you. You believe you are speaking nation
to nation and you are wrong... you are busy

flicking boogers in the chocolate... I prefer
to stay quiet in my corner than try to cover
up the sun with my hand... you are very far
from understanding the country in which we
live. I hope that you will not ever again send
any such letter to any of the Ministers nor to
the President, it is like a microbe challenging
an elephant.

Don Evaristo, his beloved grandfather who had supported
and guided him all his life, was now lost to him. And Don Evaristo was dying; he would not live to see Díaz and Limantour
sail for France and his own grandson, leader of the Revolution,
enter Mexico City in triumph, and to this day and no doubt
for many years into our future, revered as Mexico's Apostle
of Democracy.

It is perhaps of consequence in President Madero's emotional
landscape that General Huerta, who had served as secretary
to a Liberal general fighting the French and Maximilian, was,
by 1913, old enough to be his father.

*You are in the arms of Victoriano Huerta.*

Huerta fills the iconic role of Mexico's arch-villain not only
by his betrayal of Madero, but by having posed for a photograph—look for it in books and museum exhibits about the
Revolution, you'll find it—in those dark glasses and a uniform
that only lacks a swastika. Huerta wore those dark glasses
because he had cataracts. But look at a picture, any picture,
where you can see his eyes. They are not full of evil, but confusion and dread.

After the Madero brothers and Vice President Pino Suárez
had been buried, and Huerta had taken the sash of President
of the Republic, sent 84 Congressmen to jail and dissolved
Congress, he told Edith O'Shaughnessy, wife of the United
States' "confidential agent"—not ambassador, at this point there
was none—that he was not in politics "for personal ends," his
wants were few, "his habits those of an old soldier." He had a

handsome wife and eleven children, and he seemed to Mrs. O'Shaughnessy, as she reported home to her mother, "very nice."

Mrs. O'Shaughnessy also believed the story that Gustavo Madero had not been beaten and blinded by a bayonet, but that, having failed to bribe his guards, "he was gesticulating in a hysterical manner," and "his nerve seemed suddenly to leave him and he began to run, whereupon one of the guards fired, hitting him in the eye as he turned to look behind him... Doubtless had Gustavo kept his nerve, instead of trying to run, he would be alive today." (Let us hope Mrs. O'Shaughnessy did not buy too much swampland in Florida.)

Porfirio Díaz knew all about people who could be "very nice." He was a world-class expert at keeping them in line by "bread or stick" and ye olde divide and conquer—and, as we know, it worked. Until it didn't.

And this brings me back to the problem of transitions.

When *The Last Prince of the Mexican Empire* came out in 2009 and in Spanish in 2010, two reactions surprised me. First, that many readers, especially younger ones, were disturbed by the photograph, a formal *carte-de-visite*, of the little prince. Agustín de Iturbide y Green was a beautiful child, with a cupid's mouth, and he looked more like, say, an English prince than a typical Mexican. Those readers would make a twisted face, asking, "Why is he in a girl's dress?" (Well, folks, that's how they dressed aristocratic little boys back then.) Second, that so many marveled at my having spun a novel out of "a little footnote." Except for misinterpreted snippets, the story of Agustín de Iturbide y Green in the court of Maximilian may have been forgotten in the archives until I dug it out but it was no mere footnote. In a monarchy, the heir presumptive, though he be in a dress and diapers, is the living guarantee of the regime's future, and more: he is the living symbol of his future people—his subjects.

Would Mexicans be subjects, creatures born to obey—or citizens, men and women who with their full rights participate in creating their own polity? This had been Mexico's bitter and bloody question for the whole of the nineteenth century.

In telling the prince's story, from the high-noon of the Second Empire in 1865 to its collapse, and his return to his parents in Washington in 1867, I was telling the story of the fall of Mexican monarchism, a powerful idea up until that time, asserting the mystical embodiment of all Mexicans in the person of a hereditary sovereign. To be honest, in sorting out Mexico's most convoluted and transnational episode, it took me more time than I would like to admit to boil my aim down to so few words. And so, in fairness, I should not have been surprised by the reaction of those readers, for whom (as it was for me) monarchism is just a quaintly ridiculous thing preserved in the formaldehyde of textbooks or the syrup of entertainment, and where still living, as in Spain and the U.K., its royal families harmless fodder for the sorts of magazines one reads at the hairdressers.

Before Madero's lifetime, the monarchists had been definitively vanquished, in part thanks to Porfirio Díaz himself, one of President Benito Juárez's ablest generals in the fight to bring down Maximilian and eject the French. But Díaz's own decades-long reign, with his continual re-election to the office of President of the Republic, was democratic in form, not substance.

As a campesino might say, Don Porfirio threw a saddle on a billy goat and declared it a horse. One doesn't have to be a Spiritist to imagine Benito Juárez's consternation from beyond the grave.

Don Evaristo, of all people, should have recognized what was at stake for his country and his family as Porfirio Díaz descended into old age without a strategy for transition to a new regime. Without its strongman, Mexico could evolve into something greater than it was—a true republic—or once again sink into the mire of civil war and become prone to foreign invasion. If not another less capable Díaz (Limantour, General Reyes), was there anyone, anyone willing to step forward, better to lead Mexico than his grandson Francisco? And outside the inner circles of Díaz's cronies and military men, anyone who could count on the backing of such as crackerjack operator Gustavo and so many of the Madero clan? Provincial and in many ways limited as the Maderos may have been, I find it quite impossible to imagine any of the other revolutionary leaders emerging around the same time, from Abraham González to Pascual Orozco, Pancho Villa and Emiliano Zapata, able to so thoroughly articulate their platform as Madero did with *La sucesión presidencial en 1910.* Nor was there anyone with the sheer courage coupled with organizing skills, nor the wherewithal to engineer financing (yes, Madero spent his own capital, but much more was needed) or even think to hire the likes of Washington fixer Sherburne G. Hopkins (a performer of high wire wonders, if not outright miracles). And we must not overlook the many dedicated and talented activists around Madero, such as the González Garza brothers, Federico and Roque—and a long list of others. Furthermore, though not everyone welcomed him, Francisco Madero, already an experienced businessman and manager, was that *rara avis* who could reach across class lines to address his fellow citizens, whoever they might be, with charisma and ease.

But old men are not known for welcoming the new, nor for willingly ceding their status to the young. They see their death in such things.

### Window Into a Life

Madero's *Manual espírita* is, precisely, a book about life—its author's understanding of the nature and relationship of life and the afterlife. Kardec's tomes were unwieldy and out-of-date; there was half a century of psychic research and many new ideas to incorporate, plus a touch of Hermetica and the Bhagavad-Gita. Madero's *Manual espírita* filled what the Permanent Board of the Second Spiritist Congress considered an urgent need: an up-to-date Spanish language catechism, sufficiently ample to cover all the basic concepts, but small enough for a bedside table or to carry in a purse, a portfolio, a knapsack. In short, it was intended to serve both the converted and to evangelize as wide a public as possible. We know he printed those thousands of copies, and another edition was published by Casa Editorial Maucci in Barcelona in 1924. But as I have already detailed, for most historians of the past century, the *Manual espírita* remained sunken in almost complete obscurity.

Those who have troubled to read my novel will find, at the very end of the acknowledgements, my thanks to two mediums. So I slip that in here as well near the end of what I have to say. To clarify: I have never been a member of nor in any way involved with any Spiritist or Spiritualist church or organization. I was baptized Catholic but when I was a teenager in California I decided to take a lifelong vacation from the whole church thing. In writing my novel I recurred to the mediums because, though I had researched every little bit I possibly could in books and articles and archives, a couple of characters had me flummoxed. In a word I was stuck. I can almost hear some of you:

*Total waste of money. Like believing in angels.*

*Interesting. Is your wallet thinner now?*

As an artist, I say, hey, whatever works! Stand on your head! Play Mozart, blast Nina Hagen!

Maybe, in those communications—fantastic thought!—I really was hearing from the dead. Maybe not. I don't go through life with the need to wave around the cudgel of an answer for everything. My point is that these mediums communicated information that unjammed my block, for which I am profoundly grateful. One example: A communication in answer to my question put to Angel de Iturbide, the second son of the Emperor Iturbide and father of the little prince, Agustín de Iturbide y Green. In 1865, in Chapultepec Castle, along with his wife and siblings, Don Angel had signed the contract that handed over his only son to Maximilian. I asked, Why?

I believe there were manifold answers to that question. And of course, I cannot know—this delves into telepistemology—I was not in Don Angel's head on that day in 1865, nor can I know if the medium was really hearing from his spirit, from a poseur's, or simply retailing a fantasy; nor, assuming it were Don Angel's spirit, can I know if he were self-aware enough or, in any event, willing to reveal the truth to me. I had thought about his motivations for such a long time. But one that had not occurred to me—a headslapper that it had not, I admit—was that, even before and especially after Maximilian arrived in Mexico, Don Angel had been so afraid. On the other end of the telephone, this Virginia-based medium who, as far as I knew, did not speak Spanish, nor know anything about Mexican history, tumbled out a terrible story that included Don Angel's being followed and of seeing a neighbor marched out of his house in handcuffs in the night.

I realized, Don Angel must have been afraid for years. After all, he was a little boy when his father, "The Liberator," was executed by a firing squad in 1824. From my novel, Don Angel's point of view:

> He is, if by nature a stylish man, meticulous and guarded. He was glad to serve his country as a diplomat in Washington, but he has never sought to be a public man. Many are dazzled by the glamor of it. But he has always known, public life is riddled with indignity. You lose your humanity and become a thing, a puppet to be loved, or bashed, slandered, decapitated. Your fate depends on men who can be noble friends or, when you least expect it, murderous ingrates. Whether emperor or president, you and your family are the property of the nation, and the nation a Janus-faced beast.

Well, as I understood Don Angel, he was a gloomy guy.

Francisco Madero, the anything-but-gloomy guy.

In the Mexican political arena of his time, Francisco Madero was indeed a great warrior. And if he fell we should not judge him as weak or inept any more than we would a gladiator, being of flesh and blood, in the ring with a pack of hungry lions—plus, charging out of right field, a rhino. Then, gates up, the rest of that rabid menagerie.

We need to see Madero in context.

One does not have to be a Spiritist to champion freedom and democracy but for Madero, Mexico's Apostle of Democracy, metaphysics and politics were inseparable. And rather than ignore his beliefs, or titter at them, or sensationalize them, or argue about their validity (haul out the theoretical quantum physics and the consciousness studies and Near Death Experience literature and /or get all Jungian about it), or label them as plumb crazy, I ask you, dear reader who has read this far, to simply acknowledge that Madero was a Spiritist, to understand what that means, to appreciate the rich esoteric matrix from which his philosophy sprang, and why and how it informed what he did and did not do—and how some friends and some enemies saw him—as leader of the 1910 Revolution and as President of Mexico, in that comet-like moment when, with a heart full of love, he blazed into Mexican history and so profoundly changed it.

## Mexican History, Mexican Metaphysical, and the Maderos

Acosta, Ray. *Revolutionary Days: A Chronology of the Mexican Revolution*. Editorial Mazatlán, 2010.

Aguirre Benavides, Adrián. *Madero El Inmaculado: Historia de la Revolución 1910*. Editorial Diana, 1962.

Bell, Edward I. *The Political Shame of Mexico*. McBride, Nast & Company, 1914.

Beezley, William H. *Judas at the Jockey Club and Other Episodes in Porfirian Mexico*. University of Nebraska Press, 1987.

Bigelow, John, *Retrospections of an Active Life*. 3 vols, Baker and Taylor, 1909.

———. "The Heir-Presumptive to the Imperial Crown of Mexico: Don Agustín de Iturbide". *Harper's New Monthly Magazine*, April 1883.

Blasio, José Luis. *Maximiliano íntimo*. UNAM, 1996.

Buchenau, Jürgen. *Plutarco Elías Calles and the Mexican Revolution*. Rowman & Littlefield Publishers, 2006.

Casanova, Rosa, ed. *Francisco I. Madero. Entre imagen pública y acción política, 1901-1913*. Instituto Nacional de Antropología e Historia / Museo Nacional de Historia de México, 2012.

Collado Herrera, María del Carmen and Laura Pérez Rosales. *Sara Pérez de Madero: Una mujer de la Revolución*. Secretaría de Educación Pública, 2010.

Creelman, James. "President Díaz, Hero of the Americas." *Pearson's Magazine*, March 1908.

Cumberland, Charles. *Mexican Revolution: Genesis Under Madero.* University of Texas Press, 1952.

Fernández Güell, Rogelio. *La Revolución mexicana, episodios.* Editorial Costa Rica, 1973.

——. *El moderno Juárez. Estudio sobre la personalidad de Madero.* Tipografía artística, 1911.

Frías, Heriberto. [Transl. Barbara Jamison]. *The Battle of Tomochic: Memoirs of a Second Lieutenant.* Oxford University Press, 2006.

Garciadiego, Javier. "1910: el viejo al nuevo estado mexicano." In *México en tres momentos: 1810-1910-2010*, ed., Alicia Mayer. Universidad Nacional Autónoma de México, vol. 1, 2007.

——. *Rudos contra científicos. La Universidad Nacional durante la Revolución Mexicana.* El Colegio de México / UNAM, 1996.

Gardner, Dore. *Niño Fidencio: A Heart Thrown Open.* Museum of New Mexico Press, 1999.

Garner, Paul. *Porfirio Díaz: Profiles in Power.* Pearson Education Limited, 2001.

Gillow, Eulogio. *Reminencencias del Ilmo y Rmo Sr Dr D Eulogio Gillow y Zabalza, arzobispo de Antequera (Oaxaca).* Los Angeles, California, 1921.

González Garza, Federico, *La Revolución Mexicana. Mi contribución político-literaria.* A. del Bosque, 1936.

——. *El Testamento político de Madero.* Imprenta Victoria, 1921.

Grinberg-Zylberbaum, Jacobo. *Pachita*. Editorial EDAMEX, 1994.

Guerra de Luna, Manuel. *Los Madero, la saga liberal*. Tudor Producciones, 2010.

——— . "Semblanza de un adepto" in *Cuadernos espíritas 1900-1908*, vol. VI, ed. Alejandro Rosas, *Obras Completas*. Clío, 2000.

Guzmán, Martín Luis. *Febrero de 1913*, in *Obras completas*, vol. III. Fondo de Cultura Económica, 2010.

——— ."Arenga del Presidente Madero a los alumnos del Colegio Militar, en la mañana del 9 de febrero de 1913," in *Madero y Pino Suárez en el cincuentenario de su sacrificio 1913 – 1963*, ed. Arturo Arnáiz y Freg. Secretaría de Educación Pública, México, 1963.

Hart, John Mason. *Revolutionary Mexico: The Coming and Process of the Mexican Revolution*. University of California Press, 10th edition, 1997.

——— . *Empire and Revolution: Americans in Mexico Since the Civil War*. University of California Press, 2002.

Hernández y Lazo, Begoña Consuelo. *Gustavo A. Madero: De activo empresario a enérgico revolucionario, 1875-1913*. Editorial los Reyes, 2013.

Holden, William Curry, *Teresita*. Stemmer House, 1978.

IMIS. *Una ventana al mundo invisible. Protocolos del IMIS*. Editorial Antorcha, 1960.

Iturbide [y Green], Agustín de. "Mexico Under President Díaz." *The North American Review*, June 1894.

Johns, Michael. *The City of Mexico in the Age of Díaz*. University of Texas Press, 1997.

Katz, Friedrich. *The Secret War in Mexico: Europe, the United States, and the Mexican Revolution*. University of Chicago Press, 1981.

Knight, Alan. *The Mexican Revolution I: Porfirians, Liberals, and Peasants*. University of Nebraska Press, 1990.

———. *The Mexican Revolution II: Counter-revolution and Reconstruction*. University of Nebraska Press, 1990.

Krauze, Enrique. *Francisco I. Madero. Místico de la libertad*. Fondo de Cultura Económica, 1987.

———. *Siglo de caudillos*. Tusquets, 1994.

Krumm-Heller, Arnoldo. *Conferencias esotéricas*. 1909.

———. *El zodiaco de los incas en comparación de los aztecas*. 1910.

———. *No fornicarás*. Biblioteca Ocultista, 1912.

——— . *Für Freiheit und Recht: Meine Erlebnisse aus dem Mexikanischen Bürgerkriege*. Otto Thiele, 1916.

———. *El Tatwámetro o las vibraciones del éter*. 1926.

———. *Del incienso a la osmoterapia*. 1934.

Leyva, José Mariano. *El ocaso de los espíritus. El espiritismo en México en el siglo XIX*. Ediciones Cal y Arena, 2005.

Limantour, José Yves. *Apuntes sobre mi vida pública*. Editorial Porrúa, 1965.

Madero, Francisco I. *La sucesión presidencial en 1910*. El Partido Nacional Democrático, 1908.

———. *Epistolario 1900-1909*. Secretaría de Hacienda y Crédito Público, 1985.

———. *Epistolario 1910*. Secretaría de Hacienda y Crédito Público, 1985.

———[pseud. Bhîma]. *Manual espírita*. 1911.

———. *Estudio sobre la conveniencia de la construcción de una presa en el Cañon de Fernández para almacenar las aguas del Río Nazas.* 1907.

———. *La Revolución espiritual de Francisco I. Madero. Documentos inéditos y poco conocidos.* Presentación del Lic. Joaquín E. Henricks Díaz; Introducción del Dr. Jaime Muñoz Domínguez Prólogo y comentarios de Manuel Arellano Zavaleta. Gobierno del Estado de Quintana Roo, 2000.

Márquez Sterling, Manuel. *Los últimos días del presidente Madero*. Imprenta Nacional de Cuba, 1960.

Mayo, C.M. *The Last Prince of the Mexican Empire*. Unbridled Books, 2009.

Oconitrillo García, Eduardo. *Rogelio Fernández Güell: escritor, poeta y caballero andante*. Editorial Costa Rica, 1980.

O'Shaughnessy, Edith. *A Diplomat's Wife in Mexico*. Harper & Brothers Publishers, 1916.

Pérez Montfort, Ricardo. "El doctor Arnold Krumm-Heller en México, 1910-1935. Entre el esotericismo, el nacionalismo y la osmoterapia." in *Cotidianidades, imaginarios y contextos. Ensayos de historia y cultura en México, 1850-1950*. Centro de Investigaciones y Estudios Superiores en Antropología Social, 2008.

Romo, David Dorado. *Ringside Seat to a Revolution: An Underground History of El Paso and Juárez: 1893-1923*. Cinco Puntos Press, 2005.

Rosales, José Natividad. *Madero y el espiritismo. Las cartas y las sesiones espiritas del heroe*. Editorial Posado, 1973.

Rosas Robles, Alejandro. "Un adepto llamado Bhîma." *Periodos de la historia*, wikimexico.com, March 10, 2012.

———. "Los diarios espiritistas de Francisco I. Madero." *Letras Libres*, February 1999.

——— ed. *Las dos caras de la historia. Revolución Mexicana, el tiempo del caos*. Grijalbo Mondadori, 2010.

——— ed. *Obras completas de Francisco Ignacio Madero*, 10 vols. Clío, 2000.

Ross, Stanley R. *Francisco I. Madero*. Columbia University Press, 1955.

Sabazius. *Dr. Arnoldo Krumm-Heller, 1876-1949*. Ordo Templi Orientis, 1997.

Saborit, Antonio. *Los doblados de Tomóchic: un episodio de la historia y la literatura*. Cal y Arena, 2010.

———, compilador. *Febrero de Caín y de metralla. La Decena Trágica*. Cal y Arena, 2013.

Solares, Ignacio. *Madero, el otro*. Joaquín Mortíz, 1989.

———. *Presencia de lo invisible.* Taurus, 2011.

Tello Díaz, Carlos. *El exilio: un relato de familia.* Cal y Arena, 1993.

Tenorio-Trillo, Mauricio. *I Speak of the City: Mexico City at the Turn of the Twentieth Century.* University of Chicago Press, 2012.

Tortolero Cervantes, Yolia. *El espiritismo seduce a Francisco I. Madero.* Senado de la República, second edition, 2004.

Tovar de Teresa, Guillermo. *La primera gran revolución del siglo XX: Un imaginario de la revolución mexicana.* Proceso, 2010.

Tsadhe, H.S. *Krumm Heller, el Rosa Cruz.* www.gnosis2000.com undated PDF file, downloaded August 2013.

Turner, John Kenneth. *Barbarous Mexico.* Charles H. Kerr, 1910.

Urrea, Luis Alberto. *The Hummingbird's Daughter.* Little, Brown 2005.

———. *Queen of America.* Little, Brown, 2011.

Wilson, Henry Lane. *Diplomatic Episodes in Mexico, Belgium and Chile.* Doubleday, Page & Company, 1927.

Valadés, José C. *Imaginación y realidad de Francisco I. Madero,* 2 vols. Antigua Librería Robredo de José Porrúa e Hijos, 1960.

Vanderwood, Paul. *The Power of God Against the Guns of Government: Religious Upheaval in Mexico at the Turn of the Nineteenth Century.* Stanford University Press, 1998.

Vasconcelos, José. *Estudios Indostánicos.* Ediciones Bota, 1938.

——. *Ulises Criollo*. Ediciones Bota, 1937.

Villalpando, José Manuel. *La Decena trágica*. Diana, 2009.

von Feilitzsch, Heribert. *In Plain Sight: Felix A. Sommerfeld, Spymaster in Mexico, 1908-1914*. Henselstone Verlag, 2012.

Zavaleta, Antonio, and Alberto Salinas, Jr. *Curandero Conversations: El Niño Fidencio, Shamanism and Healing Traditions of the Borderlands*. University of Texas at Brownsville, 2009.

## Metaphysical, History and Contemporary (Non-Mexican)

Ackroyd, Peter H., with Angela Narth. *A History of Ghosts: The True Story of Séances, Mediums, Ghosts and Ghostbusters.* Rodale Books, 2009.

Albanese, Catherine L. *A Republic of Mind & Spirit: A Cultural History of American Metaphysical Religion.* Yale University Press, 2007.

Alexander, Eban. *Proof of Heaven: A Neurosurgeon's Journey into the Afterlife.* Simon & Schuster, 2012.

Anderson, George, and Andrew Barone. *Walking in the Garden of Souls.* Penguin, 2002.

Bamford, Christopher. *An Endless Trace: The Passionate Pursuit of Wisdom in the West.* Codhill Press, 2003.

Besant, Annie. *Hints on the Study of the Bhagavadgita.* The Theosophical Publishing House, Revised Second Edition 2001.

——. [Trad. J.M.Ch.] *Karma.* 2a edición. Barcelona, 1911.

——. [trad. del inglés por Carmen Mateos de Maynadé] *Doctrina del Corazón.* Biblioteca Orientalista, 1904.

——. [trad. del inglés por D. José Melián] *El Poder del pensamiento. Su dominio y cultura.* Barcelona, 1901.

Besant, Annie, and C.W. Leadbeater. *Thought-forms.* Theosophical Publishing Society, 1905.

——. *Lives of Alcyone,* 2 vols. Theosophical Publishing House, 1924.

Bhagavad Gîtâ. [Trad. J, Roviralta Borrel]. Barcelona, 1896.

Bhagavad Gîtâ. [Transl. from the Sanskrit by Mohini M. Chatterji]. Houghton Mifflin Company, 1887.

Bigelow, John. *The Mystery of Sleep.* Harper and Brothers Publishers, 1905.

Blavatsky, Helena Petrovna. *Isis Unveiled.* Theosophical Publishing House, 1997.

——. *The Secret Doctrine.* Abridged and annotated by Michael Gomes. Jeremy P. Tarcher / Penguin, 2009.

Blum, Deborah. *Ghost Hunters: William James and the Search for Scientific Proof of Life After Death.* Penguin, 2006.

Bragdon, Emma. *Kardec's Spiritism: A Home for Healing and Spiritual Evolution.* Lightening Up Press, 2004.

Brandon, Ruth. *The Spiritualists: The Passion for the Occult in the Nineteenth and Twentieth Centuries.* Knopf, 1983.

Brennan, Barbara. *Hands of Light: A Guide to Healing Through the Human Energy Field.* Bantam, 1988.

Britten, William. Art, *Magic, Spiritism or, Mundane, Sub-Mundane and Super-Mundane.* Progressive Thinker Publishing House, 1898.

Brower, M. Brady. *Unruly Spirits: The Science of Psychic Phenomena in Modern France.* University of Illinois Press, 2010.

Bruce, Robert. *Astral Dynamics: A NEW Approach to Out-of-Body Experience.* Hampton Roads, 1999.

Bryan, Jessica. *Psychic Surgery and Faith Healing: An Exploration of Multidimensional Realities, Indigenous Healing, and Medical Miracles in the Philippine Lowlands.* Weiser Books, 2007.

Buchanan, Lyn. *The Seventh Sense.* Gallery Books, 2003.

Burnham, Sophy. *The Art of Intuition: Cultivating Your Inner Wisdom.* Tarcher, 2011.

Carrington, Hereward, *Eusapia Palladino and Her Phenomena.* B.W. Dodge and Company, 1909.

Cayce, Edgar, and Mark Thurston, ed. *The Essential Edgar Cayce.* Tarcher, 2004.

Conan Doyle, Arthur. *The Edge of the Unknown.* Crowborough, 1930.

———. *The History of Spiritualism.* Cambridge Scholars Publishing Classic Texts, 2009.

Cross, Whitney R. *The Burned-Over District: The Social and Intellectual History of Enthusiastic Religion in Western New York 1800-1850.* Cornell University Press, 1981.

Davis, Andrew Jackson. *The Principles of Nature, Her Divine Revelations and a Voice to Mankind.* S.S. Lyon and Wm. Fishbough, 1847.

Delanne, Gabriel. [Trad. Juan Juste y Cararach] *El fenómeno espiritista. Testimonio de los sabios.* Barcelona, 1893.

———. *Le Spiritisme devant la science.* 1885

DeMarco, Frank. *The Cosmic Internet.* Rainbow Bridge Books, 2001.

DeMarco, Frank, and Rita Q. Warren. *The Sphere and the Hologram: Explanations from the Other Side.* Hologram Books, 2009.

Denis, Léon. *Après la mort.* Jean Meyer, 1890.

———. [Traducido por un estadista mexicano (Ignacio Mariscal)]. *Después de la muerte.* 1906.

———. *Pourquoi la Vie?* Librairie P.-G. Leymarie, 1899.

Dufaux, Ermance. *Jeanne d'Arc par elle-même.* Desrues, 1855.

Encausse, Gérard [pseud. Papus]. *L'Occultisme en le Spiritualisme.* Paris, 1902.

Evans, Henry Ridgley. "Madame Blavatsky." *The Monist,* vol, 14, 1904.

———. *Hours with the Ghosts or Nineteenth Century Witchcraft.* Laird & Lee Publishers, 1897.

———. *Adventures in Magic.* L. Rullman, 1927.

———. *Old Georgetown on the Potomac.* The Georgetown News, 1933.

Flammarion, Camille. *Les Habitants de l'autre monde, révelations d'outre-tombe.* 2 vols. Ledoyen, 1862.

———. *La Pluralité des mondes habités.* 4ᵉ edition. Paris, 1865.

Frances, J.R. *The Encyclopedia of Death and Life in the Spirit World: Opinions and Experiences from Eminent Sources.* The Progressive Thinker Publishing House, 1900.

Freke, Timothy, and Peter Gandy. *The Hermetica: The Lost Wisdom of the Pharaohs.* Tarcher, 1999.

Friedrich, Paul. *The Gita Within Walden*. State University of New York Press, 2009.

Fuller, John G. *Arigo: Surgeon of the Rusty Knife*. Thomas Y. Crowell Company, 1974.

Geley, Dr. Gustave. *L'Être Subconscient*. Paris, 1905.

Godwin, Joscelyn. *The Thesophical Enlightenment*. State University of New York Press, 1994.

Goldberg, Ken, ed. *The Robot in the Garden: Telerobotics and Telepistemology in the Age of the Internet*. MIT Press, 2001.

Goldsmith, Barbara. *Other Powers: The Age of Suffragism, Spiritualism, and the Scandalous Victoria Woodhull*. Harper Perennial, 1999.

Grant, Joan. *Speaking from the Heart: Ethics, Reincarnation and What It Means to Be Human*. Overlook Press, 2007.

Green, Penelope. "Clearing More Than Cobwebs." *New York Times*, June 5, 2013.

Gurney, Edmund, Frederic W.H. Myers, and Frank Podmore. *Phantasms of the Living*. 2 vols. 1886.

Harkness, Deborah. *John Dee's Conversations with Angels: Cabala, Alchemy, and the End of Nature*. Cambridge University Press, 1999.

Hartmann, Franz. *Occult Science in Medicine*. Samuel Weiser, 1975.

——. [Traducido del inglés por A.F.G.] *Ciencia Oculta en la Medicina*. Biblioteca Orientalista, 1902.

Hermans, H.G.M. *Memoirs of a Maverick: Andrija Puharich, M.D., LL.D.* Pi Publications, 1998.

Hess, David. *Spirits and Scientists.* Pennsylvania State University Press, 1991.

——. *Samba in the Night: Spiritism in Brazil.* Columbia University Press, 1983.

Home, Danniel Dunglas. *Incidents in My Life.* Carleton, 1863.

Horowitz, Mitch. *Occult America: The Secret History of How Mysticism Shaped Our Nation.* Bantam Books, 2009.

Judge, William Quan. "The Esoteric She: The Late Mme Blavatsky, A Sketch of Her Career." *The New York Sun*, September 26, 1892.

Jung, Carl. *Memories, Dreams, Reflections.* Vintage, 2011.

Kachuba, John. *Ghost Hunters: On the Trail of Mediums, Dowsers, Spirit Seekers, and Other Investigators of America's Paranormal World.* New Page Books, 2007.

Karagula, Shafika. *The Chakras and Human Energy Fields.* Quest, 1989.

——. *Breakthrough to Creativity: Your Higher Sense Perception.* Devorss Publications, 1967.

Karagula, Shafika, and Viola Pettit Neal. *Through the Curtain.* DeVorss Publications, 1983.

Kardec, Allan. *The Book on Mediums: Guide for Mediums and Invocators.* Translated by Emma A. Wood. Samuel Wieser, 1978.

———. *Spirits Book*. Translated by Anna Blackwell. George Redway, 1898.

Kendig, Irene. *Conversations with Jerry and Other People I Thought Were Dead*. Grateful Press, 2010.

Kripal, Jeffrey J. *Authors of the Impossible: The Paranormal and the Sacred*. University of Chicago Press, 2010.

Kübler-Ross, Elizabeth. *On Life After Death*. Celestial Arts, 2008.

Lachapelle, Sophie. *Investigating the Supernatural: From Spiritism and Occultism to Psychical Research and Metaphysics in France, 1853-1931*. Johns Hopkins University Press, 2001.

Lambroso, César. *El Hipnotismo*. Madrid.

Leadbeater, C.W. [Trad. del inglés D. Federico Climent Terrer] *Las últimas treinta vidas de Alcione. Rasgaduras en el velo del tiempo*. Barcelona, 1912.

Leonard, Todd Jay. *Talking to the Other Side: A History of Modern Spiritualism and Mediumship*. iUniverse, 2005.

Lutyens, Mary. *Krishnamurti: The Years of Awakening*. John Murray, 1975.

———. *Krishnamurti: The Years of Fulfillment*. Farrar, Strauss and Giroux, 1985.

———. *Krishnamurti: The Open Door*. Farrar, Strauss and Giroux, 1988.

———. *To Be Young: A Memoir of Childhood and Young Love by the Daughter of the Great Architect Sir Edward Lutyens*. Corgi, 1989.

Mack, John. *Abduction: Human Encounters with Aliens.* Ballentine Books, 1994.

Majewski, Adrien. *Mediumnité Guérissante par l'application des fluides électriques magnétiques et humains.* Paris.

Martin, Harvey. *The Secret Teachings of the Espiritistas: A Hidden History of Spiritual Healing.* Metamind Publications, 1998.

Maspero, G. *Histoire ancienne des pueples de l'orient.* 7ᵉ editión. Paris, 1905.

McMoneagle, Joe, and Charles T. Tart. *Mind Trek: Exploring Consciousness, Time, and Space Through Remote Viewing.* Hampton Roads, revised edition, 1997.

Monroe, John Warne. *Laboratories of Faith: Mesmerism, Spiritism, and Occultism in Modern France.* Cornell University Press, 2008.

Monroe, Robert. *Journeys Out of the Body.* Doubleday, 1971.

Moody, Raymond A. *Life After Life.* Bantam Books, 1975.

Moses, William Stainton. *Spirit Teachings.* Memorial Edition. London Spiritualist Alliance, 1898.

———. [Trad. par X.] *Enseignments Spiritualistes.* Paris, 1899.

Myers, Frederic W.H. *Human Personality and Its Survival of Bodily Death.* 2 vols. Longmans, Green, and Co., 1903.

———. [Trad. Javier Osorno y Alberto Leduc] *La Personalidad humana. Su supervivencia, sus manifestaciones supranormales.* Librería de la Vd. De Ch. Bouret, 1906.

Myss, Carolyn. *Anatomy of the Spirit.* Crown Publishing Group, 1996.

Noeggerath, Rufina. *La vida de ultratumba (La survie).* 2 vols. Barcelona.

Olcott, Henry S. *People From the Other World.* American Publishing Company, 1875.

Oppenheim, Janet. *The Other World: Spiritiualism and Pyschical Research in England, 1850-1914.* Cambridge University Press, 1985.

Orbegoso, Arturo. "Espiritismo, Locura e Intelectuales del 900." *Revista de Psicología,* 14 (1), 2012.

Owen, Alex. *The Place of Enchantment: British Occultism and the Culture of the Modern.* University of Chicago Press, 2004.

Peebles, J.M. *Seers of the Ages*: *Embracing Spiritualism Past and Present.* Progressive Thinker Publishing House, 1903.

Pendleton, Don and Linda Pendleton. *To Dance with Angels: An Amazing Journey to the Heart with the Phenomenal Thomas Jacobson and the Grand Spirit, "Dr. Peebles."* Pendleton Artists, Kindle edition, May 2012.

Pomés Vives, Jordi. "Diálogo Oriente-Occidente en España de finales del siglo. El primo teosofismo español 1888-1906 un movimiento religioso heterodoxo bien integrado en los movimientos sociales de su época," *Revista HmiC 2006, Historia Moderna i Contemporanea,* Universitat de Barcelona.

Prel, Baron Carl du. [Traduit d'allemand par Mme Agathe Hoemmerlé]. *La Mort l'au delà, La Vie dans l'au delà.* Biblioteque Chacornac, 1905.

Puharich, Andrija. *Uri: A Journal of the Mystery of Uri Geller.* Anchor Press, 1974.

Radin, Dean. *The Conscious Universe: The Scientific Truth of Psychic Phenomena.* Harper, 2009.

Roberts, Jane. *Seth Speaks: The Eternal Validity of the Soul.* Bantam Books, 1972

Rose, Jonathan S. *Swedenborg's Garden of Theology: An Introduction to Emanuel Swedenborg's Published Theological Works.* Swedenborg Foundation, 2010.

Rosetree, Rose. *Aura Reading through All Your Senses.* Women's Intuition Worldwide, second edition, 2004.

Rubin, Nancy. *The Reluctant Spiritualist: The Life of Maggie Fox.* Harcourt, 2005.

Rudolph, Kurt. *Gnosis: The Nature & History of Gnosticism.* Harper San Francisco, 1987.

Sage, M. *Le Sommeil Naturel et L'Hypnose.* Paris, 1904.

———. *Madame Piper et la Societé Anglo-Americaine pour les recherches psychiques.* 10e edition. Paris, 1902.

———. *La Zone-frontière entre l'Autre Monde et celui-ci.* Paris, 1903.

Schucman, Dr. Helen, and Dr. William Thetford. *A Course in Miracles.* Foundation for Inner Peace, revised, 2008.

Schuré, Édouard. *Les Grands Initiés. Esquisse de l'histoire secrète des religions,* 1908.

Sharp, Lynn L, *Secular Spirituality: Reincarnation and Spiritism in Nineteenth-Century France.* Lexington Books, 2006.

Sheldrake, Rupert. *Morphic Resonance: The Nature of Formative Causation.* Park Street Press, revised and expanded edition, 2009.

Star, Ely. *Les mystères de l'être.* Chacornac Broché, 1902.

Steiner, Rudolph, *Spiritualism, Madame Blavatsky, and Theosphy: An Eyewitness View of Occult History.* Anthroposophic Press, 2001.

———. *Staying Connected: How to Continue Your Relationships with Those Who Have Died: Selected Talks and Meditations,* ed. Christopher Bamford. Anthroposophic Press, 1999.

Swedenborg, Emanuel, *The Useful Life: A Crown to the Simple Life.* Edited and introduced by John Bigelow. Charles Schribner's Sons, 1905.

Tannoja, Antonio. *The Life of St. Alphonsus Maria de Liguori, Bishop of St Agatha of the Goths and Founder of the Congregation of the Holy Redeemer.* John Murphy & Co, 1855.

Tehrani, Kathleen. "Dr William Tiller: Interview and Insights." examiner.com, November 14, 2009.

Tiller, William. *Psychoenergetic Science: A Second Copernican-Scale Revolution.* Pavior, 2007.

Twain, Mark. "Mental Telegraphy." *Harper's Magazine.* December 1891.

Tymn, Michael. *Resurrecting Leonora Piper: How Science Discovered the Afterlife.* White Crow Books, 2013.

——. *The Afterlife Revealed: What Happens After We Die.* White Crow Books, 2011.

Van Der Naillen, A. *Dans Le Sanctuaire. Faisant Suite a dans les Temples de L'Himalaya.* Librarie P.-G. Leymarie, 1897.

Van Praag, James. *Talking to Heaven: A Medium's Message of Life After Death.* Signet, 1999.

Vernon, Roland. *Star in the East: Krishnamurti, the Invention of a Messiah.* Sentient Publications 2002.

Vivekananda, Swami. [Tradución por José Granes]. *Filosofía yoga: Conferencias dadas en Nueva York en el invierno de 1895 y 96.* Biblioteca Orientalista, 1904.

Wallace, Alfred Russel. *Miracles and Modern Spiritualism.* George Redway, 1896.

Weisberg, Barbara. *Talking to the Dead: Kate and Maggie Fox and the Rise of Spiritualism.* Harper Collins, 2004.

Wicker, Christine Wicker. *Lily Dale: The True Story of the Town that Talks to the Dead.* HarperSanFrancisco, 2003.

Williams, Lisa. *Life Among the Dead.* Gallery Books, 2008.

Yates, Frances A. *Giordano Bruno and the Hermetic Tradition.* University of Chicago Press, 1998.

Yeats, W. B. *The Trembling of the Veil.* T. Werner Laurie, 1922.

# $Spiritist \ Manual$

**by Bhîma**

**(Francisco I. Madero)**

Mexico, 1911

Translated by C.M. Mayo

# TABLE OF CONTENTS

By the author's express wishes this work is the property of the Permanent Board of Mexico's Second Spiritist Congress,* which is now empowered to reproduce this work in whole or in part, or translations into foreign languages, on the sole condition that all reproductions be true to the text and the translations accurate. In this way the author's objective and the Committee's wish, that is, to make the most propaganda possible, will be achieved.

*The original work is now in the public domain.
—Translator's Note

## DEDICATION

The author dedicates this modest work to the great and noble spirits who have led him out of the fogs of ignorance, opening his eyes to splendors and vast horizons, and made his heart, once cold with selfishness, tremble for humanity's miseries.

It is to these noble sentiments inspired by such elevated beings, that the author owes his desire to spread the light and consolation that enhalo the Spiritist Doctrine.

Aided always by his invisible friends, he has written this manual to satisfy this desire.

May it bring light to consciences; peace and tranquility to hearts; may it serve to wipe away many tears; to guide many souls to the path of goodness—and the author's desires shall be satisfied!

Mexico, August 1909*

BHÎMA

*While the dedication is dated 1909, the book was completed and delivered to the printer in 1910 and published in 1911.
—T.N.

# INTRODUCTION

Written at the request of the Permanent Board of Mexico's Second Spiritist Congress, this work is intended for young people, workers, and the general population who have not yet felt materialism's devastating influence.

We therefore address ourselves to the young people who have not yet begun to live, who have not yet imbibed from the impure fountains of materialism, who are open to admiring all that is great and beautiful; to those whose hearts have not fallen into the clutches of distressing skepticism, and who, with passion and enthusiasm, cherish noble ideals and generous feelings.

We also and equally address the worker, destitute of fortune, to whom there is no consolation in what his reason rejects; who finds no justice in materialism because it only demonstrates the triumph of the strongest, awarding the prize to the one most apt in struggle; and to the one considered the weakest, the least apt in this unending struggle of the fittest, and who does not believe it just that his destiny should be to perish, after a miserable and hard-working life, who does not believe it just to have come into this world only to enrich others and, by his privations, provide them such abundance that they may live in idleness while he is brought to his knees by work.

Thus we intend this work for those workers who also have pure hearts, and whose consciences have not yet been polluted by materialism. Here they will find the foundations of a very lofty philosophy to satisfy their most noble aspirations, and explain the meaning of life, the reasons for their sad situation, and which will show them the law of retribution, open their minds to new and vast horizons, make them understand that our lives do not play out in the miserable patch of an earthly existence, but for time they have Eternity, for space, the Universe; and finally, it will put them in a better condition to sustain their struggle for life, a struggle ever more ferocious given the selfishness of the rich and the ignorance of the poor.

To achieve our objective we will offer a brief overview of the Spiritist Doctrine. It is so beautiful and so simple that it will be easily admired and understood.

We will not make lengthy arguments nor cite numerous proofs in support of this doctrine, for the most demanding can find such arguments and proofs in specialized works.

Moreover, lengthy arguments generally serve to obscure the points we wish to clarify.

For these reasons, we shall focus on presenting proofs that can be understood by all and making simple arguments, those most appropriate for a true impression.

Our work will be to sow a seed in the furrow; that of our readers, to carefully cultivate the plant that germinates until it yields ripe fruit.

THE AUTHOR

**CHAPTER I**

# A Brief Overview of the Spiritist Doctrine

*Q. What is understood by Spiritism?*
A. Spiritism is the science concerned with investigating the powers of the human spirit, its past before arriving in this world, and its fortune upon abandoning it.

ANIMATING FORCES
*Q. Can you tell me what powers animate our spirit?*
A. These powers are enormous. In the first place there are intelligence and will, which, combined with service to higher spirits, can transform the world, as indeed it has been transformed by Buddha, Moses, Christ, and many other great men.

These spirits possess a very clear intelligence which has guided them in fulfilling their mission, and great will which empowered them with the energy to continue on their paths, though these were strewn with a thousand obstacles.

*Q. What other powers does the spirit possess?*
A. Intelligence and will in greater or lesser degrees may or may not be attributes of incarnate spirits, but in all human personalities there exist in embryo other powers susceptible to great development. These are called mental or psychic powers (from "psyche," soul.)

These powers are not of an exclusively spiritual origin, but neither are they of material origin, and their complex and mixed nature admirably serves to demonstrate that our material body is ruled by a spiritual entity.

*Q. How can you prove the existence of these powers?*
A. By means of the phenomena they produce: magnetism, hypnotism, suggestion, telepathy, somnambulism, and ecstasy.

*Q. Are these the only powers available to the human spirit?*
A. There are others which I cannot classify as mental because they only manifest with the cooperation of spirits that inhabit space; for this reason they are called mediumistic. Spirits make use of them to communicate with the living.

*Q. And do spirits communicate with all of the living?*
A. Spirits utilize certain procedures in order to exert influence over the inhabitants of this world, though this influence goes unnoticed by the great majority. However, there are individuals endowed with special abilities which allow spirits to manifest through them. Generally these people serve as intermediaries between the spirits who inhabit space and those living in this world, which is why they are called mediums. (Intermediaries.)

REINCARNATION
*Q. Can you tell me something about the state in which our spirit finds itself before coming into this world and about the fate that awaits our spirit upon leaving it?*
A. The life of a spirit is eternal. Its origin is lost in the night of time, and its future is glorious and eternal. The spirit reincarnates a considerable number of times on our planet, until it acquires the knowledge and virtues necessary to pass into a higher world.

Each time the spirit incarnates in this world, it brings with it the virtues and experiences it has acquired, in the form of intelligence, aptitudes, and character.

All of a spirit's earthly existences relate to the others; and just as the present incarnation is the result of previous incarnations, our future state will be determined by our current actions. In this way, we alone are responsible for our situation, whether happy or unfortunate, and we owe our intelligence, will, and virtues to our past efforts. No effort we make will be wasted, and as it comes to fruition, sooner or later, all of us will benefit.

SUMMARY OF THE SPIRITIST DOCTRINE

**Q. *In a few words, can you summarize the teachings of this chapter?***

A. Spiritism, supported by scientific experiments, both mental and mediumistic, and by aid of cold reason, and guided by Spiritist revelation, have proven that our spirit is a higher entity than our body, and that its life is not limited to one earthly incarnation, but it has had and will have numerous incarnations. In each incarnation, the spirit gains wisdom and virtue, and there comes a moment in which, highly evolved, it finds the physical wrapping tight and so radiates outwards, producing the various mental and spiritist phenomena of which I have spoken.

The spirit's future is glorious, for its evolution is a divine law, an immutable law which will be upheld no matter how many obstacles it encounters on its path. As the spirit evolves, its perceptions and its reasons for happiness increase, and it forgets the sufferings caused by its previous imperfections.

Evolution is slow and difficult, but it depends on us to make it faster, freeing ourselves more quickly from the causes of our sufferings, and increasing those that produce our happiness.

## CHAPTER II

# Historical Background

*Q. You have told me that the Spiritist Doctrine comes in part from revelation, and this moves me to ask, what should we understand by revelation?*

A. All of we beings who inhabit this world are creatures of God, who, as a loving Father, always watches over us and, like a powerful magnet, draws us to Him, to encourage our evolution.

To achieve His objective, He has fomented a great solidarity among all His creatures, obliging them to help each other. Thus, each of us helps, offering a hand to those behind us, as each is helped and pulled along by those who go ahead.

Just as in every family power converges to its natural head, the father, in the churches it converges to the priest, and in nations to the head of the government, so the world is governed by great spirits who, although invisible, exercise a decisive influence upon the destinies of humankind.

While these great spirits remain in space, they do not always influence incarnate beings as efficiently as they would like, and in certain cases, they incarnate in this world in order to accelerate their evolution, directing it along paths known to them.

In general, they have come to draw back the veil on the mysterious Beyond, revealing the origin and destiny of souls, and the means for achieving supreme happiness. By their self-less example, they have preached virtue and its effectiveness in curing the sicknesses of the soul; by their powerful will and superior intelligence, they have helped humanity toward its great destiny, showing it the path it must take to evolve more rapidly and achieve this purest happiness, humanity's greatest longing, which is found only by knowing and adhering to divine law.

**Q. Given that this is the origin of divine revelation, why are there so many differences among the many religions?**
A. These differences are superficial and unimportant. The essence of all religions is the same, but the teachings and doctrines of the great masters, the divine missionaries who have visited this world, though the same in essence, have suffered large changes made by the peoples who have adopted them. The truth is always the same, but each people sees it through the lens of their customs and concerns, and each gives it its own tint. This is why we observe that the same religion is interpreted in different ways by each of the peoples or races that has adopted it. Thus, for example, Christianity is observed in very diverse ways among the different Protestant sects and the Catholics.

With Spiritism something similar happens, as the English and Anglo-American Spiritists do not accept the doctrine of reincarnation, which is the foundation of Spiritism on the European continents and in the Latin American Republics.

Buddhism has numerous sects, very different one from another, according to the different Asian people that have adopted it. While some profess the purest Spiritism, others have descended into materialism.

**Q. Can you tell me which are the divine missions that have exercised the most influence over humanity?**
A. History begins with Rama, the head of the Aryan race that invaded, conquered, and civilized India. Undoubtedly, however, those that have exercised the most influence over humanity are Krishna, Hermes, Moses, and Jesus.

KRISHNA

**Q. I beg you to give me a brief explanation of the doctrine of Krishna.**

A. About 5,000 years ago, Krishna, son of the virgin Devaki, appeared in India. He taught that there is one God and that the soul is immortal, progressing through multiple reincarnations, and from these teachings, he deduced the purest morality.

GOD

Krishna said that God occupied the entire universe, but that "only the infinite can comprehend the infinite and space, and that only God can comprehend God."

IMMORTALITY OF THE SOUL

As for the immortality of the soul, he said: "The body, envelope of the soul and its dwelling, is a finite thing while the soul itself is invisible, imponderable, incorruptible, and eternal. Earthly man is triple, as divinity reflects: intelligence, soul, and body. If the soul unites with the intelligence, it achieves wisdom and peace; if it remains unsteady between the intelligence and the body, it is overcome by passion and swings from object to object around a viscious circle; if it abandons the body, it falls into madness, ignorance, and death in time."

REINCARNATION

The doctrine of reincarnation is as follows:

"After death, the soul obeys this above stated law, which determines the mystery of reincarnations: As the depths of Heaven open before the shimmering stars, so the profundities of life are illuminated by the light of this truth. When the body has dissolved, if wisdom has predominated, the soul ascends to those regions of pure beings who possess the highest knowledge; on the other hand, if passion has predominated, the soul returns to live among those who are attached to earthly things."

In terms that should inspire serious reflection, Krishna also said: "You and I have had many reincarnations. Only I know of mine, while you do not know even one of yours. Although I am not by nature obliged to be born or to die, and am master of all creatures, and in control over my nature, I make myself visible by my own power, and each time virtue falls in this world and vice and injustice reign, I make myself visible. And so I show myself from time to time, for the salvation of the just, the destruction of evil, and reestablishment of good."

MORALITY

The morality Krishna taught can only be compared to that of Christ. I will now cite one of his precepts:

"The evils we afflict upon our fellow man follow us as our shadow follows our body. Works motivated by love for our fellowman must aspire to justice, for these are the ones that weigh the most in the celestial balance.

"If you keep good company, your example will be useless; do not be afraid to live among evil men, so that you may bring them to goodness. The virtuous man is like a gigantic bodhi tree whose benevolent shadow benefits the plants that surround him, the freshness of life. As the earth supports those who leave their footprints upon it and tears its bosom in tilling it, so should we return good for evil. The good man should fall under the blows of the evil as the sandalwood tree perfumes the axe that cuts it."

HERMES

**Q. What can you tell me about the doctrine of Hermes?**
A. Hermes lived in Upper Egypt, and his name, according to the leading historians and archaeologists, is associated with the first ray of light and truth, with the first civilizing impulse that was felt in the world.[a]

UNITY OF GOD

According to Mr. Maspero,[b] an expert Orientalist and distinguished archaeologist, the affirmation of the fundamental unity of the Divine One is expressed in formal terms and with great energy in texts that predate the Christian era by thousands of years: "God is the only one who lives in substance, He is the only creator of Heaven and earth that has not been created.

"At once Father, Mother, and Son, He begets, He brings light, He exists in perpetuity. These three personas, far from dividing the nature of divinity, contribute to its infinite perfection. Its attributes are immensity, eternity, independence, Almighty will, and infinite goodness."

According to Mr. Shuré,ᶜ of God, Hermes said: "Our thinking cannot conceive of God, nor can any language define it. What is incorporal, invisible, formless, cannot be appreciated by our senses; what is eternal cannot be measured by the short ruler of time. God is ineffable. It is true that God gives to some of the elect the ability to rise above natural things, to perceive some of the rays of His supreme perfection, but these individuals do not have the words to translate into vulgar language the unearthly vision that has astonished them. They have only been able to explain secondary, fleeting things such as images of universal life; the first cause remains veiled, and we are only able to comprehend it when we pass on in death."

THE SOUL'S DESTINY; ITS IMMORTALITY; REINCARNATION
"When the adept has passed the tests of initiation, the Egyptian temple priests reveal the vision of Hermes, in the following words:

"As for man's spirit, its destiny has two phases: captivity in the material, and ascent into the light. Souls are daughters of Heaven and their journey is a test. During their incarnation, they lose the memory of their heavenly origin. Caught in the material, intoxicated by life, with voluptuous feeling, they fall like a rain of fire through all the regions of Suffering, Love, and Death, until the earthly prison, where you groan and divine life seems a vain dream.

"The lower, perverse souls remain chained to the earth for multiple reincarnations, while the virtuous souls, as if upon wings, rise toward the higher spheres, where they regain their

vision for divine things, which gives them the lucidity of consciousness illuminated by suffering, with the energy of the
will acquired by struggle. They then fill with light, for they
possess the divine in themselves, which shines forth in their
acts. So fortify your heart, oh, Hermes! and make your darkened
spirit serene by contemplating the flight of souls ascending
through the scale of spheres that brings them to the Father,
there where everything concludes, where everything is eter-
nally beginnning."

THE SECRET DOCTRINE
   *Q. The only thing you have not explained to me is
how such philosophical doctrines and elevated concepts
were understood by backward peoples, such as those who
inhabited the earth in the epoch you refer to. Furthermore,
profane history and archaeology show us that, evidently,
both the peoples of India and Egypt were idolatrous. Can
you clarify this point for me?*
A. These very elevated doctrines were only known to initiates
in the temples of India and Egypt. The initiates themselves
only learned of these doctrines gradually, to the degree that
they developed their scientific knowledge and virtue, and could
withstand the terrible tests to which they were subjected.
   The initiates did not reveal their knowledge to the multitudes. They limited themselves to guiding their evolution,
allowing them only that knowledge which was at the level of
their intelligence.
   For this reason, the ancient religions, so grandiose in their
metaphysical conceptions, were veiled from the multitudes by
a vulgar cult.

   *Q. What were the reasons the initiates hid the truth
from the masses?*
A. In revealing such doctrines to the initiates, the high priest
would say: "The veil of mystery covers the great truths. Total
knowledge cannot be revealed except to those who have come

through the same tests as we have. It is necessary to measure the truth according to intelligence; to veil it from the weak, from those who have lost their judgement, to hide it from evil-doers, those who would use it as a weapon of destruction. Keep it safe within your heart and let it reveal itself by your works. Science will be your strength, law your weapon, and silence your shield."

MOSES

Despite this, one of the initiates of the Egyptian temples, Moses—who came to earth many centuries after the appearance of Krishna and Hermes—became one of the best known divine missionaries because he was the first to reveal to humanity some of the great truths, hitherto hidden in the temples and reserved to a small group of the elect.

UNITY OF GOD

*Q. Can you tell me what were the great truths Moses revealed to the multitudes?*

A: Moses revealed to the Israelites, whom he charged with the responsibility of divulging it to the whole world, the idea of one God, condemning idolatry, according to the first commandment of the Law he received on Mount Sinai:

"I am the Lord thy God, who brought thee out of the land of Egypt, out of the house of bondage."

"Thou shalt not have strange gods before me."

"Thou shalt not make to thyself a graven thing, nor the likeness of any thing that is in heaven above, or in the earth beneath, nor of those things that are in the waters under the earth"

"Thou shalt not adore them nor serve them: I am the Lord thy God, mighty, jealous, etc."

THE SOUL'S IMMORTALITY

*Q: What did Moses say about the immortality of the soul?*

A: Moses went so far as to reveal to his people the unity of

God, and to give them an admirable set of moral laws but, with respect to the soul's immortality, he only implied this doctrine when he said, "God created man in his likeness."

MORALITY

**Q. Which are the moral precepts Moses taught?**
A. These are enshrined within the other commandments Moses received on Mt. Sinai, revealed in an extraordinary manner which deeply impressed the Israelites.

The best proof of divine origin of the Ten Commandments is that in three thousand years they have not been repealed. On the contrary: as humanity perfects itself, the better it understands each commandment, and discovers new applications.

To master the unruly Israelites, Moses promulgated many laws, some of which are still observed by modern Jews, though we may consider these other laws, some of legislative and others of hygienic character, transitory.

For these reasons, I will only refer to the ten that have such grandeur that, involuntarily, we contemplate their mysterious origin.

The commandments, including the first which I already mentioned in abbreviated form are:

1. Love God above all things
2. Never take the name of the Lord in vain
3. Respect the Holy days
4. Honor your father and mother
5. Do not kill
6. Do not commit adultery
7. Do not steal
8. Do not bear false witness against others
9. Do not covet your neighbor's wife
10. Do not covet the things of others

JESUS OF NAZARETH

**Q: And what can you say about the mission of Jesus of Nazareth?**

A: Of the missionaries to humanity, none has made such great revelations as he. Jesus did not hesitate to reveal the great mysteries, which had been, until then, the patrimony of small groups of initiates.

## UNITY OF GOD

Jesus confirmed the teachings of Moses about the existence of one God, whom he taught us to call Father and to worship in spirit and truth.

"Our Father who art in Heaven," etc., as in many other well-known passages in the New Testament.

## THE SOUL'S IMMORTALITY

The immortality of the soul follows from his teachings, and above all from his apparitions after his death.

## REINCARNATION

He and his disciples accepted the doctrine of reincarnation, as follows from these verses:

MATTHEW 16:13 "And Jesus came into the quarters of Caesarea Philippi: and he asked his disciples, saying: Whom do men say that the Son of man is?

14 But they said: Some John the Baptist, and other some Elias; and others Jeremias, or one of the prophets."

In the following verses Jesus affirms that the prophet Elias reincarnated as John the Baptist:

17:10 "And his disciples asked him, saying: Why then do the scribes say that Elias must come first?

17:11 But he answering, said to them: Elias indeed shall come, and restore all things.

17:12 But I say to you, that Elias is already come, and they knew him not, but have done unto him whatsoever they had in mind. So also the Son of man shall suffer from them.

17:13 Then the disciples understood, that he spake unto them of John the Baptist."

Jesus taught reincarnation when he said:

GOSPEL ACCORDING TO SAINT JOHN 3:1 "There was a man of the Pharisees, named Nicodemus, a ruler of the Jews:

3:2 This man came to Jesus by night, and said to him: Rabbi, we know that thou art a teacher come from God; for no man can do these signs that thou dost, unless God be with him.

3:3 Jesus answered, and said to him: Amen, amen I say to thee, unless a man be born again, he cannot see the kingdom of God."

The disciples knew the doctrine of reincarnation as can be seen in the following episode:

JOHN 9:1 "And Jesus passing by, saw a man, who was blind from his birth:

9:2 And his disciples asked him: Rabbi, who hath sinned, this man, or his parents, that he should be born blind?

9:3 Jesus answered: "Neither hath this man sinned, nor his parents; but that the works of God should be made manifest in him."

If we do not accept the doctrine of reincarnation, how can the blind man have sinned before he was born?

MORALITY

*Q. And what were Jesus' moral teachings?*

A. These were the most sublime that humanity has received. Each precept radiates that infinite tenderness which filled the Savior's soul.

The morals were contained in the following:

"Love one another," he said, but he expanded it in his teachings to his disciples and in his preaching to the people. So he said, "Love your enemies."

In the very beautiful Sermon on the Mount, directed to the people, he preached humility and charity as the most beautiful virtues; he recommended simple prayer; and he condemned the Pharisees as hypocrites who pretended great fervor and yet devoured the goods of widows.

For the meek, he offered the reign of heaven, for the oppressed, justice, and for those who repented their sins, forgiveness.

With a simple phrase, something everyone can understand, he revealed the eternal truths to the multitudes, he spoke to them of the other life, giving them hope that their suffering will be rewarded. He spoke to them of equality, saying that we are all children of God and that in His eyes the greatest are precisely the most humble.

By such gentle and persuasive words, his simple doctrines penetrated the hearts of the multitudes, and gave them the will to raise their faces to the sky in search of new horizons and forge their hearts with the heroism necessary to achieve their liberty, and especially that of their consciences, the most dear for all peoples. For this reason we see that the first Christians had no fear of confronting the greatest risks, and even death. For such sublime martyrs for their faith, there was no life but the eternal one, they knew no other satisfaction than that of fulfilling their duty, they had no ideal other than to imitate Jesus and put his teachings into practice.

REVELATION

Finally, Jesus said he was sent by God and clearly established the doctrine of revelation, as we can see in the following verses:

MATTHEW 10:40 "He that receiveth you, receiveth me: and he that receiveth me, RECEIVETH HIM THAT SENT ME."

ST JOHN 16:5 "And now I go to HIM THAT SENT ME"

ST JOHN 17:3 "Now this is eternal life: That they may know thee, the only true God, and JESUS CHRIST, WHOM THOU HAST SENT"

ST JOHN 17:4 "I have glorified thee on earth; I have finished THE WORK WHICH THOU GAVEST ME TO DO"

17:8 "BECAUSE THE WORDS WHICH THOU GAVEST ME I HAVE GIVEN TO THEM; AND THEY HAVE RECEIVED THEM, AND HAVE KNOWN IN VERY DEED THAT I CAME OUT FROM THEE, AND THEY HAVE BELIEVED THAT THOU DIDTH SEND ME."

17:23 "I in them, and thou in me; that they may be made perfect in one: AND THE WORLD MAY KNOW THAT THOU HAST SENT ME, and hast loved them, AS THOU HAST ALSO

LOVED ME."

17:25 "Just Father, the world hath not known thee; but I have known thee: and THESE HAVE KNOWN THAT THOU HAST SENT ME."

SPIRITIST REVELATION
*Q. And Spiritism, is that also a revelation?*
A. In fact, Spiritism is the last revelation that humanity has received.

The difference is that this time it was not a divine missionary who brought the Good News to the world, but a multitude of spirits who have communicated through people with special abilities whom we call mediums.

There are many of these people and by the teachings they have obtained and, in searching for agreements among the revelations, the necessary information has been compiled to formulate a Spiritist doctrine, which expands and explains what has been taught by divine missionaries about the unity of God, immortality, reincarnation of the soul or spirit, and about morality.

*Q. Undoubtedly we should believe what the great missionaries have revealed to the world, but should we also believe everything the mediums pretend to receive as revelation from the spirits?*
A. By no means should we believe everything asserted by the mediums, nor by the spirits themselves, for both are prone to errors.

*Q. How should we distinguish truth from fraud?*
A. Only our reason can guide us. All spiritist communication, even when it appears authentic, should not be accepted without first passing it through the sieve of our reason. Communications from spirits should have the same validity as the writing of a living person. Only the force of his arguments should convince us.

We should do the same with respect to the teachings of the great missionaries who have visited humanity.

We should submit their doctrines to a cold and dispassionate examination. Undoubtedly, such great spirits knew the whole truth, but they are not the ones who left us written documents. This work was undertaken by their disciples. Now then, should we believe that their disciples, the interpreters of their philosophy, clearly comprehended their teachings? Have the sacred books never been mutilated or adulterated to serve egotistical purposes? Finally, in speaking to the multitudes, the divine missionaries had to use language they could comprehend, and take into account their customs and prejudices.

For all these reasons we should only believe what our reason understands. Nevertheless, this does not permit us to deny that which we cannot understand. In the latter cases, we should consider revelations a kind of guide that directs our steps, like a torch that lights our path.

### Q. Can you tell me something about the origin of Spiritism?

A. Spiritism is as old as the world, for its philosophical doctrines, like the phenomena upon which they are based, were known to the divine missionaries and by groups of initiates that practiced these doctrines.

Thus Krishna said to his disciples:

"Long before throwing off their mortal shell, the souls that have practised goodness aquired the ability to communicate with those who have come before them in spiritual life."

ST. JOHN THE EVANGELIST 4:1 "Dearly beloved, believe not every spirit, but try the spirits if they be of God."

The doctrines of Socrates and other Greek philosophers, as with the practices of the Druids of ancient Gaul and North America's savage Indians, demonstrate that humanity has always believed in the possibility of communicating with spirits and has always been in communication with them.

Nevertheless, the ignorance of these peoples did not permit Spiritism to be widely divulged; it was reserved for our modern rational spirit of criticism and analysis to take from spiritist phenomena the deductions that have formed the Spiritist doctrine.

Modern Spiritism had its origin in the many clamorous phenomena that appeared simultaneously in various parts of the world.

It was not until the opportune time that a phalanx of spirits knocked at the door of our material world, to prove to us their existence, and thereby demonstrate the soul's immortality, and give the fatal blow to the immoral materialist doctrines that had begun to reign in the world.

The old religions, overloaded with useless rituals, having lost their esoteric tradition, forgetting their essence, and having converted themselves into instruments of domination instead of serving as refuge for the helpless, lost their prestige and power, and were unable to stop materialism's dreadful advances.

Then the Supreme Being, alert to the evolution of the worlds, decided to reveal Spiritism to humanity.

The phenomena that appeared spontaneously could very soon be invoked, thus permitting their study. Expert investigators observed the laws these phenomena obeyed and from their deductions the Spiritist doctrine of which I have already made a brief review resulted. I will endeavor to further develop this doctrine in the following chapters.

Among these experts, the name of Allan Kardec stands out. A notable philosopher who lived in France in the middle of the previous century, he was the founder of the Spiritist doctrine and its principal proponent by means of a series of notable works titled *What Is Spiritism; Spirits' Book; The Book on Mediums; The Gospel Explained by the Spiritist Doctrine; Heaven and Hell;* and *Genesis,* which I recommend you read.

# CHAPTER III

# Spiritist Phenomena

**Q. The antiquity of Spiritism and the fact that it formed the basis of the great religions is evidence of its authenticity. Despite this, our century is not satisfied with abstract demonstrations. It requires proofs that fall within the bounds of physical senses. Can you give me some of these proofs?**

A. Spiritism's strength is precisely in the phenomena that serve as the foundation of its doctrines, phenomena that, for those willing, are easy to observe.

**Q. I would be grateful if you would explain the most important phenomena.**

A. I am delighted to grant your request:

I begin by making a distinction between mental and spiritist phenomena.

Mental phenomena are produced by the forces of our soul; the spiritist, by discarnate spirits that appear, under appropriate conditions, by combining their energies with those of incarnate beings.

Mental phenomena serve to demonstrate the existence of the soul as an entity independent of the body, and therefore immortal for, being independent from the body, it is not subject to illnesses or death.

Spiritist phenomena corroborate the above, putting us in contact with spirits that have departed this world.

MENTAL PHENOMENA

The most important and well-observed mental phenomena are the following: magnetism, hypnotism, suggestion, telepathy, sleepwalking, clairvoyance, astral projection, and ecstasy.

**Q. Can you explain to me, what is magnetism?**

A. Magnetism is the vital fluid that serves as the intermediary between the soul and the body. When this fluid weakens, sickness appears; when it runs out, death. In addition, the latter can occur when the vital fluid encounters obstructions in the channels in which it circulates, as happens with serious injuries or similar cases.

The vital fluid, or magnetism, can become subject to the force of will and therefore, whoever exercises his will over his fluids—a magnetizer—can send part of his fluid to other people, what we call "magnetizing them."

When the fluid is very abundant, the subject (the magnetized) falls asleep, entering a more or less lucid dream, depending on the will and the abilities of the magnetizer. During this dream, certain phenomena are produced, such as suggestion, hypnotism, sleepwalking, etc., which we can study.

Magnetism's most common and usual effect is to heal the sick. Sending healthy and vigorous fluid to a debilitated organism provokes a reaction in the latter's fluids, which very rapidly alleviates physical ailments.

**Q. I beg you to tell me, is it very difficult to heal by using magnetism?**

A. On the contrary, it is easy. The only requirements are GOOD INTENTIONS AND THE VEHEMENT DESIRE TO HEAL THE SICK WITHOUT TAKING ANY CONSIDERATION OF ONE'S EGO. With these desires, and the intention of sending your fluids to the sick person, place your hands on the afflicted part of the patient's body, and wait calmly in peace and quiet and concentration. Very soon you will feel the magnetic current running down your arms, producing various effects. In some cases, your arms will begin to tremble more or less strongly; in others, the magnetizer will feel a headache or great fatigue. All of this happens the first time, but persevere in your intentions and you will soon cease to feel any discomfort and give healings more rapidly and effectively.

When you have developed your ability to heal you will no longer need to use your hands. It will be enough to make ten passes above and below from a distance. These passes help the action of the magnetizer and, in most cases, are recommended.

Finally, once you have been convinced that you have influence over someone, you can magnetize water or sugar granules and send these, assured that you will obtain the same result. Water and sugar are magnetized in the same way you magnetize a person.

The water can be used to drink or in a compress to heal ulcers, sores, wounds, etc.

I advise you to not be discouraged by failures at first. These are usually due to two causes: first, because not everyone can heal the first time they attempt it; second, because even the most powerful magnetizers have no influence over certain people, especially members of their own family.

### Q. What proofs can you give me about the existence of magnetism?

A. What better proof do we have than that you yourself confirm the existence of this phenomenon?

Nevertheless, I will give you a means to obtain another proof, but this you cannot do until you are sure of your ability to heal, or if you have the help of someone who has it.

The proof consists of placing your hand on a photographic plate for twenty minutes, keeping it in a bath of hydroquinone. Then, fix it in a solution of sodium hyposulfite and you will have an impression of your luminous hand on the plate. Make the experiment in several ways: with your entire hand or the fingertips to one side of the collodion or the other, making sure in this last case that the plate does not touch the bottom of the pan, so as not to separate the collodion.

These experiments should be carried out in a darkroom or one lit only weakly with a red light.

### Q. What can you tell me about hypnotism?

A. There is a strong analogy between magnetic and hypnotic phenomena, as they are produced by the same forces, combined in different measures. For this reason it is difficult to find the exact lines that divide the spheres of hypnotism and magnetism.

In principle, I will say that magnetic phenomena are reduced almost exclusively to the transmission of vital fluid from one organism to another, while hypnotism is the control the hypnotist exercises over the will of the hypnotized. So it is not only the transmission of fluid working on its own, but the energetic imposition of the hypnotist's will, which works according to the intentions that guide it.

Nevertheless, the magnetizer, in sending his fluid, must make a certain mental effort; similarly, in order to exercise one's power over the subject, the hypnotist needs to put him to sleep, and to do that, he uses his fluids.

Hypnotism is no longer doubted by anyone of average education, as it has been accepted by official academies.

I will only tell you that its use is dangerous and has few practical applications. The only thing it could be used for is inducing catalepsy in order to perform surgical operations without anesthesia, but for that there are serious difficulties.

The main phenomena produced by hypnotism are: catalepsy; insensitivity, to the degree that the hypnotist can injure the subject without his feeling any pain or drawing blood; suggestion, making the subject sense what the hypnotist suggests. There is also suggestion over time, when the hypnotist causes the subject to verify in a more or less long period of time, according to his influence, some action, ridiculous or not, but sufficient to demonstrate that he obeys some strange suggestion.

**Q. Can you tell me something about suggestion?**
A. Suggestion is widely practiced with hypnotism and that is its main foundation, however it also exists independently, and appears in multiple forms.

Suggestion is generally exercised by superior men who suggest by their conviction, conveying it to others; speakers who arouse crowds, and pull them along behind them; and heroes who inspire their followers to heroism. Suggestion is exercised by use and by will. A person who has a powerful idea can communicate it to others. Generally people with strong character impose their way of thinking on weaker people.

Suggestion, being an attribute exclusively of the soul, is held by it, and can be exercised even after departing the mortal shell, but in this case, suggestion falls within the domain of the spiritist phenomena, which we will study later.

**Q. And what can you tell me about telepathy?**
A. Telepathy is the transmission of thoughts over distance by means of mental images.

A person finds himself in a stressful situation and he communicates his anxiety to a loved one, no matter how distant. Thus, when someone has a serious accident, the image representing that accident is transmitted to one of his family or friends, who perceive it clearly. These cases are much more frequent at the moment of death. There are many cases of entire families that, in this way, have learned of the death of one of their members.

The transmission of thought can also be classified as a telepathic phenomenon. This can be produced relatively easily by an adequate use of the corresponding ability.

**Q. I am very interested in what you can tell me about somnambulism. Can you satisfy my wishes?**
A. The phenomenon of somnambulism has been known since the distant past, as oftentimes natural sleepwalking produces strange phenomena such as waking up asleep, going

through dangerous places, etc., etc. But this class of phenomena is the crudest.

If one cultivates the ability to sleepwalk, producing it by means of magnetic passes, one can achieve the following transcendent phenomena: a subject in a state of somnambulance, if he has developed great lucidity, can report with precision what is happening in a distant place; he can describe the symptoms of some illness of his own or another's; do the most detailed work with his eyes closed, and also a multitude of phenomena as curious as they are interesting.

**Q. *Now I beg you to tell me something about clairvoyance.***
A. Clairvoyance is seeing at a distance while awake—this is the only difference between somnambulism and clairvoyance. Those who can foretell the future we also call clairvoyants, but this phenomenon is difficult to prove and, above all, it cannot be evoked by means of exercises.

The only clairvoyants found in the latter category are those people of great virtue who, by intuition or internal revelation, foresee the great events of human interest. As for the clairvoyants who tell us our fortune or predict your future, you can classify these, without fear, as charlatans.

**Q. *And what is understood by astral projection? I confess I find this word strange.***
A. Indeed, this word is little known, as is the phenomena it designates, but this makes it no less interesting.

As with all the phenomena we have studied, this one has an immense variety of character according to its intensity and the person who produces it.

Thus at one end we have the projection that happens when a person is sleeping and his spirit travels to other realms, a phenomenon that is confused, on the one hand, with somnambulism or telepathy, and, on the other, material projection, given that the person who produces this phenomenon leaves his physical body in the place he is, and with his fluid body, transports himself to another place, making himself visible and even tangible to the people he visits.

### Q. But is such a peculiar phenomenon really possible?
A. If it were not, it wouldn't exist, but this phenomenon has been proven in very numerous cases.

The Catholic religion tells of this type of phenomena in which the protagonists were venerated saints.

St. Alphonsus Maria de Liguori, a priest, was in the city where he lived. One day he fell deeply asleep, and his fluid body transported itself to another city, where he followed the trial of his father, and in the moment he was condemned to death, St. Alphonsus APPEARED before the judges and with eloquence and irrefutable proof defended his father, who was innocent, and caused him to be absolved. He then disappeared without anyone present noticing, for it was only later that it was proved he was in the city where he lived at the same time that he was far away, publically speaking at his father's trial.[d]

I could cite many examples that have all the characteristics of authenticity, however, I will limit myself to telling you that, in truly unusual conditions, our modern experts have had the opportunity to prove satisfactorily some phenomena of this nature.

A young lady who was a schoolteacher had this rare ability and people who walked with her were surprised to see her frequenting the garden, cutting flowers, at the same time that she was in some other place, sitting in silence.

She produced this phenomenon unconsciously and this caused people to shun her, for they feared her power.

The sages of India affirm that this ability can be acquired by means of practice. The Hindu masters often projected in order to visit their disciples with their astral body. This has not been proven by our Western experts. But from the moment we could confirm similar phenomena, and knowing of the vast knowledge the Hindus have about such matters, we have no trouble believing it.

*Q. What you have told me about astral projection is surprising. To conclude about mental phenomena, I beg you to tell me something about ecstasy.*

A. I have little to tell you about this phenomenon, for only beings of the highest virtue can enter into ecstasy, and what they see in such a state is so sublime that they themselves have no words to describe it. Moreover, this phenomenon cannot be evoked. It is spontaneously experienced by individuals of great virtue when they are in fervent prayer.

SPIRITIST PHENOMENA

*Q. Moving now to another order of phenomena, the spiritist, which you mentioned, can you tell me what it consists of?*

A. Spiritist phenomena are extremely varied and to list them all would confuse you.

I will tell you about the most important ones, first making a large distinction between intuitive phenomena and mechanical phenomena, although the overwhelming majority appear to have a greater or lesser degree of both characteristics.

Intuitive phenomena comprise inspiration, mental suggestion, and written or spoken communication, as long as it is intuitive. In this case, the medium, aware of what he writes or speaks, receives ideas as inspiration.

Physical phenomena include:

MECHANICAL WRITING: The medium writes without realizing it; in other words, unconsciously.

DIRECT WRITTEN COMMUNICATION: The spirit writes directly on a sheet of paper or slate. In this case, the medium does not do anything except lend the fluids for the spirits to use.

TIPPING: A table or similar furniture communicates by means of a given number of knocks.

MOVEMENT OF DIFFERENT OBJECTS: By means of psychic powers combined with spiritual powers, and among these phenomena, materializations (apports) of flowers and other objects from great distances.

PERCEPTIBLE APPARITIONS: Only to certain people.

APPARITIONS OF PHANTOMS: A large number of people can perceive these; also perceptible to the point of being able to leave an impression on a photographic plate.

Also in this category of phenomena are those produced by the following mediums:

AUDITORY MEDIUMS are people who hear the spirits' voices, which give them certain information or instructions.

PHYSICAL MEDIUMS are people whose bodies are possessed by spirits in order to realize their wishes and bring us teachings and instructions.

### Q. Can you tell me something about the intuitive phenomena in general?

A. Phenomena related to intuition have existed since humanity appeared on the surface of the earth. They are the invisible threads by which the higher spirits guide humanity toward its destiny, accelerating our evolution, easing our suffering, wiping our tears, providing light and comfort.

Precisely because they are so general, these phenomena are not easily perceived by human beings, for we only notice things when there is a point of comparison.

In general all people, to some degree, closely related to their degree of advancement, receive inspiration and suggestion from spirits.

For this reason, we come to judge inspiration as one of the attributes of the human spirit, and we do not recognize the degree of our inferiority. We believe that what we produce is wholly the work of our own intelligence; we do not recognize the powerful help we receive from the invisible beings who are in perpetual communion with us, ever strengthening our brotherly ties to them.

The Christian belief in guardian angels is a very beautiful picture of love which guides us and helps the spirits who are dedicated to this task; they love us and very much deserve that we call them "our guardian angels." They work upon us by means of suggestion.

If this very consoling doctrine were untrue, how could we explain those sudden inspirations of genius of great artists, writers, poets and orators, inspirations that are so rarely repeated, and that bring them to previously unknown heights? How to explain in men of average ability and in specific moments, that overwhelming eloquence that inspires crowds to the most heroic actions, and serenely sacrifice themselves—or dampen their fury, as if by a spell?

**Q. *By what means can we verify this influence or sense it more effectively?***
A. If even when unconscious we receive such useful help from invisible beings, undoubtedly, recognizing their means of communication, and developing our own abilities in an appropriate manner, we can receive their influence with greater perception and effectiveness.

As our will exercises a decisive influence on all class of phenomena of this nature, if we ask to attract this help and persevere, we will achieve our desires.

To obtain help by a more direct means, we need to send them all of our strength, in accord with two principal forms:

First, to attract this help with our desire.

Second, to avoid that which obstructs the effectiveness of this help.

The first is achieved by persevering effort, and one can receive inspiration in writing or speaking.

The second is obtained by making our spirit dominate the body, converting it into a docile instrument. It requires constant effort to overcome, little by little, our tendencies and make our actions obey a predetermined plan, and this is granted when we find ourselves in absolute tranquility, free from the influence of any passion, desire, or worry.

For this reason, the man who is sober, temperate, generous to his fellows and of pure heart, is most likely to receive inspiration from higher spirits, and in fact, he does receive it.

As for the practical procedures for developing the ability to write, when we sit down, making our spirit serene by means of prayer, concentration, and by the rapture that results when we meditate upon the greatness of our destinies, the infinity of Creation, and the Goodness and Wisdom of God, it is only necessary to ask the invisibles' help.

Of course, in this case, it is important that the writing be toward some noble end, of interest for the community, and not merely to satisfy the ego.

**Q. Is this the only way to write with assistance from the spirits?**
A. There are other procedures, but they are in the domain of phenomena with a more material nature.

**Q. Can you tell me what are these procedures?**
A. Mechanical writing consists of the medium writing without being aware of it. In many cases the medium has written in languages unknown to him.

In this instance, the spirit's influence is not on the medium's mind, inspiring ideas, but, like a kind of hypnotic or catalytic action, utilizing the material organism of the medium, as an unconscious instrument.

In this circumstance, to develop this mediumship, it is necessary for the medium, his mind completely empty, to invoke the spirits. He then places his hand with a pencil upon a sheet of paper, and waits patiently for his hand to move by itself and begin to write.

**Q. And this result is achieved immediately?**
A. Yes, with exceptionally talented mediums, but not in most cases. For this reason, it is necessary to have great perseverance, with the goal of frequently repeating the method of experiment until obtaining satisfactory results.

*Q. Are these two kinds of mediumistic writing the only ones?*
A. These are the important types of mediumship, but there is a great variety of mediums who participate to a greater or lesser degree in these two types; for this reason they are called:
INTUITIVE MECHANICAL WRITING MEDIUMS or SEMI-MECHANICAL

*Q. Which of the two types of mediumship is best?*
A. Undoubtedly, intuitive mediumship has been of greater service, clarifying the most difficult problems, revealing in a luminous way the great truths that have made humanity progress, both in the social and the religious realms, given that there exists an intimate relation among political institutions and religious ideas.

Intuitive mediumship serves, furthermore, to guide us securely along the path for good, as the spirits, illuminating our minds, make us comprehend the evil of continuing certain behaviors. In this manner, our efforts to correct our defects will be conscious and, for this reason, more effective.

This is not the case with mechanical mediumship because, if the medium receives a communication which indicates or orders that he follow this or that moral precept, should he not be convinced of the necessity of doing so, his efforts to follow it will be very weak. In addition, if the mechanical mediums propose to follow all the instructions they receive from the spirits without having a great deal of discernment to comprehend their transcendence, they can become the prisoners of imperfect or evil spirits, who will carry them to the precipice.

As I have already repeated, the only way to distinguish truth from fraud is to pass the communications through the sieve of reason, and the intuitive messages must pass forcefully through this sieve, given that we can almost compare the intuitive medium to a translator who takes in ideas before transmitting them in another language. In the case at hand, spirits illuminate the understanding of such mediums, and they put them in a condition to better appreciate, to see clearly matters which, previously, they could not comprehend.

Nonetheless, mechanical writing mediums are of great usefulness and in fact, they are the most appropriate to verify the existence of spiritist phenomena.

### Q. Can you tell me, by which circumstance?

A. Mechanical writing mediums, when highly developed, can write very precise communications, by this means irrefutably proving the communicating spirit's identity. This is not the case with semi-mechanical or intuitive mediums, whose mediumship is not appropriate for this type of experiment.

In sum, mechanical mediumship serves to prove the material reality of spiritist phenomena, while the intuitive types have been of great service in philosophical speculations, the solving of problems of higher morality, etc.

However, there are numerous exceptions, because some mechanical writing mediums have made important revelations, and above all, semi-mechanical mediums sometimes receive messages beyond their intellectual ability to comprehend. In these cases, the greater the degree of the medium's intellectual and moral development, the more transcendent the communications he receives.

### Q. Of what does direct writing consist?

A. The spirits, by means of fluid hands that have been photographed in certain cases, write directly on a sheet of paper or between two slates which have been carefully tied together, face to face, leaving only a tiny space between them.

To produce this phenomenon, the medium can be some distance away from the slate or paper, or nearby, without touching them, but without physically influencing them. In these cases, the spirits make use of the medium's fluids.

In speaking to you about these types of mediumship I have not wanted to document my assertions with proof because it would be very lengthy and you yourself can find the proofs in specialized treatises or in experimenting on your own.

Nevertheless, apropos of this class of phenomena, I remind you that the Bible cites the celebrated feast of Belshazzar in Babylon, when a mysterious hand wrote these solemn and prophetic words upon the wall:

*God hath numbered thy kingdom and hath finished it.*

### Q. Now I beg you to tell me, what is understood by table tipping?

A. This name designates the phenomena produced by small tables, or similar furniture, in transmitting messages by means of raps, as at a door.

### Q. Of what importance is this phenomenon?

A. It was very great in the mid-nineteenth century, the first days of Spiritism, and it still serves to confirm the Spiritist phenomenon in one of its most interesting phases; but as a means of communication, it has fallen into disuse as mechanical writing mediumship has proven both easier and faster.

### Q. In enumerating these phenomena you have mentioned moving objects by means of psychic powers together with spirits' powers. Can you tell me something about this interesting phenomenon?

A. It is the same as with the little tables.

Movements of objects by means of occult powers (which, for brevity, we will call psychic or spiritist) serves to demonstrate the existence of the invisible world which surrounds us and is interested in and cares about us and takes part in our endeavors.

As materialism was extending its unhealthy influence over the world's most civilized nations, it was precisely the apparition of these very natural phenomena and others which were so clamorous in order to gain our attention. In sum, we can say that those phenomena at the origin of Spiritism were the knocks by which the spirits called at the door of our material world to announce their visit. Once we opened the door and admitted them into the house, in calmness and solemnity, they have revealed the object of their visit. They have come to tell us that our spirit is immortal, that life continues after our mortal shell has dissolved, that this life and space are one, that there is no debt that goes unpaid nor agreement that goes unfulfilled; in a word, they have revealed to us the Spiritist doctrine, as summarized in this manual.

**Q. You have spoken to me of apparitions that can be seen by a larger or smaller number of people, and of others perceptible to touch and capable of causing an impression on a photographic plate. Can you tell me, of what do these differences consist?**

A. Essentially, to a greater or lesser degree, these consist of a phantom's materialization which can be perceived by a larger or smaller number of people, given that not all have the gift of clairvoyance, or to the same degree. Some phantoms are so faint that they can only be seen by very gifted mediums. On the other hand, on occasion there are apparitions that can be seen by everyone, and they can even be touched and photographed.

**Q. Can you cite some notable cases?**

A. The apparitions of Jesus after his death before his disciples are of this character. Thomas could even touch Jesus' wounds.

The visions and voices of which Joan of Arc spoke cannot be doubted, for, if so, how to explain that an ignorant and simple shepherdess could raise the morale of the French armies and lead them to a victory that saved France from the foreign yoke?

There are many cases in the Bible, the New Testament, and in the lives of the saints. Furthermore, recently, there have been many very notable materializations which have been photographed and whose validity have been confirmed by experts, whose testimonies cannot be doubted.

*Q. These phenomena seem to me very striking. Can you tell me how they are produced?*

A. To satisfy your reasonable desire, I must enter into lengthy explanations, which I will do in the following chapter.

*Q. Of auditory mediums, what can you tell me?*

A. They are of little use, for there is no way to prove what they assert; one must take them at their word. This type of mediumship can be useful to the mediums themselves, and by means of their works, reflect goodwill toward others.

Joan of Arc heard voices that told her what to do. Only she could acknowledge these voices, but when these were heeded, and she acted upon their advice, an entire nation benefited.

*Q. And lastly, what should we understand by physical mediums and what is their usefulness?*

A. Physical mediums are as useful as writing mediums, and for the most part appear as the same types, some making specific revelations and speaking of matters entirely unknown to the medium, while others seem to be inspired and their natural intelligence united in the fire of inspiration.

Generally, we consider those who enter a kind of trance, similar to convulsions, physical mediums.

# CHAPTER IV

# Philosophy

**Q. You have shown that the Spiritist doctrine has existed since the most remote antiquity and then you have cited a series of phenomena that supports this doctrine. Can you tell me what deductions you have been able to make from these phenomena?**

A. Before answering directly I would like you to know the Spiritist doctrine more profoundly for only thus can I give you a philosophical explanation of these phenomena. I beg you, of course, to consider the doctrine I am about to expound as a hypothesis, a simple theory, which you can confirm to the degree to which you attempt to resolve a greater number of problems related to this matter.

The theory is as follows:

The human spirit slowly detached itself from the material in which it was enveloped, to pass through the kingdoms of vegetable, animal, and now human beings.

But the human spirit is not material.

I tell you that it has detached itself from the material because, before arriving at the high point of world evolution it currently occupies, and prior to passing through the vegetable and animal kingdoms, it animated the material, being the power that causes atoms to be attracted to each other and that determines the crystallization of salts in perfect geometric forms. This very symmetrical grouping of atoms demonstrates that a power, at least of rudimentary intelligence, has presided over its grouping.

Previously dispersed throughout the Universe, these atoms which have constituted our planetary system, were brought together by this power, first to form nebulae, which have become suns and inhabited worlds, in accord with the procedure accepted by modern science.

The planetary systems—I continue in the realm of hypothesis—dissolve once their cycle has completed; for example, our world will become colder little by little until it is an inert mass drifting through space. Then, the power which gave it fertility and life and held together its molecules shall have abandoned it; earth will disintegrate into dust beyond dust, into atoms, and will once again become a fluid substance, known as ether or cosmic universal material. (This theory is asserted by Hindu philosophers and verified, in part, by our astronomers.)

This inert material, when in its maximum subdivision, is once again made fertile by the divine breath: it is like an electro-magnet that has lost its power and, by means of receiving electric current, regains its power.

Thus, the scattered atoms once again receive their divine spark, which gives new life, makes them active, makes them come together again in nebulae to make new worlds and new humanities.

This is the process of creation.

Creation is constant but, undoubtedly, as with everything in nature, it obeys inflexible laws.

In order for the human spirit to reach its current level of evolution, it has had to form itself slowly, beginning its evolution when the cosmic material which gave birth to our planet, was fertilized and once again became active.

Afterwards, passing through a long series of plants and animals, in each stage acquiring new experiences and perfecting organs, this rudimentary soul could inhabit a human body, beginning this new phase of its evolution in primitive races, until, after uncounted earthly existences, reaching the highest level of civilization.

When the spirit achieves the highest degree of development it can reach on this planet, new senses begin to show themselves, with ever greater perception and sharpness: clairvoyance, etc. It seems the evolving spirit finds its mortal shell too small; to the degree of its elevation, it radiates outward, expanding over a more extensive area. This is the cause of mental and spiritist phenomena.

*Q. The doctrine you have explained to me about the genesis of the spirit and its evolution seems very wonderful, but I would be grateful if you would explain the theory of mental and spiritist phenomena in a more concrete fashion.*
A. The theory of these phenomena is very simple.

When the spirit has attained a high degree of development, it acquires a certain independence from the body.

No longer a prisoner tied by a heavy chain to the material, it is now a being free to make use of its shell according to its will.

Thus, we see that to cure by means of magnetism, the spirit has great power over its fluids and it sends them to another person to give them health and strength.

The same happens with magnetic and hypnotic phenomena. From his spirit, the magnetizer or hypnotist sends his fluids to another person.

Suggestion, telepathy, somnambulism, clairvoyance, and even ecstasy result from similar causes. Momentarily, the spirit frees itself from the body and enters into possession of the abilities it had when it was in space, before its last incarnation.

Projection is even more notable, for the spirit accompanies its perispirit, or fluid body, and from the greater part of its magnetic fluids, it abandons the body to transport itself to other places where it can become visible and even tangible.

**Q. Can you explain to me how the human spirit, in abandoning its body, can make itself visible and tangible in another place?**
A. That was precisely my intention and indeed, the same theory will serve as the foundation for explaining to you the spiritist phenomena of apparitions, phantoms, materializations, etc.

THEORY OF THE PERISPIRIT
When the vital principle or rudimentary soul animates plants, we observe that each one has its special structure; it seems that certain fluid currents give it the form that corresponds to its type; it is like a schema or energetic skeleton around which the material molecules form that the plant extracts from the soil to feed itself.

And so we observe that for each plant that arrives at its full development, there passes a constant current of material that does not alter its form.

This schema or energetic skeleton is the instrument that always accompanies the vegetable soul. From the time the soul finds itself in the tiny seed, it is already accompanied by its fluid body, which perfects itself to the degree that its vegetable soul ascends, and as this serves to determine the plant's structure, so, when it becomes an animal, it also serves to determine the structure of its new earthly shell.

Material molecules form in accord with determined currents of energy, which in turn form an invisible pattern.

Thus, these currents of energy, this invisible schema, is the fluid body, inseparable companion of the soul or spirit during its innumerable migrations through the vegetable, animal, and human kingdoms.

This body, called the perispirit, is slowly modified to the degree that the spirit ascends and it serves as the receptacle of all its experiences, which slowly transform it, making it increasingly appropriate for the spirit's needs.

THEORY OF ASTRAL PROJECTION

To produce the phenomenon of astral projection, it is sufficient, then, that the spirit can detach from its body, accompanying its perispirit and a certain quantity of material molecules, which, disseminated throughout the fluid body according to the lines of energy just mentioned, will give that body all the appearances of a human body, differing only in density, which will increase in the visiting phantom's body, or fluid double, to the degree that it diminishes that of the body. In a word, the sum of the weights of the phantom and the abandoned body will always be the same as when the living being is in his normal state.

THEORY OF THE SPIRIT PHANTOM

The spirit phantom has a similar origin. The spirit is accompanied by its perispirit when it abandons its mortal shell, when what we call death overtakes it.

In this new state, when it wants to make itself visible, it takes material molecules from the body of some persons, who consciously or unconsciously yield them. These molecules mold themselves to the phantom's perispirit in accord with the lines of energy I have mentioned, permitting the spirit to make itself visible.

The person who yields part of his material molecules so that the spirit may utilize them in his materializations, is called a medium. Generally, these mediums can also yield the same molecules, to accompany their own spirit in the phenomenon of astral projection. Consequently, most physical mediums are people who can project consciously or, more commonly, unconsciously.

From this there result serious difficulties in distinguishing projection (mental phenomenon) from the spiritist phenomenon of physical apparition. Nevertheless, methodical and constant observation can allow for a clear distinction between one and the other.

**Q. And the other spiritist phenomena, how do you explain them?**

A. In mechanical writing the spirit wills the medium to write, taking possession of his arm, and exercising a kind of hypnotic action over him. It is the same with physical mediums.

With respect to direct writing, table tipping, movement of objects, materialized objects, etc., the explanation is as follows: the spirit that wishes to produce such phenomena makes use of the medium's vital fluids and even external nervous energy. For this reason, after each session in which such phenomena are observed, the medium is often greatly exhausted.

**Q. You have told me that the mental phenomena serve to demonstrate the spirit's existence apart from the body, as well as its immortality. Can you tell me what is the reasoning that has led you to such a conclusion?**

A. I will tell you that in general the proof of the spirit's existence is only found by those who look for it within themselves, who analyze their own personality, complex and mysterious as it is, both profoundly and serenely.

In effect, who would dare to negate the existence of their spirit when THEY THEMSELVES THINK AND REASON independently from their body, as they can observe when they are absorbed in meditation, insensitive to physical necessities? Who would do so if he observes that when his body is in repose, his senses paralyzed by sleep, THE SOMETHING in him that thinks and reasons continues, active; it resolves problems he had not been able to resolve while awake; it can glimpse what is happening in other places or the future?

And who has not experienced at least one of these phenomena, or observed it in a friend or relative?

Humanity has almost always been Spiritist, but in reacting so vigorously against the religious fanaticism of the seventeenth century, by the nineteenth, the opposite extreme, the absolute negation of everything spiritual, making criteria so materialistic that when various mental and spiritist phenomena appeared to pique our curiosity, we were obliged to embark on new research that encouraged us to conclude that the soul is immortal.

The first phenomena observed in Europe in modern times were those of magnetism, healings achieved by means of this fluid and the state of somnambulism it induced.

Naturally, the following question will occur to the impartial researcher:

What is the fluid that emanates from the magnetizer's body and brings health to his patient?

The magnetizer will say: "I do not use any of my organs nor my physical senses to transmit the fluid. I only use the power of my will. What then is my will? Who is this invisible entity who, to make its influence felt at a greater or lesser distance, does not require the body? How can I make the fluid arrive at a determined place if I cannot see it with my eyes, nor direct it with my organism? Thus we have some as yet unknown senses, but they are beginning to show themselves in certain people. But these senses are not physical; they are independent of our body, given that they enable us to sense their influence beyond the reach of our physical senses."

It is the same with the phenomenon of somnambulism.

The somnambulist describes with precision what is happening in a place far from where he is.

Here the existence of this new sense is more perceptible; it has been demonstrated that people in a state of somnambulism can see what is happening in another place, without making use of their physical sight. And they not only manage to see, they can account for what they are seeing and describe it in minute and exact detail.

How can we explain this phenomenon if we do not accept the existence of an entity independent of the body which, in certain circumstances, can manifest beyond?

The most curious thing is that the subject in a state of somnambulism has an unusual lucidity for all types of matters; he shows knowledge that he has not acquired in his normal state;

he is aware of his state and affirms that he produces such phenomena because his spirit is out of his body. This affirmation should be taken seriously because of the lucidity he shows and because, undoubtedly, the subject himself is as perfectly aware of how he produces the phenomenon as are the people who observe him.

As for cases of telepathy and clairvoyance, this transmission over great distance of mental images and visions of the future, how can we explain them if we do not accept the possibility that our spirit can move outside our body in a given moment?

In the Spiritist doctrine the explanation for these phenomena is very logical, for it is said: "when someone suffers a serious accident, his main desire is to let his loved ones know, and to do this, his spirit takes advantage of his dizziness or fainting, so that it may go out and impress upon the desired person the news of what has happened." Another case: "A person dies suddenly, far from his family. He has the same desire and to achieve it, he takes advantage of the moments between the accident and death to have his spirit GO OUT and let the person know what has happened."

With respect to telepathy and clairvoyance, this is even more evident for, to foresee the future with precision or to know what is happening at a great distance, one needs such lucidity that it is impossible to concede it to material reality nor to senses that the human body does not possess.

As for hypnotic phenomena, how can we explain overpowering the will of another person, so far as to paralyze the functioning of his organs, make him numb, cause a postage stamp to raise a blister, etc?

If we were made only of material substance, why does will, which is not physical, exercise such power over it?

If a hypnotist, by his will, exercises such power over another person, would it not be logical to accept that he can also exercise it over himself? This inference is demonstrated by numerous phenomena, notably by the fakirs in India, and some healing by autosuggestion that have served as the basis for founding a religious sect called "Christian Science."ᵉ

The Indian fakirs exercise such power over themselves that they are able to remain lying on a bed of nails, which they achieve by means of making their body numb; or rather paralyzing the functioning of their organism for a long period, probably inducing a special form of catalepsy which allows them to BE BURIED ALIVE, and remain buried for several months.

As for "Christian Science," which is based on healing oneself by autosuggestion, or others by suggestion, this has spread through the United States and Europe in so impressive a fashion that we cannot but believe in the success of this procedure in least some of these healings.

Indeed, these phenomena produced by autosuggestion are very similar to the multitude of phenomena produced by us unconsciously that we can observe every day. For example, by means of our organism's slow work, of which we are unaware, injuries we receive scar over by themselves. Similarly, unconsciously, we direct the circulation of our blood, our growth, digestion, nutrition, etc., etc.

Thus there exist many normal phenomena that demonstrate the possibility of the above mentioned anormal phenomena and that reveal, in each of us, the existence of an entity that is, to a certain point, independent of the physical body and that has the ability to ORGANIZE MATTER.

For this reason, rather than assume the physical body exercises power over the nonphysical, it is very logical that our physical body depends upon this latter entity, which we can call, provisionally, "the unconscious."[1]

If will exercises such power over the physical body, should we not accept that will comes from an entity that is higher than or independent from the body?

Undoubtedly, the human entity is a compact WHOLE and there exist constant influences and reactions between the spirit and the body. But this does not take away from the fact that the spirit can make itself numb to the necessities and sufferings of the body, whether because it is absorbed in intense intellectual labor or because it exercises autosuggestion, that is to say, the direct power of its will over the organism.

Finally, how can we explain to the materialists the admirable phenomenon of astral projection?

They feel impotent before it and they deny it. But it is impossible to deny a phenomenon known since the most remote antiquity, from which we have the testimonies, perfectly well confirmed in the lives of some Catholic saints, as well as others frequently observed in India and that have even been confirmed by European experts, upon whose opinion no doubt can be cast, as the majority of these were materialists—or, at least before they observed the first phenomena.

In reality, without accepting the Spiritist theory, it is impossible to satisfactorily explain how a person can project, leaving a part of his physical body in deep stupor, transport himself with this other body of fluid, which accompanies the spirit, and can be made visible and even tangible, to other places. In most of the cases observed, this other body is accompanied by the spirit, by the intelligent being, as in the previously mentioned case of St. Alphonsus Maria de Liguori, which demonstrates the ability of the spirit to detach from the body and the coexistence of the two elements which, although continually reacting one upon the other, have a relative independence, and so proves that the soul can live independently from the body.

**Q. Now that you have concluded the analysis of the mental phenomena, deducing from these proofs of the soul's immortality, I ask you to pass now to the spiritist phenomena for which, as you have affirmed, we will find even more conclusive proofs.**

A. Following the order in which I set out these phenomena, I must first speak to you of the intuitive phenomena.

In some cases, for the mediums themselves, when they do not know the greatness, clarity and concision of the thoughts, writing, or speaking that occur to them in certain circumstances, such phenomena can constitute proof of the Beyond.

Nonetheless, the nature of these phenomena do not lend themselves to experimentation, nor supply the proofs required by the modern spirit which is so skeptical and materialist.

Now we will continue on to physical phenomena.

## MECHANICAL WRITING

By means of this mediumistic ability it has been possible to prove the identity of many discarnates, because from their communications it has been possible to recognize their handwriting, signature, style, or particular ideas. This has been confirmed in conditions impossible to misrepresent.

Now then, how to explain that a person, without having known the spirit in life, can evoke that spirit, imitate his handwriting, his signature, and know his style or particular ideas? Such a medium, if not truly directed by the spirit, must have prodigious abilities, at once incomprehensible and inexplicable given that, with his own mind, the evoker would have had to come up with everything he wrote, and then coordinate it himself with such great speed and precision.

But this very implausible supposition is insufficient to explain all the phenomena, given that, with certain mediums, it has been possible to prove the revelation of events about which the evokers themselves, and those around them, knew nothing. Upon investigation, these revelations, to general amazement, have been found to be exact.

By means of the phenomena of direct writing or table tipping, similar proofs have been found. Although, in general, the communications obtained from these procedures have been completely banal and in many cases analogous to the incoherence of ordinary dreams, this does not diminish their value as truly transcendental communications that unquestionably reveal the identity of the communicating spirit.

With respect to the phenomena of moving objects, these have also been observed in conditions impossible to misrepresent.

Indeed, the movements of these objects are understood to obey a predetermined plan, that is, an intelligent force that combines with them to be able to transmit its thoughts to the people who are present.

These phenomena have the special characteristic of appearing spontaneously, although, for some time until now, powerful mediums have been able to produce them at will.

From the time the first phenomena of this nature appeared in the United States, the people who have observed them have not doubted that they were produced by the spirits of those who passed on before us, and who constitute an invisible world around us.

APPARITIONS OF VISIBLE AND TANGIBLE PHANTOMS
This phenomenon is the most conclusive of all. Even if it is true that there may have been some confusion with the medium's fluid double, this confusion disappears immediately when one investigates with method and patience.

The medium's double always has the same height and features as the medium himself, while phantoms or materializations are larger or smaller and with different features.

An English expert, Mr. W. Crookes,[f] was able to confirm this circumstance perfectly, as during three years he experimented with a famous medium and was able to prove that the materialized phantom was taller than she was, had a different heartbeat, different physiognomy, and spoke of matters unknown to the medium. He was even able to photograph the medium and the phantom at the same time. In this photograph the differences in the height and features of both subjects are clear.

These phenomena are such nature that the people who have observed them, including experts of such note as Crookes, Aksakov,[g] Richet,[h] Flammarion,[i] etc., have been left with no doubt as to the reality of the Spiritist phenomenon.

In summary, all the phenomena we have covered can only be explained by the Spiritist doctrine.

According to this doctrine, the human personality is directed by the spirit, which has the power to organize and disorganize material and to momentarily abandon its earthly shell, transporting itself to other places. Given that the spirit is independent of the physical body, it is logical to accept that the spirit can live without the body and that the death of the body does not affect it, only signifying the dissolution of the ties which had bound it.

**Q. These arguments for the survival of the soul seem to me very conclusive, but can you give me another type of reason to support your thesis?**
A. Ever since humanity had use of reason, this very important point has been discussed and the topic should have been exhausted. But it is not so: every day there are new skeptics and also new defenders of the truth.

The principal argument the materialists use to deny the soul's immortality is that they cannot feel it; it is not in the domain of their physical senses. But how can they physically feel something spiritual? Reason: do they feel that or perceive that? They only observe its effects and they attribute its functions to the brain. They think the brain secretes thought, as the mouth secretes saliva.

The analogy is rude and imprecise, nevertheless, I accept it and say the following: Saliva is secreted by mucous-making glands of the mouth, but it is not produced by them. Saliva is made in the mysterious laboratory of the human body, with a clearly determined end: facilitating digestion. But who directs this laboratory?

One could say the same about thought: it is emitted by the brain, or more precisely, the brain serves as the organ to emit it, but whom does the organ serve? Who produces thought?

If the brain or the brain's cells were the ones producing thought, why do they cease to produce it at the moment the individual departs from that SOMETHING that is life? That SOMETHING can disappear violently without directly affecting the brain, and nonetheless, why can this physical mass no longer think?

The materialists' great argument runs as follows: the brain is made of various nerves which produce thought. The proof of this is that if we mutilate some of these nerves, we will cause the individual to cease thinking; he becomes an idiot or perhaps we will make him lose the memory of verifiable events in a certain period of his life, or we reduce some intellectual ability, corresponding to the nerve or area that has been altered.

This argument is very easy to answer.

The brain is an instrument which serves the spirit to manifest its thought. This is a precision instrument that has been developed by the spirit according to its requirements. The brain, just as the body, is formed in the perispirit according to determined energy lines. If by a mechanical lesion you destroy or mutilate an organ, the spirit will not make use of it or will make imperfect use of it.

If you tie or cut the arms of a very strong man, he will continue to be as strong as before, he will have the same potential, but he cannot show it, nor can he make use of it.

The same happens with a person whose brain has been mutilated: his spirit has the same potential, but he does not have the means to manifest it, nor organs to emit his thought or evoke the memory of the past, etc.

In truth, the materialists observe the manifestations of life in the human body, such as thought, but they cannot explain the mysterious agent that presides over each personality.

We find the proof that something independent of material reality exists by observing ourselves intimately.

From whence come these internal struggles between the imperious voice of our conscience that orders us to comply with our duty and the physical appetites that tempt us to satiate them?

Do we not see in these daily struggles the conflict between two distinct elements: the spiritual, attracted to the heights, toward the Creator, and the material, always insatiable and only concerned with satisfying its appetites?

The origin of these two elements is the following: during our very long pilgrimage through the lower realms of nature, we had a purely animal life, concerning ourselves only with satisfying the all-consuming necessities of life. When we acquired the sufficient qualities to be able to subsist in this world, we passed into humanity, where we begin to sense more elevated aspirations, which we find in constant struggle with the inveterate habits acquired in our animal past.

The origin of these higher aspirations cannot be explained by materialism, while Spiritism offers a very satisfactory explanation, attributing them to the unconscious memory of interplanetary existences between each incarnation and the previous one, just as with the influence by means of suggestion exercised by the discarnate spirits over those who inhabit this world.

Only Spiritism can provide this very logical explanation. Materialism must rely on complicated and implausible theories and nevertheless does not satisfactorily explain this problem.

In general materialists believe that our conscience and noble sentiments generate beautiful but useless utopias and, according to them, a rational person should combat these tendencies.

Another one of these very weighty arguments, in which the materialists attempt to support their theory, and which at the same time they use to support their explanation of evolution, is the law of inheritance.

They assert that there is a close relationship between our intelligence and brain activity; and they assert that, just as in England horse breeders can predict the abilities their colts will have, of given parents, we can deduce the qualities of their children.

Undoubtedly, inheritance greatly influences the physical organism, and children will always resemble their parents, not only in physical respects, but also in moral respects, for they have received from their parents the brain through which their thoughts will be emitted, and although each spirit forms itself according to its necessities, its influence cannot be exercised beyond certain limits. Another reason the child resembles its parents is the education it receives from them. But as far as character goes, the ressemblance does not hold; it cannot be deduced that this is inherited because observation demonstrates how different the characters of parents and children are.

Moreover, Spiritism explains in a very satisfactory manner the similarity between the character and tendencies of parents and children in the following manner: the affinity of tendencies attracts some spirits to others, causing them to come together into families, societies, and even nations, that these tendencies may be expressed. This is notable even in this world: those who tend toward the realization of some mercantile or industrial enterprise come together in business societies; while those who pursue some political ideal organize themselves into clubs and political parties; those who pursue some altruistic end, in philanthropic societies for temperance, etc. In contrast, those affected by alcohol congregate in taverns, etc.

For these reasons, we can say that the ties of affinity are stronger than those of family relation, for the latter only strongly tie family members to each other when there is affinity among them; whereas, if no affinity exists among members of a family, it seems some members are exotic plants and they only find their true environment and happiness when surrounded by a circle of friends with whom they feel affinity.

We human beings always try to find other people with whom we feel affinity, especially when we begin some difficult undertaking. Therefore it is logical to assume that when we resolve to embark upon the very delicate undertaking of incarnating into this world, we try to arrive accompanied by a group of spirits with whom we feel affinity, and who probably have accompanied us in previous incarnations, so that we know, when the moment of truth comes, what we can expect from them.

Generally, superior men have mediocre parents and they almost never have descendants who inherit their great virtues.

The materialist theory, in supposing that our intelligence is a product of material evolution, asserts a principle it will never be able to prove because FROM LESS THERE CAN NEVER FOLLOW MORE.

Although there exist many arguments that support this thesis, I believe I have presented a sufficient number to illustrate the issue and—unless you have some strongly held preconceived idea to the contrary—form your conviction that our soul survives our body.

REINCARNATION

**Q. Can you tell me something in support of the doctrine of reincarnation?**

A. This doctrine has been accepted by the greatest philosophers of antiquity and preached by the great missionaries, as I explained in the historical part, and I should like to underline similarities among the doctrines as taught by Krishna in India, Hermes in Egypt, and Christ in Judea, as with other great philosophers, and, since the middle of the past century, by the uncounted spirits that have come to communicate with humanity. This doctrine is not only supported by revelation in accord with the great missionaries, but it is the most rational philosophical doctrine and for all the problems as yet unexplained by other philosophical doctrines, it presents the most logical explanation.

**Q. Can you tell me what those problems are?**

A. A great number of issues remain obscure when we analyze them through the lense of other doctrines. For example: the very notable inequality among human beings, some rich, others poor, some happy, others melancholy; some born with illnesses that accompany them to the grave and make their life miserable, while others, full of health, seem to enjoy smiling fortune in everything.

In the same way we observe that many men who, during their lives, commit great crimes do not seem to receive punishment before leaving this world, while others are inevitably their victims and suffer all kinds of vexations without seeing justice in their lifetime.

Another problem other philosophical doctrines leave unresolved is the satisfactory explanation for the birth of children who, from earliest infancy, show themselves to be true geniuses and demonstrate extraordinary talents, whether for music, or some branch of science, etc.

Lastly, no religion nor system of philosophy has been able to satisfactorily explain why children of the same parents sometimes have such different characters, ideas and tendencies.

The materialist view does not offer a satisfactory explanation for these phenomena for, being logical in its principles, it must assume chance determines the qualities of each individual at birth, not only from the moment he begins to have consciousness, but some years after his birth, and so he has a wealth of qualities, good and bad, which he did not acquire himself, nor did his parents attempt to transmit in the moment of conception.

If chance is what determines each human being's aptitudes, we would not see that very harmonious and concordant similarity among the works and teachings of the great men, who by mysterious and various paths, have accelerated humanity's evolution toward progress and happiness.

Neither would we observe that admirable opportunity by which, in the most propitious moments, superior men have come to earth, whether to save humanity from grave dangers or lead it on a new path.

According to Catholicism and the Protestant sects, human life begins at birth and the qualities it has are given by the grace of God, who, being omnipotent and creator of all that exists, assigns to each creature its abilities at the moment of birth.

This doctrine is simple and simply monstrous, for it makes God fundamentally unjust.

In contrast, with the doctrine of reincarnation all the above mentioned difficulties disappear. It is no longer by chance nor divine caprice that qualities of each human being are determined; it is the very same being who brings into each incarnation the qualities and aptitudes it acquired in previous incarnations, whether in the planetary or the interplanetary.

With this theory the inequality among living beings is

perfectly explained. We bring all the knowledge acquired in our previous existences in the form of greater intelligence; experiences; in the form of character—and so it is that, in each new earthly or interplanetary existence, we gain more knowledge, develop our intelligence, and strengthen our character, which is only formed through life's struggles, overcoming the innumerable obstacles we encounter on our path.

With respect to differences in fortune, unpunished crimes, or unrewarded virtues—all obscure problems for materialism—these are illuminated by the daylight of Spiritism which says, our life does not unfold in the miserable patch of an earthly existence, but develops over uncounted planetary and interplanetary existences, all soldered as in a chain to one another for, if in one existence we are poor, in another we will be rich; if in one we were oppressors, in another we will be oppressed, etc. This doctrine is also more in accord with divine than Catholic justice, which makes our circumstances in eternity depend upon our actions in this very short earthly existence, without considering the immense differences under which we struggle even in the case of our all being born equal, given the differences in the environments into which we are born and in which we develop. We will always be better off when our parents are virtuous than when they are evil.

With respect to child geniuses, according to materialism, they are explained by a kind of disequilibrium and, according to Catholicism, they are favored by divine grace; while according to Spiritism, they are highly evolved spirits who visit our planet once in a while to accelerate humanity's evolution.

Finally, just as Spiritism explains in such a satisfactory fashion the similarity of character and tendencies among members of the same family, it also equally well explains exceptions such as when one member of the family does not have the same ideas or get along with the others: from before the time he was born, this individual did not have affinity with the members of the family in whose bosom he was to incarnate and his incarnation, in such conditions, had the objective of expiating some fault, erasing some old hate or accelerating his progress. In this instance, the law of inheritance must rely on explanations that are in no way satisfactory.

Another type of phenomena that cannot be satisfactorily explained by these other philosophical systems is the lucidity of somnambulists, who, in finding themselves in this state, reveal knowledge very superior to that which they have in their normal waking state, and that they have not acquired during their current incarnation.

Neither materialism nor Catholicism nor Protestantism can explain this phenomenon. They are completely unable to give any explanation.

However, by the doctrine of reincarnation, all is made clear. The extraordinary knowledge revealed by a person in a state of somnambulism was acquired in his previous existences; and as somnambulism permits the spirit relative freedom, it may manifest, if not with the totality of his knowledge, but in conditions superior to his normal state.

In incarnating, spirits lose the memories of their previous existences, and they bring to earth their previous knowledge only as a form of intelligence that helps them cultivate, with greater ease, the same branches of science they have already studied.

For this reason, the spiritual entity has greater knowledge than the mere human personality. The spirit remains the same, while in incarnation represents a new personality.

Another important problem is, how to explain the complicated functioning of the human organism? We digest, taking in food which must nourish us and, should we suffer an injury, we heal it ourselves with a scar, and all of this we do without consciousness of the procedure.

Could it be possible that such a complicated mechanism could be directed by an entity independent of ourselves? No. The most logical thing is to assume that the entity that directs the functioning of organic life forms part of our personality. But what is that entity?

Materialism asserts that it is the organism and that this is the result of material evolution, in which it limits itself to expounding in vague terms an observed fact, without demonstrating the theory upon which it is founded.

Indeed, each person's physical organism is constituted by the substance he has assimilated from his food, which belongs to the realms of animal and vegetable.

Thus constituted, the organism renews most of itself every three months, and every seven years down to the last atom.

Being thus, what is the material that has evolved? What is it that has come to constitute a conscious being? How is it possible that the material of which plants are made, only by means of serving as food for man, is transformed into intelligence? Thus, who would ascertain that transformation?

If there is a constant flow of material through the human body, which does not alter its form, who then conserves that form?

If it is physical material which evolves to the point of transforming into intelligence, how can it ascertain that evolution?

The experience that material acquires in a vegetable or animal family: how can this ascend to the next level?

For example, how can the material intelligence of a monkey ascend to that of a human organism?

Spiritism, however, provides a very clear explanation: in the lower realms of nature, the spirit has acquired the necessary knowledge on how to feed itself, digest, heal wounds, etc.

This knowledge has been the fruit of thousands and thousands and maybe millions of years, during which each effort repeated thousands of times has come to engrave itself into a line of energy, and these lines, each time more numerous and pronounced, constitute the perispirit or schema of the human body.

In order to acquire each of these abilities, the spirit has labored for thousands of years, but once in possession of them, the perispirit is modified, and afterwards functions unconsciously, without the spirit's taking notice of them.

It is the same with all the movements we learn from the time we are born. For example: the first steps we take with difficulty, but once we learn how to walk, our spirit does not pay attention to the efforts that must be made to maintain equilibrium.

To learn the position of the keys, the pianist or typist must focus all his attention to those movements; but after a certain amount of practice, he can make these movements unconsciously, without the spirit taking notice of them.

All of this can be corroborated, for according to the doctrine of reincarnation, it is not material substance that evolves, but rather the energy behind it, which passes from realm to realm, until arriving at that of man. Material substance only serves as a dressing or vehicle for the animating MENTAL power, to facilitate its evolution. The mental power is the one that, by means of evolution, eventually constitutes individualities of spirits. Compared to that affirmed by the doctrines of the materialists, this is the more logical and rational explanation.

Finally, materialism does not offer a logical explanation for the phenomena of materialization or apparitions. It is content to deny them, declaring them impossible. Catholicism and other religions consider them miracles, that is, outside the laws of nature.

In asserting that said phenomena are impossible because they are outside the laws of nature, materialism presumes that these laws are all already known. And Catholicism, in calling these phenomena a miracle, and for this reason outside those same laws, also presumes that these laws are known. In both cases, the explanations are presumptuous and demonstrate very little prudence, as new phenomena, which revolutionize our knowledge, are constantly being discovered.

Spiritism presents a very simple explanation for these phenomena. When a spirit wishes to appear before living beings, it pulls in physical molecules from people who have this ability to allow this and, at once, these molecules form around the perispirit, according to the lines of energy of which I have spoken. This is why, when a spirit appears, it takes the form of a human being, but its density is different and variable, as this depends on the number of physical molecules it has been able to attract.

It is similar in the case of astral projection, the only difference being that, not needing them from other people, the spirit takes on molecules from its own body, as is the case with beings who inhabit space, when they materialize.

In sum, the theory of reincarnation is the most logical of all, as it is the only one that is capable of simply and satisfactorily explaining all the phenomena we have examined.

Furthermore, it has been revealed to humanity by higher beings, and it is the most consoling and moral and that which best corresponds to our noble ideals. It is moral and consoling because, convinced of our character and intelligence, and also our current circumstances, which we owe to our own efforts, we are no longer subject to the weaknesses of those who attribute their defects and misfortune to blind fatality or to divinity, whose justice cannot be explained. We know that the reason we suffer in our current existence is to purge faults committed in previous existences, and that if our intelligence is not well developed, it is because in previous incarnations we wasted time and we have not dedicated ourselves to developing it.

Lastly, Spiritism makes us understand that we are responsible for our own actions; and that the consequences of each evil act will follow us like our own shadow through numerous incarnations, while each act of good will, invariably, yield fruit. And so, with faith in the great future that awaits us, we no longer need to worry about the immediate results of our works, and we find the tranquility to wait for results to develop on their own.

Although I could provide more arguments, I believe I have given a sufficient number for you to understand that your life is immortal, that your evolution is realized over innumerable incarnations, that YOUR CURRENT SITUATION IS THE RESULT OF YOUR PAST ACTIONS, AND THAT YOU CANNOT CHANGE IT QUICKLY BUT YOUR FUTURE BELONGS TO YOU AND YOU CAN CREATE IT AS YOU WISH.

I will give you an example so that you may better understand me. A person who, in his youth, did not study will become an ignorant adult. If he studies medicine, he will be a doctor and will have to continue practicing this profession, unless he resolves to adopt another, in which case he will have to make a new effort, but in the moment of conceding to that desire, he cannot immediately change his circumstances; the only thing he can do is work toward his goal little by little, so that some years later, he may obtain his result.

GOD

**Q. Before concluding this philosophical part, can you tell me something about the existence of God?**
A. All the Spiritist philosophical systems and all religions accept the existence of God. Only atheism and modern positivism do not accept the existence of God, but neither do they dare to negate it.

Although each religion accepts God's existence, each one has shaped a god according to its ideals.

The Hebrews had a God, as the Bible says, an image and likeness unto ourselves; for this reason, they attributed to God all of our defects and passions, making him cruel and vengeful.

Catholicism also has a very imperfect conception of divinity, because Catholicism really dates from the Middle Ages, a period of great corruption among certain Catholic clergy, who conceived of a God as unyielding and vengeful, like the cruel inquisitors.

Just as they believed that to kill or burn a heretic was pleasing to God, they imagined that for whatever mistakes humans committed, God would become angry and condemn them to eternal suffering.

In reality, this dogmatic idea is not held by every Catholic; each forms an idea of God with the highest attributes of which he can conceive.

Undoubtedly, many saints, persons of great virtue, held a very different conception of divinity, as can be seen in their prayers, which have become an example for Christianity.

In India, during the times of the Brahmins, there was an idea of divinity so elevated that it was forbidden to mention it.

Spiritism has never attempted to define divinity. It limits itself to considering God as the Creator of all that exists, like an all powerful Being, all good and all love for His creation in general and for each one of His creatures in particular.

It seems that God is the spirit of the Universe and that the material of the cosmos, the nebulae and the innumerable suns and planets, constitute a living body, the part of God that is material and visible.

Thus, the Milky Way is like an artery through which circulates the life which which has given birth to a great part of the Universe and constantly renews it. Of course, this conception of divinity is the greatest which our intelligence, in its current state of development, can conceive of, but undoubtedly, as we evolve, our understanding will become finer, our senses will open to our intelligence as yet unknown and ever more vast horizons, and then our conception of the divine will evolve, coming increasingly closer to reality.

The proofs of the existence of God are clear. Only passion can blind certain people to what, for the majority of humanity, is as clear as the midday sun.

Indeed, our intelligence is so small, our knowledge so little, that we cannot explain even the functioning of some of our organs.

Neither can we explain how, in a tiny seed's sprout there is not a tree but thousands and thousands of gigantic trees, capable of populating the earth. If our ignorance is such, if we have the consciousness of being at the mercy of the elements and that life can escape from us at any moment, how can we deny our smallness and proudly call ourselves kings of the earth? How can we not accept that we have not created ourselves, for, if that were the case, would we not have realized it and would we not know how and when we were created?

Since we have not spontaneously created ourselves, it is

logical to believe that we were created by a superior Being.

Moreover, the admirable harmony with which the heavenly bodies move in their orbits, the marvelous laws of the planetary systems, all make us understand that this Being is One and infinitely great, as great the space in which it exercises its activity is infinite; infinitely good, as is shown by the untiring care for all beings that exist. To Him we owe our life. Since we cannot imagine that He has a beginning or end, we believe Him to be eternal.

Lastly, the increasingly profound research into nature makes us admire the order we find everywhere, and astronomy, in demonstrating that the number of planetary systems is incalculable, allows us to glimpse the infinity of the Universe and its Creator.

To conclude, I will say that when we address ourselves to Him with devotion, each of us senses the hand of God.

Undoubtedly, He does not remove the obstacles in our path, for we must overcome these in order to develop our powers, But when we address ourselves to Him with fervor, we receive, like a bath of heavenly perfumes, what fortifies and nurtures us. In addition, prayer brings us closer to God, it puts us in intimate communion with Him and it increases our assurance that, in working according to His laws, that is, according to the Divine Plan, we can count on innumerable beings who support our efforts. In knowing that we are children of God, that our destiny is glorious, and the potential of our forces is immense, our efforts in any given moment are hundreds of times more powerful.

# CHAPTER V

# Spiritist Morality

**Q. What should we understand by morality?**
A. This is the totality of rules for directing man on the path of righteousness.

**Q. What are these rules?**
A. According to their dogma, each religion has its own rules, all with the goal of happiness, which will be enjoyed by those who obey them.

The materialists also have their moral rules, with the goal that man may know how to conduct himself in this world and be happy in it.

As I have already told you, although the religions are very similar in their origins and fundamental principles, with the fanaticism, ignorance, and ambition of their respective clergies, the founders' pure moral teachings have been corrupted, mixed up with innumerable rules that are intended to allow followers to easily achieve glory by means of religious practices, rather than by overcoming their own passions.

**Q. What is the objective of morality?**
A. So you can understand from what I have just explained, morality is meant to give man the rules by which he may be happy, whether in this life or in space, according to his respective beliefs.

## Q. What is the basis of Spiritist morality?

A. Spiritist morality has a very firm foundation, which is entirely philosophical and rational, as I will now explain to you:

Spiritism affirms that the only true happiness that can be found is in fulfilling one's duty, that is, obeying the Divine Law, summed up by Jesus Christ is the following words: "that you love one another."

It is true indeed that in loving our fellow man we find happiness; people who live and work only for themselves are very rare. The overwhelming majority of beings who inhabit this world feel happiest in the company of their fellows and when the object of their work, their worries, and many times even including their crimes, is to achieve their loved ones' well-being.

Selfishness, vanity, anger, sloth, lust, gluttony, and craving for intoxicating liquors can put human beings' noble sentiments for their fellow men to sleep.

Therefore to be happy we must make our love radiate as far as possible, and we must make our greatest, most constant efforts to expand it.

## Q. Can you tell me a little more about what is understood by happiness according to Spiritism?

A. I have already said that happiness is only found in abiding by the law, indeed, humanity has always tried to find felicity in material pleasures, riches, etc.

Many people, tired of life, have turned to drunkenness to forget their sorrows, for they do not have the courage to bear them, nor sufficient strength to struggle against adversity.

Happiness cannot be found on these paths. It is found in the joys of the spirit by upright men, those of moderate habits and who are therefore awake, their spirits lucid, and admiring all that is truly great and beautiful. And so we see those people delighting in contemplating the beauties of nature, the more notable works of art, and the works of superior men who reveal to humanity glimpses of the life Beyond. Finally, these admirers of all that is good, aided by reading and study, are constantly in touch with select spirits who have visited the earth. They emulate these higher beings, and follow in their footsteps. Whenever they dedicate themselves to study, to increasing their knowledge so they may better comprehend the laws of Universe, they feel such pure joy, that only those who have experienced it can understand.

The man who takes pleasure in studying will always be happy in this world, for no human power can impede his study. He will also be assured of his happiness in space for, when his spirit is free from its physical shell, with greater lucidity and greater appetite, he can devote himself with even greater dedication to study.

In increasing the sphere of our knowledge, studying makes us more sensitive to all the beauties of nature and it increases our enjoyment in contemplating them.

Another one of the important benefits of studying is that it acquaints us with the divine laws and so enables us to adapt our actions in accord with them.

Naturally, the man who is studious and good, free of passions, serene, of profound knowledge, and a lover of the beautiful, will always find in his fellow men something to admire, something that inspires his love for them, even if it is only their resignation to suffering.

Individuals who have achieved this level have expanded their love in a considerable fashion. They love not only their family, not only the inhabitants of their country, but all human beings and even animals.

In sum, happiness is only found in study and in doing good, in loving our fellow men.

According to the revelations of the spirits (and it is perfectly logical to believe it), human beings, in departing the flesh, live in space for a more or less long time, until once again they incarnate on earth.

The period that separates one incarnation from the next is longer to the degree that the spirit has evolved and is capable of developing itself in a purely spiritual environment.

When a spirit has acquired all the experience it can on earth, it will no longer incarnate on its surface, but will remain in space for a long period or incarnate on planets where more evolved spirits reside.

On the other hand, we see that among the less evolved humans only physical necessities will cause them to develop their intelligence. For these beings, life in space has no attraction or use and sadly, they waste their time, so to them it is more attractive to incarnate in this world where they search for happiness by satisfying minor necessities, for this requires certain efforts, forms their character, and in this manner prepares their spirit to develop itself in higher spheres.

Spirits who are a little more advanced in science but not in virtue, having given free rein to their passions and used their knowledge only to exploit their fellow men, do not find happiness in space either.

People who are accustomed to idleness or indulging in material pleasures cannot find any satisfaction in life nor in space, and when they arrive there they will suffer terribly for they cannot carry on the life to which they were accustomed on earth.

I will give you two examples so that what I want you to understand may be more deeply impressed upon your imagination:

Undoubtedly, music is one of the more beautiful manifestations of art. Nevertheless, not all music can be appreciated by the general population. If you take a person who does not have a very developed artistic sensibility to a concert of the best music, alas, he will not understand, nor can he appreciate its beauty, and instead of enjoying it, he will find it boring.

So you see, even to appreciate the beauty of music, one needs to have a highly cultivated taste for it. And it is the same with all the beauties of Nature: only cultivated spirits can appreciate and admire them.

Another example I would like to give you of how different people have different aptitudes is the following: If a youth is destined for life as a soldier, as an engineer, or for some profession that obliges him to live in the countryside and work to the point of exhaustion, it is most apt for him to have, from earliest childhood, a special education so that he may find pleasure and satisfaction in complying with his duties, even when he is older.

Great expeditions, hard labor, etc., are very attractive to people who are used to them. On the other hand, they are intolerable to those who have been educated differently.

Thus, if we always live with an eye to our happiness in space, which is a lasting happiness, we must educate ourselves in this sense, directing all our efforts toward that objective. Without a doubt, the human being finds pleasure in satisfying his habits, but it is also the case that these can be changed by means of constant effort.

For this reason, if we want to be happy in the other life we must direct all our efforts toward becoming accustomed to finding pleasure in study and in good works.

The former can be cultivated by avoiding idle conversations and banal reading; the latter, by cultivating love for a noble cause to the degree that we identify with it.

There are a great variety of different causes, and for each, each person has different aptitudes.

Some people develop by making discoveries to benefit humanity, others in organizing charitable societies, in founding institutions for good works, or in fighting for a people's freedom. Philosophers, legislators and even warriors can work toward their people's progress and well-being by means of the enormous efforts to promulgate wise laws.

In all of these ways one can do good for humanity, and our love for our fellow men may be measured by our efforts.

People who embrace one of these ideas will become so identified with it that they will love it more than life. Thus, we see how many experts have fallen victims to their own discoveries; how many of humanity's benefactors have found death in the midst of these same causes to which they have dedicated their lives; how many patriots have fallen in achieving independence, liberty, and just laws for their country.

When they assume such noble sentiments, human beings are happy in this world because, for them, there is no happiness other than the satisfaction of knowing they fulfill their duties, that they do what they must for their cause to triumph. The setbacks that discourage most mortals carry no weight for them, for their souls' greatness makes them disdain the trivialities of this world. Thus, poverty, sickness, death—none of these discourage them or make them miserable. Their enthusiasm always sustains them and their faith makes them keep their eye upon the ideal they pursue. For them, this ideal will be achieved sooner or later, for they are convinced that humanity's progress is an inescapable law.

With all the above, you see how, to be happy, is it necessary to imitate the example of the great men who have visited humanity.

In this way you will be happy, not only in this life, but in space, where you will have full rein for your love for learning and where you will find yourself working for the triumph of a cause with which you have identified yourself, and unlike less evolved beings, you will not miss material satisfactions so much, because you will not be accustomed to them.

**Q. I beg you to tell me what are the rules by which, according to Spiritist morality, one can achieve happiness.**
A. To achieve this objective, you must always keep in mind complying with the law of God and consider this your highest duty.

In this respect, duty has no limits and it increases to the degree that the spirit ascends. Duty begins with duty to oneself; then it extends to family, to country, to humanity, and to God.

**Q. Can you tell me what are the duties the human being has to himself?**
A. Man must carefully observe what it is that impedes his satisfaction and happiness; he must painstakingly study his senses, so that he may know exactly which are those actions that most pleasantly and lastingly impress him, and which are

only fleeting and which have painful consequences; and once he has identified those that cause suffering, or to some degree diminish his happiness, he should make a constant effort to eliminate them.

### Q. Can you tell me which are the acts that impede man's happiness?

A. All the low passions cause suffering for the human being. The man who is quick to anger is a victim of his bad temper because he is always quarreling with those around him; when he finds himself in trouble, there is no one to offer him a hand; furthermore, his choleric character affects his organism, causing him to suffer physical pains.

The prideful and the vain can never be happy for their very pride and vanity isolate them and make those around them, who see very clearly how unfounded are their pretensions, want to tear them down.

Pride makes men blind to the point where they commit the greatest crimes. A man who has stained his conscience by spilling the blood of another will never be happy; at the bottom of his soul, he will always have that gnawing worm and, before his eyes, there will always be the tragic picture of his crime. Moreover, the prideful man cannot be happy even in this life for, despite his pretension in believing himself superior to others, in every moment he is humiliated, whether by men or by nature, which is inflexible for all.

The man who succumbs to animal pleasures, who eats too much and drinks himself into a stupor, is the most miserable on earth, for, in such moments, by his own doing, he sinks to a level lower than even animals, because a drunk loses even the instinct for self-preservation.

With these vices, he quickly loses his health and will and the organs which serve to manifest his intelligence atrophy. These men, looked down upon by society, pitied by their families, little by little fall into such degradation that they become numb to all the pleasures of the human spirit.

On a smaller scale, the use of alcohol paralyzes the soul's noble impulses, it blinds intelligence and makes the character irritable; thus we see how people who, while not under the influence of alcohol, are benevolent and enjoy great lucidity, but once they drink something, even without becoming intoxicated, suffer a rapid transformation: they become irritable, violent and insensitive to the great, the noble and the beautiful, and to them, everything seems inexplicable and gloomy. In a word, with alcohol, their optimism is converted to pessimism, and their joy to sadness.

Selfishness, to think only of oneself under the influence of low passions, is also one of the great enemies of man's happiness.

The selfish man thinks only of his material pleasures, in enriching himself and never worrying about the sufferings of others.

Therefore, on the day the selfish person gets into trouble, he finds no one to offer him a hand.

The saddest thing is that even in space, selfish people feel completely isolated and indeed, that is where they will most keenly feel the dismal consequences of thinking only of themselves.

In this world, to a point, material satisfactions can make one forget the need for love for one's fellow men; however, in space, where it is not possible to satisfy these needs, what one will feel is an immense vacuum.

In this way, our bad deeds follow us beyond the grave and, even into our future incarnations, we harvest the bitter fruit.

Finally, sloth is the mother of all vices because the inactive man, when he does not dedicate himself to any mental or physical labor, is very strongly influenced by suggestions, and inevitably, he will feel drawn to satisfy those desires whose realization requires the least effort. Thus we will see him dedicate himself to gambling, overeating, drinking, etc., etc.

In general terms, these are the main enemies of man's happiness.

**Q. *Would you please tell me in more detail about man's duties toward himself?***

A. Once you have understood what I have already told you, you will be able to clearly deduce which are these duties. Man must struggle constantly and resolutely to overcome his evil inclinations, and given that laziness favors the development of all the vices, it follows that activity is the principal means to combat them. Determine then to be always occupied, dedicating yourself to some useful work, some labor, whether intellectual or physical, that obliges you to concentrate your attention, for even the latter requires constant attention to what you are doing and keeps the spirit from being taken prisoner of evil thoughts that should be avoided at all cost. No work can be undertaken without having first been fashioned in the mind. Be, then, active and hard-working. Dedicate your hours of rest, whether to the pure satisfactions found in the home or in study, and flee from wicked places as if from your worst enemy.

The active and studious man is in an excellent position to progress and to elevate himself, for with these virtues he can go far.

However, study and work must be pursued with a higher aim. If we only work to increase our fortunes and accumulate riches, we will very easily become overwhelmed by pride and vanity, these almost inseparable companions of wealth, and at the same time, we will feel compelled to give free rein to all our passions. Wealth in itself is good, as is everything that exists in nature, but it is evil to employ it wrongfully.

If we consider wealth as a means to execute works of general interest this is good; however, if we only think of acquiring wealth to provide personal satisfactions, then it is evil.

In all of the above you will see how man must always observe certain rules of conduct so that he will not lose himself on the innumerable paths upon which his passions constantly attempt to thrust him.

In addition to being active and studious, man must be indulgent with those around him; he must try to love them with his heart.

He should be frugal in eating and drinking; he should be chaste; he should do no harm to anyone.

In sum, man should always be looking to lift himself up, increasing his knowledge and virtues and expanding his realm of beneficent action.

In observing the rules of conduct I have given you, your intelligence will always be lucid, your spirit serene, and very soon you will feel capable of undertaking the greatest enterprises, for your clear intelligence will reveal the means to achieve them; the purity of your habits will help you to never lose heart, knowing that you will always receive help more or less directly from the invisible ones, and you will have a greater influence upon the people around you.

The greatness of the soul has always characterized the superior men who have made humanity progress rapidly, even when they sacrificed their lives, as has happened with most of humanity's liberators and redeemers.

But what is life to one of such men? He only considers it one face of his existence, like a stage of his eternal life, and he uses it to perfect his spirit and fulfill his duties in this world, duties to which he feels irresistibly attracted, because he has come to identify with some higher and noble cause.

In conclusion, for his own self, man must constantly work toward his elevation, increasing his virtue and knowledge of science.

### Q. Can you now tell me, what are the duties of man to his family?

A. Children should love and respect their parents, for whom they should have immense gratitude. It is difficult for children to appreciate how very much they owe them.

Our parents are the guides God has put on our path to lead our first steps, to mold our tender hearts and engrave upon them the better sentiments, the virtues that, later in life, will make us men who can be useful to ourselves, our family, and society.

The love our parents have for us attracts the help of the invisible ones who inspire them with the best ways to direct us. A son should always be respectful to his parents, and when they become old, he should understand that, when in his youth, his parents constantly concerned themselves with helping and supporting him, so he should help and support them when they no longer have the strength to overcome the most pressing needs in life.

Brothers should help one another and be loving, for they have been born into the same family to love one another and to find strength in fraternal union.

The main factor that determines into which family one incarnates is the nature of ties created by previous incarnations.

It seems the same families come together each time they undertake a new pilgrimage to earth and, before resolving upon this very dangerous journey, the spirits come together in small groups of beings among whom there is great affinity and great sympathies created in previous existences in which they have suffered and worked together and, together, achieved triumphs or suffered defeats.

In no case should a man be selfish, and even less so with his brothers, for if because of his selfishness he becomes distant from them, he will find himself weak in his struggle against the vicissitudes of life and in danger of succumbing.

The father of the family has an immense responsibility for the respect he should show his wife and the education he must give his children.

He should consider his wife the weaker part of himself, but at the same time his equal, and he should understand that she has the same rights as he does, that if she is weaker physically, in contrast, she has a greater moral strength, given that, for suffering, she has an admirable resistance and when it comes to the health of her husband and children, she forgets herself completely, thinking only of her loved ones, whom she attends with a tenderness and care of which only she is capable.

Consequently, the husband must be loving and faithful to his wife. In this way happiness will always reign in his home.

The woman, in turn, must treat her husband with love and respect and she should never irritate him because, after all, he is the stronger one and an irritated man forgets his duties.

By means of persuasion and love, the woman should do everything possible to increase her influence over her husband.

Finally, parents must understand that their mission is to lead their children on the path to good, and their duty, to help them progress. For this reason they should help their children from their earliest age to develop the inclination to work, for order, activity, and modesty, and also the love for their fellow men and for the country in which they were born.

But affection should not be an excuse to spoil their children, forgive their faults or provide excessive comforts, for there is always the danger that, from the time they are young they can acquire problematic tendencies and become accustomed to luxury or ostentation.

As for children, from their earliest infancy, they should be treated as if they were grown men: they should never be teased nor frightened. When they are scolded or punished for some mistake, they should be made to understand what it was they did wrong, for if they are not convinced, they will believe they have been wrongly punished and they will never learn. Children have a very precise idea of justice and they will only change their behavior when convinced that their punishment is just.

Instead of worrying about leaving great wealth to their children, parents should try to leave them good habits; they should mold their character so they can make their way in life, and satisfy their needs.

The parent should lead his child and help him overcome the obstacles he encounters in his path, not remove them. The child must get used to struggling with and overcoming them by himself, otherwise, when he grows up, he will have to remain under paternal instruction and, on the day that that falters, resign himself to succumbing.

While some parents strive to remove all kinds of obstacles for their children and in so doing encourage their defects, others, with a more violent character, scold their children for any and all mistakes, and they hit them hard. With this, they only harden their hearts.

These children, having suffered so much since infancy and accustomed to receiving blows, learn to treat their fellow men the same way.

In conclusion, it is as much a disservice to a child to spoil him as it is to be overly strict.

### Q. Can you tell me now what are the duties of a man toward his country?

A. As I told you at the beginning of this chapter, man is essentially social; he tends to live with his fellow men. For this reason, he has formed large population centers, and because collective effort is more effective than the individual's, as these centers expand, they provide superior conditions for their residents.

Consequently, it is in the interest of each member of the collective to work for its development and well-being, as everything that concerns one member is felt by the others.

In order for these human groupings to become large cities and develop normally, the inhabitants have had to come together and name their representatives to proclaim the laws to which all subject themselves.

Laws are meant to guarantee individual liberty for all, recognizing the rights of the individual and his duties toward the constituted government, as the latter, to satisfy the needs of the collective and defend it against external attack, relies on the support of all members, according to their resources and abilities.

Population centers, dispersed and weak at first, have been growing and, by the mutual attraction of cities with the same language, same religion, and same tendencies, coming together to constitute nations, which are more or less great and powerful.

The nations thus constituted have had to undergo both internal struggles, in order that the principles of liberty and progress may triumph, and external struggles, to defend their independence against other nations that would impose their yoke.

The efforts and internal strife of each nation have increased the solidarity among those who live there, for nothing brings men together like struggling and suffering together.

Such histories have marked each people and have formed their special character. Indeed, the memory of the acts of their great men and the most important episodes constitutes each nation's history. A people remembers its ancestors' heroic acts because they know that a country that has provided great men is likely to continue providing them. For a people, the past is a guarantee of the future.

We enjoy the results of our ancestors' efforts; we know that our independence and our laws cost them rivers of blood, so we must preserve this precious inheritance and pass it on to our children intact or even greater.

It is the duty then, of all men, to love the country in which they were born and to always be ready to defend it whenever some foreign nation attempts to attack it.

Independence is the most precious thing a people can enjoy, for the condition of subjugated peoples is very sad. For the conquered there are no guarantees of any kind, they are not permitted to work for the betterment of their compatriots, nor nourish altruistic feelings, nor may they be allowed any liberty at all, and for this reason all progress remains paralyzed.

For all citizens it is also an unfailing duty to work toward the progress of their country, making it ever stronger, and so avoid conquest by a foreign nation.

Patriotism is not only shown on the battlefield when the country is in danger, but also in avoiding these dangers, in working for the development of public education, of agriculture, etc., in a word, toward the progress of all compatriots, for the more they progress and the higher the level of its members, the stronger and more respected will be the nation.

To achieve this, all inhabitants must concern themselves with public life. They should participate, whether directly or indirectly, by means of their vote and in recognizing the transcendental importance that the laws and rights of everyone be respected, for when there is an abuse against a member of the collective, it is an abuse against all. From the moment a government ceases to respect the law, there is no rule, only discretion.

Law is the solemn pact governments celebrate with the governed and to which all inhabitants of a country are subject. He who infringes upon it, whether a commoner or the highest public official, commits a crime against his country for to infringe upon the law it is necessary to resort to violence and this brings discord and civil wars.

The only way to avoid these disturbances is for each person to respect the rights of others. No one who wants the best for his country should ever forget that admirable saying of the Great Juárez: "Respect for the rights of others is peace."[j]

In conclusion, one should never lose sight of the matters of public interest out of petty self-interest, for it is not only our obligation to concern ourselves with all the members of the collective that constitutes our country, but a necessity, for the abuses commited against some of our compatriots can very soon be committed against our own selves. For this reason, no one should spare expense nor effort in serving his country, whether in defending it against foreign invaders or working vigorously toward laws that may be more egalitarian and progressive, so that these may be respected by both the government and the governed.

### Q. And the duties of the individual toward humanity, can you can tell me of what they consist?

A. The only way to raise ourselves up, to come closer to God and achieve our evolution, is to increase the extent of our activity and our influence in benefitting others.

Progress can only be made by working for the progress of others, for our level, whether more or less elevated, depends on our capacity to do good.

The belief that certain rites and practices of a more or less religious character can speed an individual's progress is, in most cases, mistaken. No practices have such an effect except for those that help raise the spirit precisely by increasing the extent of good deeds that benefit other men.

We must therefore work for all that is for humanity's good, whether for its material, intellectual, or moral progress. This is achieved by promoting associations that pursue good works and, as far as we are able, to share the knowledge that can help raise humanity's intellectual and moral level.

Furthermore, these results are obtained by promoting useful inventions, research aimed at discovering the laws behind the various phenomena of nature and human destiny, as well as sharing those we already know, in the manner appropriate to the various social levels.

Lastly, we must work toward erasing the borders between nations, so that we may extinguish hatreds between neighbors, as well as those barbarous customs that result in settling disputes on the battlefield.

The love for country must not blind us to our neighboring nations' merits, and we must combat that narrow provincialism that makes our compatriots consider their own country the best in all and everything.

The love for one's country is not opposed to the love for humanity any more than the love for one's family is opposed to that for one's country, or love for oneself for one's family.

Each country's progress and discoveries redound in benefit for all, which shows that there is strong solidarity among all nations. We must, then, strive to make this solidarity ever greater.

This is our duty to humanity.

MAN'S DUTIES TOWARDS GOD

**Q. Lastly, I ask you tell me, what are man's duties to God?**
A. You will find man's duties to God in the first commandment of the Law of Moses: "Love God above all others."

**Q. How does one love God?**
A. God is a Being so abstract and infinitely great that it is impossible for us, in our current state of development, to form even a vague idea of Him.

Because of this, it is very difficult to love God as we love some cherished person or some good cause, and in fact, it is impossible for us to love God directly, although we can love His works. God needs nothing from us and therefore we cannot pay him any tribute. As a loving Father, the only thing he desires is that we be happy, and so that we may achieve it, he has given us His laws. For this reason, what is most pleasing to God is that we obey His laws, so that we may find in them our good fortune, which consists in working together toward the happiness of humankind. When we love our fellow men, when we do as much good as possible and identify with some noble cause, we therefore love God and worship Him in spirit and in truth.

In spirit, for we do not look for crude images that represent Him, but worship Him by obeying His law and trying to be in harmony with His plan, which consists of accelerating human evolution. In truth, for our devotion is sincere and part of a profound and honorable conviction.

PRAYER
In spite of the above, we must make the effort to raise our spirit toward God by means of prayer.

But prayer must be an intimate talk with our Heavenly Father in which we tell all our mishaps, we paint our weaknesses, we ask for strength to struggle and light for the path we must follow, and which permits us to clearly understand our duties. In few words, prayer should ask God for light and strength to continue serenely on the path which He made for us.

However, to direct ourselves toward God in this way, we must have a high degree of virtue and a very clear idea of the laws that determine the world's evolution.

For this reason, Jesus of Nazareth gave us an example of how we should pray. He left us the Lord's Prayer, a very beautiful prayer that sets forth our true duties toward God and humanity, and at the same time, it teaches us what we can ask of our Father.

In this prayer, Jesus makes us understand that God is our Father, and with this, he has taught us that we are all creatures of God, we are all His children, and He loves us all equally.

When such a conviction impresses itself deeply upon our soul, our consciousness of our own value increases; we understand that all men are equal, that we possess the seeds of all virtues and all powers, and we need only make the effort and we can attain the level of the most elevated men. With such faith, each act of goodness has a value far greater than all the world's riches and all the world's glitter.

The men in whose hearts this idea has sunk deep roots have had the courage to defy the wrath of the powerful, to valiantly struggle for the triumph of truth and justice, and thus accelerate humanity's progress. This constitutes true faith. To have faith is to cherish an absolute conviction that we are children of God and that, while we observe His law, while we direct our efforts toward the good of humanity, we have absolute assurance that God must help us in our enterprise and our efforts will yield fruit.

It is not for this that I tell you that God will personally intervene to help us; no, our efforts will be supported and directed by higher spirits who dedicate their activity and energies to working for the good of humanity, and supported by those men who are dedicated to good, arousing new aid, clearing the obstacles from their mission's path, and keeping at bay the dangers that could menace their work. The spirits exercise their influence on humans by means of suggestion and many times they make the person they want to help unconsciously remove himself from danger. They might even suggest an idea to some other person who is sympathetic, and aware of machinations against him, so that he can slow or even stop them.

As I have told you, Jesus left us the legacy of the Lord's Prayer that the great majority of Christians recite without meditating upon the meaning of each of its verses. I will now give you an explanation of each one, so that you can more profoundly comprehend the greatness contained in this prayer and so better comprehend your duties.

"OUR FATHER WHO ART IN HEAVEN,
HALLOWED BE THY NAME."

I have explained the great significance of considering God as our Father. From the moment we say, "Hallowed be thy name," we show our desire that all of humanity know that He is our Father and adore Him in spirit and in truth, by means of good works. In sending out this desire, it must be sincere and profound. We must think seriously about the value of our words, in the significance of the desire, in the effort demanded of us in working toward its realization.

So then, in desiring that humanity adore God and work in harmony with His law, we must show humanity this law, we must work by whatever means we can so that this law be known to all.

We must work in the same way toward humanity's progress. To achieve this goal, we need great self-denial and to throw off all the trivialities of this world and keep our gaze fixed on the highest ideals and work resolutely toward their triumph. In practical terms, this means we must improve public education, urging people to combat their vices and helping them cultivate their virtues.

This is achieved by passionately propagandizing of all types of progressive and beneficial ideas, joining associations and groups that are dedicated to altruistic works of all kinds—though at times, efforts in these spheres are insufficient and it is necessary to act on thornier ground, fighting against bad rulers who slow down any altruistic works, who oppress people, permitting them no liberty, not even to work for their own betterment.[2]

The first freedom one must conquer above all others is that of thought, for man is a free being with rights the Creator has given him at birth. These he must protect as his most precious inheritance, for they are indispensable for his evolution and progress.

When a people does not enjoy liberty it is because they are governed by violence and caprice. Those who govern by these means do so in view of satisfying their passions and in no way concern themselves with the progress and well-being of the governed. For these reasons man should fight so that the people where he lives may enjoy complete liberty. He should fight against those who violate liberty, against bad governments that usurp the rights of the people—and without concern for his own life, for we must always be ready to sacrifice ourselves for the common good, in this way imitating the example of Jesus and of so many martyrs and heroes who have shed their blood for humanity.

"THY KINGDOM COME"
In saying this, we express the desire that God reign on Earth, that is to say, that there may reign His law—love, justice, equality—in the relationships among individuals and among nations, and that "might makes right" and the rule of the strongest be forgotten, so that justice reigns on earth.

"THY WILL BE DONE ON EARTH, AS IT IS IN HEAVEN."
The will of God is that we comply with His law, that we be happy, that we dedicate all our efforts to developing our virtues, and that we recognize no hierarchies other than merit and virtue.

This thought becomes a corollary to the others, completing and explaining them.

"GIVE US THIS DAY OUR DAILY BREAD"
In asking God to give us our daily sustenance, we are not referring only to ourselves and physical food. We ask for material,
intellectual, and spiritual food, and not only for ourselves; for
all humanity. The meaning of this phrase becomes the following: "I wish that all the poor who are hungry may find food,
that the teachings and knowledge of the truth may come to
all those who are submerged in ignorance, so that they may
understand the divine laws and find happiness working in
accord with them."

For ourselves specifically, we should ask for spiritual enlightenment, so that we may develop our intelligence and, more
effectively, receive help from the invisibles, so that we may
multiply our efforts—as long as they have the aim of working
for the good of our fellow men.

Naturally, to achieve this, it is necessary to involve oneself in
public life, so that the highest positions in government may be
occupied by people who pursue the same ideals, who concern
themselves with the good of the people and improving their
material, intellectual, and moral conditions, which are the only
foundation for the greatness of nations.

Peoples who have great laws and virtuous children have left
a glorious memory for posterity, and we try to follow in their
footsteps, while peoples who have enjoyed material greatness
without concern for the virtue of citizens, have left us nothing
but memories of pomp, their potentates' vices and subjects'
misery.

"LEAD US NOT INTO TEMPTATION AND DELIVER US
FROM EVIL."
To receive the help of the invisibles by means of inspiration—
since this influence is the most effective—we must keep
ourselves completely pure, both in thought and in works,
committing no acts that impede the elevation of our spirit to
higher spheres. Only thus can we work in an effective manner

to achieve the very beautiful ideals I have expressed here and for whose triumph superhuman efforts are required.

To achieve this objective, we must ask our Heavenly Father for His help.

"FORGIVE US OUR TRESPASSES, AS WE FORGIVE THOSE WHO TRESPASS AGAINST US."

This phrase, so clear and understandable—how many people repeat it unconsciously! How many people not only do not forgive those who have trespassed against them, those who have offended them; they treat and judge them with excessive severity; they show great bias toward their fellow men, even those who neither owe them nor have offended them! And these wretched men, without realizing what they are doing, ask God to apply "an eye for an eye" and because they have shown no mercy to their fellow men, so their Father, when He judges them, should be unyielding.

Instead of saying, "forgive our trespasses as we forgive those who trespass against us," would it not be a thousand times better to say, "My God, my soul lacks the necessary greatness to forgive those who have trespassed against me; I ask that you grant me the generosity necessary to forgive them, so that I myself may merit the forgiveness for my faults"? In my view, this is the true meaning of the phrase and it should be understood thus.

Jesus Christ told us: "with what measure you mete, it shall be measured to you again." If we want to be forgiven for our faults, we must forgive those of our fellow men, forgetting their offenses against us, and judging them with benevolence.

Instead of scorning evil men for their conduct, we should consider them as backward beings who wallow in ignorance, and we should have compassion for them and, with love and care, help them rise up from their sad situation to a higher level.

# CHAPTER VI

# *Summary*

*Q. In a few words, can you tell me what is the objective for which man comes into this world and his duties, and what are the rules of conduct he should observe?*
A. Man comes into this world as a child to a school: to study and develop his abilities.

In order to progress, the spirit needs to encase itself in flesh, for by remaining in space without needs to satisfy he cannot progress. It is only necessity that obliges us to work and advance our intelligence and ingenuity, so that we may overcome the innumerable obstacles we encounter on our path. For the great majority of beings, this is the reason for incarnation.

However, truly elevated beings do not incarnate for their evolution; they can progress in space. It is not need that obliges them to study, but love for study and for science and their very ardent wish to discover the laws behind the evolution of humanity and the worlds.

The end of evolution is happiness and true happiness is only found in complying with the law, that is, in developing the self by means of virtue and science.

This is the happiness evolved spirits find in study and doing good works for humanity. The spirits who have arrived at such a highly evolved level live in unceasing activity and always dedicate their efforts to some useful work, whether they are incarnated or in space.

In space they are better able to do research. Their senses are more developed; therefore, they can undertake more concientious and profound studies.

On the other hand, when these spirits incarnate in this world, although their senses are less developed than in space, these are sharper than those of normal people, and their aim is to promote humanity's progress.

Very often these superior beings go unrecognized by the world, which treats them badly and makes them suffer humiliating deaths. This does not frighten the illustrious group of higher superior spirits who constantly work for humanity's progress and incarnate in this world whenever they are called.

As for the less evolved spirits who comprise the great majority of the earth's inhabitants, for the most part they live without thinking of eternal life, ignoring the objective for which they have come into this world. For such people, evolution is more difficult than for those who know the destinities of the soul beyond death and the reason for incarnation.

Among those ignorant of their destiny there are several classes: the intellectual, the wealthy, and the proletarian.

Those in the first class dedicate themselves assiduously to study, finding their happiness in their work and although in many cases they profess mistaken ideas, when the moment is right, their constant, disinterested effort toward developing their intelligence can result in rapid evolution.

As for those spoiled with a fortune, those who possess immense riches, for them it is more difficult to see the light of truth, for in addition to the fact that riches foment vices and serve to unleash passions, the wealthy are generally surrounded by people who adulate them and so make denser the veil that hides the truth.

Christ said it is more difficult for a rich man to go to Heaven than for a camel to pass through the eye of a needle.

Because riches are so agreeable and provide for so many satisfactions, he who has no ambition for them is very unusual. This ambition is shared by the great majority of spirits before incarnating in our world, for they want the test of possessing riches, imagining that they will be able to comply with the rich man's mission. Unfortunately, most of those who take the test succumb, for instead of dedicating their wealth for the good of their fellow men, they simply satisfy their own material desires.

For this reason, it is not good to be ambitious for riches. Each person should be content with what he has and try to satisfy only his needs without yearning for luxuries and other superficial things on this earth.

Material well-being is necessary so that the spirit may feel more tranquil and not worry only about struggling for a living, but be able to dedicate himself to study and work that raises his level.

Oftentimes the worker dedicated to rude labors is unhappy with his lot, but his unhappiness is unjustified, for he must realize that improving it depends upon him. It is enough that he not spend anything on things he doesn't need, above all on intoxicating beverages that make not only the one with the vice but all his family suffer so terribly. Moreover, by working hard and responsibly, it is unusual for any worker not to achieve a higher salary and a better position, assuming greater responsibilities, for all watch-men, or at least employees of a certain category, are recruited from among the most responsible and capable.

Above all, workers should never despair of their luck and the circumstances they find themselves in, for it is the result of their previous incarnations and cannot be changed quickly. The present moment is the product of the past and it is not in our power to change it; however, the future depends on us and we can change it according to our desires.

If a worker's circumstance is sad, he can improve it by means of continual and persevering effort. Violence achieves no practical result. But what should most sustain the worker in his constant struggle is the conviction that he is not alone, he is not defenseless, for there is always some spirit at his side who asks to guide him, help him, and sustain him, and above this spirit there is God, Father of all mortals, who has reserved for him the same destiny.

The difference among positions in this world is only important from a material point of view, and if we suppose that our present life is the only life we enjoy.

On the other hand, considering this from the point of view of multiple existences, whether on earth or in space, such differences lose all importance, for admirable recompense is inherent in everything.

When he leaves this world, he who has dedicated himself to satisfying material pleasures will find no way to satisfy them in space. His spirit is unprepared for other types of activities, he cannot enjoy them, and he finds himself in a very painful situation, which can become truly distressing and terrible for those hard-hearted ones who have thought only of themselves.

In space, the unrepentant criminal and the despot suffer cruel punishment and are constantly pursued by visions of their victims.

In general, as Jesus said, "the last shall be first," explaining that the humble, the simple, those who lead the quietest of lives, those who have always lived in harmony with divine law, will be first in space, they will occupy the highest positions and enjoy the greatest happiness, while the proud will be humiliated, even if on earth they have enjoyed a fortune.

This law of retribution and progress of the spirit through multiple incarnations should console all the afflicted, making them understand the Creator's admirable justice, making them wait for the prize for every effort made with some noble end in mind.

In this manner all the inhabitants of this world can scorn life and its trivialities, as we dedicate ourselves with ardor to developing our virtues and our intelligence and to working for the progress of humanity, with the firm conviction that numerous high-ranking spirits guide and support us. With these beliefs the human spirit will forget its pessimism, its lack of faith, and will be inspired by optimistic ideas that nurture and bring cheer to our noble hearts to undertake the most arduous enterprises.

Having glimpsed part of the truth, our enthusiasm will multiply our ardor to carry on our studies, and along the way, we will put aside everything that impedes the free development of our spirit.

We will only sleep as needed to replenish our strength (eight or nine hours for young people and seven to eight for adults.)

We will eat only what we need to conserve our bodies' vigor and among foods, we will select the most nutritious and healthy (the best being those from the vegetable kingdom, for from the animal kingdom, only milk and its derivatives have the required properties). We will be methodical in the way we manage our time so that there is enough for everything and we will faithfully comply with our daily duties and, at the same time, we will dedicate some periods to study and meditation.

We will exercise strict discipline in all our behavior. For this we will especially concern ourselves with controlling our thoughts, always focussing on some useful work, for we cannot perform any good or bad act if we have not previously prepared it in the laboratory of our minds. We will never allow any impure thought to take hold of our mind; on the contrary, we will always think of useful things and only when there is nothing important to distract us will we permit ourselves to wander through the fields of the ideal, dreams, even the most unrealistic ones, as long as they have a noble end.

In this way your spirit will always have noble tendencies and these apparently unachievable dreams will be achieved much sooner than you think for in the end you yourselves will feel impelled to work for their triumph.

Finally, from the time you are young, try to select your companion, for in married life you will find true happiness and, for men, this is the best way to avoid falling onto the paths of vice.

The obligations of the married man and father of a family make him have a higher conception of life and of himself; they make him more serious, more circumspect, and give his resolutions more gravity.

In sum, a man's existence is ennobled when he dedicates his efforts to the well-being of his dear companion and their cherished children.

Bachelorhood is only appropriate for those self-sacrificing beings who have come into this world to undertake a special mission which requires precisely this sacrifice.

Fortunately, in order to remain pure, these beings do not require the brake of conjugal life, nor do they need a family to ennoble their efforts, for they are dedicated to the betterment of humanity. These missions are only undertaken by selected spirits.

To conclude, I will not tire of recommending that you direct all your efforts to your betterment, always keeping in your sights the great destiny your Creator has in store for you. Pray to Him often, asking Him to light your path, and that your strength may never falter on your long and arduous journey.

# ENDNOTES

[1]We present our theory of the "unconscious" later in this chapter in the section on the philosophy of reincarnation.

[2]I have not hesitated to state these bold ideas because I wish to combat the selfishness which, in most religions, generally accompanies mystics and believers.

The author believes that the true believer must take a broad view, identifying himself with the general aspirations of the people where he lives, and he must take an important part in their struggles to improve the situation of the collective, for the progress of an isolated individual does not exist; the degree of elevation of each being is measured precisely by the extent of his good works.

The desired objective is obtained by taking active part in enterprises of public interest. In a word, the true believer must not vacillate in adhering to the political parties that best respond to his aspirations, the goal being to work in the most efficient manner for the progress of humanity.

Undoubtedly, if all good men put aside their selfishness and involve themselves in public matters, people would be governed wisely and men of greatest merit and virtue would occupy the highest positions. And it is natural that such men work for the good and accelerate humanity's evolution. This is not the case with evil men who so often occupy such positions, for apart from governing only in their own interests, they give a pernicious example to the masses who only see crime behind success and this both promotes evil tendencies and serves as an obstacle to virtue because in such conditions the good and virtuous man is a victim of all kinds of persecutions while the bad one adapts to the situation and is rewarded.

In sum, in a country governed by perverse men, crime is rewarded and virtue persecuted, and this has a powerful influence on the morale of the great majority who numbly accustom themselves to considering practical and convenient all that tends to harmonize with such a situation, while everything that signifies noble and higher tendencies they consider dreams, utopias, madnesses, etc.

In such conditions, instead of progressing, people fall into decadence and their evolution is considerably retarded.

# TRANSLATOR'S NOTES

[a]This was Thoth, a mythical Egyptian sage and inventor of hiero-glyphic writing, who is represented as a scribe with the head of an ibis. The Greeks called him Hermes, conflating Thoth with the Greek god Hermes. He was also known as Hermes Trismegistus (Thrice-Great).

[b]Gaston Maspero (1846-1916) was a French Egyptologist and the author of *L'égyptologie* and *L'archéologie egyptienne*, among other works.

[c]Édouard Schuré (1841-1926), French philosopher and playwright specializing in esoteric subjects, was a contemporary of Helena Petrovna Blavatksy, and a friend of both Richard Wagner, the composer, and Rudolph Steiner, founder of Anthroposophy. Among Schuré's many works are *Les Grands Initiés* (The Great Initiates) a phenomenally popular book first published in 1889.

[d]St. Alphonsus Maria de Liguori (1696-1787), a Neapolitan lawyer-turned-priest known for his missionary work among the poor and many miraculous healings and a levitation, was canonized in 1839. See *The Life of St Alphonsus Maria de Liguori, Bishop of St Agatha of the Goths and Founder of the Congregation of the Holy Redeemer* (1855).

[e]Christian Science was founded by Mary Baker Eddy in 1879. Now with churches in some 130 countries, the headquarters is the Mother Church, First Church of Christ, Scientist, in Boston, Massachusetts.

[f]Sir William Crookes (1832-1919) was a leading English chemist and physicist who, apart from his research on gases, electricity, diamonds, and more, conducted research on some of the best known mediums of the nineteenth century, including D.D. Home. The University of Oxford's Chemistry Department offers an extensive biography of this "Victorian man of science" which, however, neglects to specify the nature of his psychical research.

http://www.chem.ox.ac.uk/icl/heyes/lanthact/biogs/crookes.html

gAlexandr Nikolayevich Aksakov (1832-1903), Russian journalist, translator, and avid psychic researcher specializing in mediums, translated several works by Swedish mystic Emmanuel Swedenborg and also authored several books about Swedenborg's philosophy and revelations.

hCharles Robert Richet (1850-1935) was a professor of physiology on the Faculty of Medicine in Paris and the winner of the 1913 Nobel Prize. His psychical research focused on mediums, most notably Eusapia Palladino, and in 1922 he published *Traité de Métapsyche*, which was translated as *Thirty Years of Psychical Research* in 1923.

iCamille Flammarion (1842-1925) was a leading French intellectual, science journalist, novelist, and astronomer.

jBenito Juárez led the Republican struggle against the French Intervention of 1861-1867. He served as President of Mexico from 1861 until his death in office in 1872 of a heart attack.

# Index

Visit www.cmmayo.com

*For many resources for researchers,*
*including interviews and podcasts with C.M. Mayo*

CPSIA information can be obtained at www.ICGtesting.com
Printed in the USA
LVOW05s1648051114

412175LV00020B/1242/P